Preface

3rd Nephi 23:1

1 And now, behold, I say unto you, that ye ought to search these things. Yea, commandment I give unto you that ye search these things diligently; for great are the words of Isaiah.

I have always striven to heed the words of our Lord and Savior, Jesus Christ in His instructions to those of the Nephi civilization almost two millennia ago. As I progressed along my own independent study of this magnificent work of art and scripture, a deep yearning to share my study with my children and friends. This book and others in this series are the result.

For this particular project, I provide the reader with a "Harmony" view of the book of Isaiah by comparing the King James Version (KJV), Joseph Smith Translation (JST) and all of the Isaiah chapters and verses that are quoted with the Book of Mormon (BOMV). My intention is that this Harmony view will aid the reader to see where the texts align and where they diverge. As a student of the scriptures, we can learn from both of the convergences and divergences that occur across these three versions of this wonderful book of scripture.

Why these three versions specifically? The English version of the King James Version published by the Church of Jesus Christ of Latter-Day Saints is considered the canonized version for faithful members of the Church and as a result should be taken as the base set of scriptures that we rely on and look to when conducting any serious scripture study. Joseph Smith, recognizing some errors in the KJV version during his day, set out to create a revision of both the Old and New Testaments. It has been referred to as the Joseph Smith Translation. As a result of his work and effort, we now have available to us his inspired version of these two great bodies of scripture. In my study of his inspired version of both the Old and New Testaments over the last 3 decades of my life, I have found great insight and understanding. As such, it only seemed fitting to compare what where this text aligns with or diverges from the canonized KJV. Finally, Joseph Smith also translated the Book of Mormon through the power of God in these latter days. As part of this new volume of scripture introduced to us in our day, many of the ancient prophets quoted from and relied heavily on the words of Isaiah to help the people of their time understand both the covenants of God with the people and the current and future fulfillment of them. Accordingly, some of these verses align exactly with the KJV and/or JST and others do not. Equally insightful are these moments over alignment or divergence.

I have intentionally not included any of my insights or understandings in this particular volume of work, though I do hope to in my final book of this series. Instead, I am taking you along on a journey that I have been on. The first stop was to set up the harmony in this way. I am therefore providing the reading the harmony version to save you the time and work to create this but allowing you the space to ask your own questions and seek for your own answers as to why certain words are used, added or taken away in some versions and not others. In the end, your experiences, insight, and understandings will be uniquely yours and the hope of the author in publishing this work.

Table of Contents:

Chapter 1................................3
Chapter 2................................8
Chapter 3................................12
Chapter 4................................16
Chapter 5................................17
Chapter 6................................23
Chapter 7................................25
Chapter 8................................29
Chapter 9................................33
Chapter 10................................37
Chapter 11................................43
Chapter 12................................46
Chapter 13................................47
Chapter 14................................51
Chapter 15................................56
Chapter 16................................58
Chapter 17................................61
Chapter 18................................64
Chapter 19................................65
Chapter 20................................70
Chapter 21................................71
Chapter 22................................74
Chapter 23................................78
Chapter 24................................81
Chapter 25................................85
Chapter 26................................87
Chapter 27................................91
Chapter 28................................93
Chapter 29................................98
Chapter 30................................108
Chapter 31................................114
Chapter 32................................116
Chapter 33................................119

Chapter 34................................124
Chapter 35................................127
Chapter 36................................129
Chapter 37................................133
Chapter 38................................140
Chapter 39................................144
Chapter 40................................146
Chapter 41................................151
Chapter 42................................156
Chapter 43................................160
Chapter 44................................165
Chapter 45................................170
Chapter 46................................175
Chapter 47................................177
Chapter 48................................180
Chapter 49................................185
Chapter 50................................191
Chapter 51................................194
Chapter 52................................198
Chapter 53................................201
Chapter 54................................204
Chapter 55................................207
Chapter 56................................209
Chapter 57................................212
Chapter 58................................215
Chapter 59................................219
Chapter 60................................222
Chapter 61................................227
Chapter 62................................229
Chapter 63................................232
Chapter 64................................235
Chapter 65................................238
Chapter 66................................243

King James Version (KJV)	Joseph Smith Translation (JST)	Book of Mormon Version (BOMV)
Isaiah: Chapter 1	**Isaiah: Chapter 1**	
[1] The vision of Isaiah the son of Amoz, which he saw concerning Judah and Jerusalem in the days of Uzziah, Jotham, Ahaz, and Hezekiah, kings of Judah.	[1] The vision of Isaiah, the son of Amoz, which he saw concerning Judah and Jerusalem in the days of Uzziah, Jotham, Ahaz, and Hezekiah, kings of Judah.	
[2] Hear, O heavens, and give ear, O earth: for the LORD hath spoken, I have nourished and brought up children, and they have rebelled against me.	[2] Hear, O heavens, and give ear, O earth, for the Lord hath spoken; I have nourished and brought up children, and they have rebelled against me.	
[3] The ox knoweth his owner, and the ass his master's crib: but Israel doth not know, my people doth not consider.	[3] The ox knoweth his owner, and the ass his master's crib; but Israel doth not know; my people doth not consider.	
[4] Ah sinful nation, a people laden with iniquity, a seed of evildoers, children that are corrupters: they have forsaken the LORD, they have provoked the Holy One of Israel unto anger, they are gone away backward.	[4] Ah, sinful nation, a people laden with iniquity, a seed of evildoers, children that are corrupters; they have forsaken the Lord; they have provoked the Holy One of Israel unto anger; they are gone away backward.	
[5] Why should ye be stricken any more? ye will revolt more and more: the whole head is sick, and the whole heart faint.	[5] Why should ye be stricken any more? Ye will revolt more and more; the whole head is sick, and the whole heart faint.	

[6] From the sole of the foot even unto the head there is no soundness in it; but wounds, and bruises, and putrifying sores: they have not been closed, neither bound up, neither mollified with ointment.

[7] Your country is desolate, your cities are burned with fire: your land, strangers devour it in your presence, and it is desolate, as overthrown by strangers.

[8] And the daughter of Zion is left as a cottage in a vineyard, as a lodge in a garden of cucumbers, as a besieged city.

[9] Except the LORD of hosts had left unto us a very small remnant, we should have been as Sodom, and we should have been like unto Gomorrah.

[10] Hear the word of the LORD, ye rulers of Sodom; give ear unto the law of our God, ye people of Gomorrah.

[11] To what purpose is the multitude of your sacrifices unto me? saith the LORD: I am full of the burnt offerings of rams, and the fat of fed beasts; and I delight not in the blood of bullocks, or of lambs, or of

[6] From the sole of the foot even unto the head there is no soundness in it, but wounds, and bruises, and putrefying sores; they have not been closed, neither bound up, neither mollified with ointment.

[7] Your country is desolate; your cities are burned with fire; your land, strangers devour it in your presence, and it is desolate, as overthrown by strangers.

[8] And the daughter of Zion is left as a cottage in a vineyard, as a lodge in a garden of cucumbers, as a besieged city.

[9] Except the Lord of hosts had left unto us a very small remnant, we should have been as Sodom, and we should have been like unto Gomorrah.

[10] Hear the word of the Lord, ye rulers of Sodom; give ear unto the law of our God, ye people of Gomorrah.

[11] To what purpose is the multitude of your sacrifices unto me? saith the Lord; I am full of the burnt offerings of rams and the fat of fed beasts; and I delight not in the blood of bullocks, or of lambs, or of

he goats.

[12] When ye come to appear before me, who hath required this at your hand, to tread my courts?

[13] Bring no more vain oblations; incense is an abomination unto me; the new moons and sabbaths, the calling of assemblies, I cannot away with; it is iniquity, even the solemn meeting.

[14] Your new moons and your appointed feasts my soul hateth: they are a trouble unto me; I am weary to bear them.

[15] And when ye spread forth your hands, I will hide mine eyes from you: yea, when ye make many prayers, I will not hear: your hands are full of blood.

[16] Wash you, make you clean; put away the evil of your doings from before mine eyes; cease to do evil;

[17] Learn to do well; seek judgment, relieve the oppressed, judge the fatherless, plead for the widow.

[18] Come now, and let us reason together, saith the LORD: though your

he goats.

[12] When ye come to appear before me, who hath required this at your hand, to tread my courts?

[13] Bring no more vain oblations; incense is an abomination unto me; the new moons and sabbaths, the calling of assemblies, I cannot away with; it is iniquity, even the solemn meeting.

[14] Your new moons and your appointed feasts my soul hateth; they are a trouble unto me; I am weary to bear them.

[15] And when ye spread forth your hands, I will hide mine eyes from you; yea, when ye make many prayers, I will not hear; your hands are full of blood.

[16] Wash ye; make you clean; put away the evil of your doings from before mine eyes; cease to do evil;

[17] Learn to do well; seek judgment; relieve the oppressed; judge the fatherless; plead for the widow.

[18] Come now, and let us reason together, saith the Lord. Though your sins

sins be as scarlet, they shall be as white as snow; though they be red like crimson, they shall be as wool.

[19] If ye be willing and obedient, ye shall eat the good of the land:

[20] But if ye refuse and rebel, ye shall be devoured with the sword: for the mouth of the LORD hath spoken it.

[21] How is the faithful city become an harlot! it was full of judgment; righteousness lodged in it; but now murderers.

[22] Thy silver is become dross, thy wine mixed with water:

[23] Thy princes are rebellious, and companions of thieves: every one loveth gifts, and followeth after rewards: they judge not the fatherless, neither doth the cause of the widow come unto them.

[24] Therefore saith the Lord, the LORD of hosts, the mighty One of Israel, Ah, I will ease me of mine adversaries, and avenge me of mine enemies:

be as scarlet, they shall be as white as snow; though they be red like crimson, they shall be as wool.

[19] If ye be willing and obedient, ye shall eat the good of the land;

[20] But if ye refuse and rebel, ye shall be devoured with the sword; for the mouth of the Lord hath spoken it.

[21] How is the faithful city become a harlot! It was full of judgment; righteousness lodged in it, but now murderers.

[22] Thy silver is become dross, thy wine mixed with water;

[23] Thy princes are rebellious, and companions of thieves; everyone loveth gifts and followeth after rewards; they judge not the fatherless; neither doth the cause of the widow come unto them.

[24] Therefore saith the Lord, the Lord of hosts, the Mighty One of Israel, Ah, I will ease me of mine adversaries and avenge me of mine enemies.

[**25**] And I will turn my hand upon thee, and purely purge away thy dross, and take away all thy tin:

[**26**] And I will restore thy judges as at the first, and thy counselors as at the beginning: afterward thou shalt be called, The city of righteousness, the faithful city.

[**27**] Zion shall be redeemed with judgment, and her converts with righteousness.

[**28**] And the destruction of the transgressors and of the sinners shall be together, and they that forsake the LORD shall be consumed.

[**29**] For they shall be ashamed of the oaks which ye have desired, and ye shall be confounded for the gardens that ye have chosen.

[**30**] For ye shall be as an oak whose leaf fadeth, and as a garden that hath no water.

[**31**] And the strong shall be as tow, and the maker of it as a spark, and they shall both burn together, and none shall quench them.

[**25**] And I will turn my hand upon thee, and purely purge away thy dross, and take away all thy tin;

[**26**] And I will restore thy judges as at the first and thy counselors as at the beginning; afterward thou shalt be called the city of righteousness, the faithful city.

[**27**] Zion shall be redeemed with judgment, and her converts with righteousness.

[**28**] And the destruction of the transgressors and of the sinners shall be together, and they that forsake the Lord shall be consumed.

[**29**] For they shall be ashamed of the oaks which ye have desired, and ye shall be confounded for the gardens that ye have chosen.

[**30**] For ye shall be as an oak whose leaf fadeth and as a garden that hath no water.

[**31**] And the strong shall be as tow and the maker of it as a spark; and they shall both burn together, and none shall quench them.

2
[1] The word that Isaiah, the son of Amoz, saw concerning Judah and Jerusalem.

[2] And it shall come to pass in the last days, that the mountain of the LORD's house shall be established in the top of the mountains, and shall be exalted above the hills; and all nations shall flow unto it.

[3] And many people shall go and say, Come ye, and let us go up to the mountain of the LORD, to the house of the God of Jacob; and he will teach us of his ways, and we will walk in his paths: for out of Zion shall go forth the law, and the word of the LORD from Jerusalem.

[4] And he shall judge among the nations, and shall rebuke many people: and they shall beat their swords into plowshares, and their spears into pruninghooks: nation shall not lift up sword against nation, neither shall they learn war any more.

Chapter 2
[1] The word that Isaiah, the son of Amoz, saw concerning Judah and Jerusalem:

2:2 And it shall come to pass in the last days, when the mountain of the Lord's house shall be established in the top of the mountains, and shall be exalted above the hills, and all nations shall flow unto it,

2:3 And many people shall go and say, Come ye, and let us go up to the mountain of the Lord, to the house of the God of Jacob; and he will teach us of his ways, and we will walk in his paths; for out of Zion shall go forth the law, and the word of the Lord from Jerusalem;

2:4 And he shall judge among the nations and shall rebuke many people; and they shall beat their swords into plowshares and their spears into pruning hooks; nation shall not lift up sword against nation; neither shall they learn war any more.

(2nd Nephi 12-24)
12:1The word that Isaiah, the son of Amoz, saw concerning Judah and Jerusalem:

12:2And it shall come to pass in the last days, when the mountain of the Lord's house shall be established in the top of the mountains, and shall be exalted above the hills, and all nations shall flow unto it.

12:3And many people shall go and say, Come ye, and let us go up to the mountain of the Lord, to the house of the God of Jacob; and he will teach us of his ways, and we will walk in his paths; for out of Zion shall go forth the law, and the word of the Lord from Jerusalem.

12:4And he shall judge among the nations, and shall rebuke many people: and they shall beat their swords into plow-shares, and their spears into pruning-hooks— nation shall not lift up sword against nation, neither shall they learn war any more.

[5] O house of Jacob, come ye, and let us walk in the light of the LORD.

[6] Therefore thou hast forsaken thy people the house of Jacob, because they be replenished from the east, and are soothsayers like the Philistines, and they please themselves in the children of strangers.

[7] Their land also is full of silver and gold, neither is there any end of their treasures; their land is also full of horses, neither is there any end of their chariots:

[8] Their land also is full of idols; they worship the work of their own hands, that which their own fingers have made:

[9] And the mean man boweth down, and the great man humbleth himself: therefore forgive them not.

[10] Enter into the rock, and hide thee in the dust, for fear of the LORD, and for the glory of his majesty.

2:5 O house of Jacob, come ye, and let us walk in the light of the Lord; yea, come, for ye have all gone astray, everyone to his wicked ways.

2:6 Therefore, O Lord, thou hast forsaken thy people, the house of Jacob, because they be replenished from the east and hearken unto soothsayers like the Philistines, and they please themselves in the children of strangers.

2:7 Their land also is full of silver and gold; neither is there any end of their treasures; their land is also full of horses; neither is there any end of their chariots;

2:8 Their land also is full of idols; they worship the work of their own hands, that which their own fingers have made.

2:9 And the mean man boweth not down, and the great man humbleth himself not; therefore, forgive them not.

2:10 O ye wicked ones, enter into the rock, and hide ye in the dust; for the fear of the Lord and his majesty shall smite thee.

12:5O house of Jacob, come ye and let us walk in the light of the Lord; yea, come, for ye have all gone astray, every one to his wicked ways.

12:6Therefore, O Lord, thou hast forsaken thy people, the house of Jacob, because they be replenished from the east, and hearken unto soothsayers like the Philistines, and they please themselves in the children of strangers.

12:7Their land also is full of silver and gold, neither is there any end of their treasures; their land is also full of horses, neither is there any end of their chariots.

12:8Their land is also full of idols; they worship the work of their own hands, that which their own fingers have made.

12:9And the mean man boweth not down, and the great man humbleth himself not, therefore, forgive him not.

12:10O ye wicked ones, enter into the rock, and hide thee in the dust, for the fear of the Lord and the glory of his majesty shall smite thee.

[11] The lofty looks of man shall be humbled, and the haughtiness of men shall be bowed down, and the LORD alone shall be exalted in that day.

[12] For the day of the LORD of hosts shall be upon every one that is proud and lofty, and upon every one that is lifted up; and he shall be brought low:

[13] And upon all the cedars of Lebanon, that are high and lifted up, and upon all the oaks of Bashan,

[14] And upon all the high mountains, and upon all the hills that are lifted up,

[15] And upon every high tower, and upon every fenced wall,

[16] And upon all the ships of Tarshish, and upon all pleasant pictures.

2:11 And it shall come to pass that the lofty looks of man shall be humbled; and the haughtiness of man shall be bowed down; and the Lord alone shall be exalted in that day.

2:12 For the day of the Lord of hosts soon cometh upon all nations, yea, upon every one, yea, upon the proud, and lofty, and upon everyone who is lifted up; and he shall be brought low.

2:13 Yea, and the day of the Lord shall come upon all the cedars of Lebanon, for they are high and lifted up, and upon all the oaks of Bashan,

2:14 And upon all the high mountains, and upon all the hills, and upon all the nations which are lifted up,

2:15 And upon every people, and upon every high tower, and upon every fenced wall,

2:16 And upon all the ships of the sea, and upon all the ships of Tarshish, and upon all pleasant pictures.

12:11And it shall come to pass that the lofty looks of man shall be humbled, and the haughtiness of men shall be bowed down, and the Lord alone shall be exalted in that day.

12:12For the day of the Lord of Hosts soon cometh upon all nations, yea, upon every one; yea, upon the proud and lofty, and upon every one who is lifted up, and he shall be brought low.

12:13Yea, and the day of the Lord shall come upon all the cedars of Lebanon, for they are high and lifted up; and upon all the oaks of Bashan;

12:14and upon all the high mountains, and upon all the hills, and upon all the nations which are lifted up, and upon every people;

12:15and upon every high tower, and upon every fenced wall;

12:16and upon all the ships of the sea, and upon all the ships of Tarshish, and upon all pleasant pictures.

[17] And the loftiness of man shall be bowed down, and the haughtiness of men shall be made low: and the LORD alone shall be exalted in that day.

[18] And the idols he shall utterly abolish.

[19] And they shall go into the holes of the rocks, and into the caves of the earth, for fear of the LORD, and for the glory of his majesty, when he ariseth to shake terribly the earth.

[20] In that day a man shall cast his idols of silver, and his idols of gold, which they made each one for himself to worship, to the moles and to the bats;

[21] To go into the clefts of the rocks, and into the tops of the ragged rocks, for fear of the LORD, and for the glory of his majesty, when he ariseth to shake terribly the earth.

[22] Cease ye from man, whose breath is in his nostrils: for wherein is he to be accounted of?

2:17 And the loftiness of man shall be bowed down, and the haughtiness of men shall be made low; and the Lord alone shall be exalted in that day.

2:18 And the idols he shall utterly abolish.

2:19 And they shall go into the holes of the rocks and into the caves of the earth, for the fear of the Lord shall come upon them; and the glory of his majesty shall smite them when he ariseth to shake terribly the earth.

2:20 In that day a man shall cast his idols of silver and his idols of gold, which he hath made for himself to worship, to the moles and to the bats,

2:21 To go into the clefts of the rocks and into the tops of the ragged rocks; for the fear of the Lord shall come upon them, and the majesty of the Lord shall smite them when he ariseth to shake terribly the earth.

2:22 Cease ye from man, whose breath is in his nostrils. For wherein is he to be accounted of?

12:17 And the loftiness of man shall be bowed down, and the haughtiness of men shall be made low; and the Lord alone shall be exalted in that day.

12:18 And the idols he shall utterly abolish.

12:19 And they shall go into the holes of the rocks, and into the caves of the earth, for the fear of the Lord shall come upon them and the glory of his majesty shall smite them, when he ariseth to shake terribly the earth.

12:20 In that day a man shall cast his idols of silver, and his idols of gold, which he hath made for himself to worship, to the moles and to the bats;

12:21 to go into the clefts of the rocks, and into the tops of the ragged rocks, for the fear of the Lord shall come upon them and the majesty of his glory shall smite them, when he ariseth to shake terribly the earth.

12:22 Cease ye from man, whose breath is in his nostrils; for wherein is he to be accounted of?

3

[1] For, behold, the Lord, the LORD of hosts, doth take away from Jerusalem and from Judah the stay and the staff, the whole stay of bread, and the whole stay of water,

[2] The mighty man, and the man of war, the judge, and the prophet, and the prudent, and the ancient,

[3] The captain of fifty, and the honourable man, and the counseller, and the cunning artificer, and the eloquent orator.

[4] And I will give children to be their princes, and babes shall rule over them.

[5] And the people shall be oppressed, every one by another, and every one by his neighbour: the child shall behave himself proudly against the ancient, and the base against the honourable.

Chapter 3

3:1 For behold, the Lord, the Lord of hosts, doth take away from Jerusalem and from Judah the stay and the staff, the whole staff of bread, and the whole stay of water,

3:2 The mighty man, and the man of war, the judge, and the prophet, and the prudent, and the ancient,

3:3 The captain of fifty, and the honorable man, and the counselor, and the cunning artificer, and the eloquent orator.

3:4 And I will give children unto them to be their princes, and babes shall rule over them.

3:5 And the people shall be oppressed, everyone by another, and everyone by his neighbor; the child shall behave himself proudly against the ancient, and the base against the honorable.

13:1For behold, the Lord, the Lord of Hosts, doth take away from Jerusalem, and from Judah, the stay and the staff, the whole staff of bread, and the whole stay of water—

13:2the mighty man, and the man of war, the judge, and the prophet, and the prudent, and the ancient;

13:3the captain of fifty, and the honorable man, and the counselor, and the cunning artificer, and the eloquent orator.

13:4And I will give children unto them to be their princes, and babes shall rule over them.

13:5And the people shall be oppressed, every one by another, and every one by his neighbor; the child shall behave himself proudly against the ancient, and the base against the honorable.

[6] When a man shall take hold of his brother of the house of his father, saying, Thou hast clothing, be thou our ruler, and let this ruin be under thy hand:

[7] In that day shall he swear, saying, I will not be an healer; for in my house is neither bread nor clothing: make me not a ruler of the people.

[8] For Jerusalem is ruined, and Judah is fallen: because their tongue and their doings are against the LORD, to provoke the eyes of his glory.

[9] The shew of their countenance doth witness against them; and they declare their sin as Sodom, they hide it not. Woe unto their soul! for they have rewarded evil unto themselves.

[10] Say ye to the righteous, that it shall be well with him: for they shall eat the fruit of their doings.

[11] Woe unto the wicked! it shall be ill with him: for the reward of his hands shall be given him.

3:6 When a man shall take hold of his brother of the house of his father and shall say, Thou hast clothing; be thou our ruler, and let not this ruin come under thy hand,

3:7 In that day shall he swear, saying, I will not be a healer; for in my house there is neither bread nor clothing; make me not a ruler of the people.

3:8 For Jerusalem is ruined, and Judah is fallen because their tongues and their doings have been against the Lord, to provoke the eyes of his glory.

3:9 The show of their countenance doth witness against them and doth declare their sin to be even as Sodom; they cannot hide it. Woe unto their souls! For they have rewarded evil unto themselves.

3:10 Say unto the righteous that it is well with them; for they shall eat the fruit of their doings.

3:11 Woe unto the wicked! For they shall perish; for the reward of their hands shall be upon them.

13:6When a man shall take hold of his brother of the house of his father, and shall say: Thou hast clothing, be thou our ruler, and let not this ruin come under thy hand—

13:7in that day shall he swear, saying: I will not be a healer; for in my house there is neither bread nor clothing; make me not a ruler of the people.

13:8For Jerusalem is ruined, and Judah is fallen, because their tongues and their doings have been against the Lord, to provoke the eyes of his glory.

13:9The show of their countenance doth witness against them, and doth declare their sin to be even as Sodom, and they cannot hide it. Wo unto their souls, for they have rewarded evil unto themselves!

13:10Say unto the righteous that it is well with them; for they shall eat the fruit of their doings.

13:11Wo unto the wicked, for they shall perish; for the reward of their hands shall be upon them!

[12] As for my people, children are their oppressors, and women rule over them. O my people, they which lead thee cause thee to err, and destroy the way of thy paths.

[13] The LORD standeth up to plead, and standeth to judge the people.

[14] The LORD will enter into judgment with the ancients of his people, and the princes thereof: for ye have eaten up the vineyard; the spoil of the poor is in your houses.

[15] What mean ye that ye beat my people to pieces, and grind the faces of the poor? saith the LORD GOD of hosts.

[16] Moreover the LORD saith, Because the daughters of Zion are haughty, and walk with stretched forth necks and wanton eyes, walking and mincing as they go, and making a tinkling with their feet:

[17] Therefore the LORD will smite with a scab the crown of the head of the daughters of Zion, and the LORD will discover their secret parts.

3:12 And as for my people, children are their oppressors, and women rule over them. O my people, they who lead thee cause thee to err and destroy the way of thy paths.

3:13 The Lord standeth up to plead and standeth to judge the people.

3:14 The Lord will enter into judgment with the ancients of his people and the princes thereof; for ye have eaten up the vineyard, and the spoil of the poor is in your houses.

3:15 What mean ye? Ye beat my people to pieces and grind the faces of the poor, saith the Lord God of hosts.

3:16 Moreover, the Lord saith, Because the daughters of Zion are haughty and walk with stretched-forth necks and wanton eyes, walking and mincing as they go, and making a tinkling with their feet,

3:17 Therefore, the Lord will smite with a scab the crown of the head of the daughters of Zion; and the Lord will discover their secret parts.

13:12And my people, children are their oppressors, and women rule over them. O my people, they who lead thee cause thee to err and destroy the way of thy paths.

13:13The Lord standeth up to plead, and standeth to judge the people.

13:14The Lord will enter into judgment with the ancients of his people and the princes thereof; for ye have eaten up the vineyard and the spoil of the poor in your houses.

13:15What mean ye? Ye beat my people to pieces, and grind the faces of the poor, saith the Lord God of Hosts.

13:16Moreover, the Lord saith: Because the daughters of Zion are haughty, and walk with stretched-forth necks and wanton eyes, walking and mincing as they go, and making a tinkling with their feet—

13:17therefore the Lord will smite with a scab the crown of the head of the daughters of Zion, and the Lord will discover their secret parts.

[18] In that day the Lord will take away the bravery of their tinkling ornaments about their feet, and their cauls, and their round tires like the moon,

[19] The chains, and the bracelets, and the mufflers,

[20] The bonnets, and the ornaments of the legs, and the headbands, and the tablets, and the earrings,

[21] The rings, and nose jewels,

[22] The changeable suits of apparel, and the mantles, and the wimples, and the crisping pins,

[23] The glasses, and the fine linen, and the hoods, and the vails.

[24] And it shall come to pass, that instead of sweet smell there shall be stink; and instead of a girdle a rent; and instead of well set hair baldness; and instead of a stomacher a girding of sackcloth; and burning instead of beauty.

[25] Thy men shall fall by the sword, and thy mighty in the war.

3:18 In that day the Lord will take away the bravery of tinkling ornaments, and cauls, and round tires like the moon,

3:19 The chains, and the bracelets, and the mufflers,

3:20 The bonnets, and the ornaments of the legs, and the headbands, and the tablets, and the earrings,

3:21 The rings, and nose jewels,

3:22 The changeable suits of apparel, and the mantles, and the wimples, and the crisping pins,

3:23 The glasses, and the fine linen, and the hoods, and the veils.

3:24 And it shall come to pass, instead of sweet smell there shall be stink; and instead of a girdle, a rent; and instead of well-set hair, baldness; and instead of a stomacher, a girding of sackcloth; burning instead of beauty.

3:25 Thy men shall fall by the sword, and thy mighty in the war.

13:18In that day the Lord will take away the bravery of their tinkling ornaments, and cauls, and round tires like the moon;

13:19the chains and the bracelets, and the mufflers;

13:20the bonnets, and the ornaments of the legs, and the headbands, and the tablets, and the ear-rings;

13:21the rings, and nose jewels;

13:22the changeable suits of apparel, and the mantles, and the wimples, and the crisping-pins;

13:23the glasses, and the fine linen, and hoods, and the veils.

13:24And it shall come to pass, instead of sweet smell there shall be stink; and instead of a girdle, a rent; and instead of well set hair, baldness; and instead of a stomacher, a girding of sackcloth; burning instead of beauty.

13:25Thy men shall fall by the sword and thy mighty in the war.

[26] And her gates shall lament and mourn; and she being desolate shall sit upon the ground.

4

[1] And in that day seven women shall take hold of one man, saying, We will eat our own bread, and wear our own apparel: only let us be called by thy name, to take away our reproach.

[2] In that day shall the branch of the LORD be beautiful and glorious, and the fruit of the earth shall be excellent and comely for them that are escaped of Israel.

[3] And it shall come to pass, that he that is left in Zion, and he that remaineth in Jerusalem, shall be called holy, even every one that is written among the living in Jerusalem:

3:26 And her gates shall lament and mourn; and she shall be desolate and shall sit upon the ground.

3:27 And in that day seven women shall take hold of one man, saying, We will eat our own bread and wear our own apparel; only let us be called by thy name, to take away our reproach.

Chapter 4

4:1 In that day shall the branch of the Lord be beautiful and glorious, and the fruit of the earth shall be excellent and comely to them that are escaped of Israel.

4:2 And it shall come to pass, they that are left in Zion and he that remaineth in Jerusalem shall be called holy, even everyone that is written among the living in Jerusalem,

13:26And her gates shall lament and mourn; and she shall be desolate, and shall sit upon the ground.

(Chapter 14)

14:1And in that day, seven women shall take hold of one man, saying: We will eat our own bread, and wear our own apparel; only let us be called by thy name to take away our reproach.

14:2In that day shall the branch of the Lord be beautiful and glorious; the fruit of the earth excellent and comely to them that are escaped of Israel.

14:3And it shall come to pass, they that are left in Zion and remain in Jerusalem shall be called holy, every one that is written among the living in Jerusalem—

[4] When the Lord shall have washed away the filth of the daughters of Zion, and shall have purged the blood of Jerusalem from the midst thereof by the spirit of judgment, and by the spirit of burning.

[5] And the LORD will create upon every dwelling place of mount Zion, and upon her assemblies, a cloud and smoke by day, and the shining of a flaming fire by night: for upon all the glory shall be a defence.

[6] And there shall be a tabernacle for a shadow in the daytime from the heat, and for a place of refuge, and for a covert from storm and from rain.

5

[1] Now will I sing to my wellbeloved a song of my beloved touching his vineyard. My wellbeloved hath a vineyard in a very fruitful hill:

4:3 When the Lord shall have washed away the filth of the daughters of Zion and shall have purged the blood of Jerusalem from the midst thereof by the spirit of judgment and by the spirit of burning.

4:4 And the Lord will create upon every dwelling place of Mount Zion and upon her assemblies, a cloud and smoke by day and the shining of a flaming fire by night; for upon all the glory of Zion shall be a defense.

4:5 And there shall be a tabernacle for a shadow in the daytime from the heat, and for a place of refuge, and for a covert from storm and from rain.

Chapter 5

5:1 And then will I sing to my well-beloved a song of my beloved touching his vineyard. My well-beloved hath a vineyard in a very fruitful hill;

^{14:4}when the Lord shall have washed away the filth of the daughters of Zion, and shall have purged the blood of Jerusalem from the midst thereof by the spirit of judgment and by the spirit of burning.

^{14:5}And the Lord will create upon every dwelling-place of mount Zion, and upon her assemblies, a cloud and smoke by day and the shining of a flaming fire by night; for upon all the glory of Zion shall be a defence.

^{14:6}And there shall be a tabernacle for a shadow in the daytime from the heat, and for a place of refuge, and a covert from storm and from rain.

^{15:1}And then will I sing to my well-beloved a song of my beloved, touching his vineyard. My well-beloved hath a vineyard in a very fruitful hill.

[2] And he fenced it, and gathered out the stones thereof, and planted it with the choicest vine, and built a tower in the midst of it, and also made a winepress therein: and he looked that it should bring forth grapes, and it brought forth wild grapes.

[3] And now, O inhabitants of Jerusalem, and men of Judah, judge, I pray you, betwixt me and my vineyard.

[4] What could have been done more to my vineyard, that I have not done in it? wherefore, when I looked that it should bring forth grapes, brought it forth wild grapes?

[5] And now go to; I will tell you what I will do to my vineyard: I will take away the hedge thereof, and it shall be eaten up; and break down the wall thereof, and it shall be trodden down:

[6] And I will lay it waste: it shall not be pruned, nor digged; but there shall come up briers and thorns: I will also command the clouds that they rain no rain upon it.

5:2 And he fenced it, and gathered out the stones thereof, and planted it with the choicest vine, and built a tower in the midst of it, and also made a winepress therein; and he looked that it should bring forth grapes, and it brought forth wild grapes.

5:3 And now, O inhabitants of Jerusalem and men of Judah, judge, I pray you, betwixt me and my vineyard.

5:4 What could have been done more to my vineyard that I have not done in it? Wherefore, when I looked that it should bring forth grapes, it brought forth wild grapes.

5:5 And now go to; I will tell you what I will do to my vineyard; I will take away the hedge thereof, and it shall be eaten up; and I will break down the wall thereof, and it shall be trodden down;

5:6 And I will lay it waste; it shall not be pruned nor digged; but there shall come up briers and thorns. I will also command the clouds that they rain no rain upon it.

15:2And he fenced it, and gathered out the stones thereof, and planted it with the choicest vine, and built a tower in the midst of it, and also made a wine-press therein; and he looked that it should bring forth grapes, and it brought forth wild grapes.

15:3And now, O inhabitants of Jerusalem, and men of Judah, judge, I pray you, betwixt me and my vineyard.

15:4What could have been done more to my vineyard that I have not done in it? Wherefore, when I looked that it should bring forth grapes it brought forth wild grapes.

15:5And now go to; I will tell you what I will do to my vineyard—I will take away the hedge thereof, and it shall be eaten up; and I will break down the wall thereof, and it shall be trodden down;

15:6and I will lay it waste; it shall not be pruned nor digged; but there shall come up briers and thorns; I will also command the clouds that they rain no rain upon it.

[7] For the vineyard of the LORD of hosts is the house of Israel, and the men of Judah his pleasant plant: and he looked for judgment, but behold oppression; for righteousness, but behold a cry.

[8] Woe unto them that join house to house, that lay field to field, till there be no place, that they may be placed alone in the midst of the earth!

[9] In mine ears said the LORD of hosts, Of a truth many houses shall be desolate, even great and fair, without inhabitant.

[10] Yea, ten acres of vineyard shall yield one bath, and the seed of an homer shall yield an ephah.

[11] Woe unto them that rise up early in the morning, that they may follow strong drink; that continue until night, till wine inflame them!

[12] And the harp, and the viol, the tabret, and pipe, and wine, are in their feasts: but they regard not the work of the LORD, neither consider the operation of his hands.

5:7 For the vineyard of the Lord of hosts is the house of Israel, and the men of Judah his pleasant plant; and he looked for judgment, but behold oppression; for righteousness, but behold a cry.

5:8 Woe unto them that join house to house, that lay field to field till there can be no place, that they may be placed alone in the midst of the earth!

5:9 In mine ears said the Lord of hosts, Of a truth many houses shall be desolate, and great and fair cities without inhabitant.

5:10 Yea, ten acres of vineyard shall yield one bath, and the seed of a homer shall yield an ephah.

5:11 Woe unto them that rise up early in the morning, that they may follow strong drink, that continue until night, and wine inflame them!

5:12 And the harp and the viol, the tabret and pipe, and wine are in their feasts; but they regard not the work of the Lord, neither consider the operation of his hands.

15:7For the vineyard of the Lord of Hosts is the house of Israel, and the men of Judah his pleasant plant; and he looked for judgment, and behold, oppression; for righteousness, but behold, a cry.

15:8Wo unto them that join house to house, till there can be no place, that they may be placed alone in the midst of the earth!

15:9In mine ears, said the Lord of Hosts, of a truth many houses shall be desolate, and great and fair cities without inhabitant.

15:10Yea, ten acres of vineyard shall yield one bath, and the seed of a homer shall yield an ephah.

15:11Wo unto them that rise up early in the morning, that they may follow strong drink, that continue until night, and wine inflame them!

15:12And the harp, and the viol, the tabret, and pipe, and wine are in their feasts; but they regard not the work of the Lord, neither consider the operation of his hands.

[13] Therefore my people are gone into captivity, because they have no knowledge: and their honourable men are famished, and their multitude dried up with thirst.

[14] Therefore hell hath enlarged herself, and opened her mouth without measure: and their glory, and their multitude, and their pomp, and he that rejoiceth, shall descend into it.

[15] And the mean man shall be brought down, and the mighty man shall be humbled, and the eyes of the lofty shall be humbled:

[16] But the LORD of hosts shall be exalted in judgment, and God that is holy shall be sanctified in righteousness.

[17] Then shall the lambs feed after their manner, and the waste places of the fat ones shall strangers eat.

[18] Woe unto them that draw iniquity with cords of vanity, and sin as it were with a cart rope:

5:13 Therefore, my people are gone into captivity because they have no knowledge; and their honorable men are famished, and their multitude dried up with thirst.

5:14 Therefore, hell hath enlarged herself and opened her mouth without measure; and their glory, and their multitude, and their pomp, and he that rejoiceth shall descend into it.

5:15 And the mean man shall be brought down; and the mighty man shall be humbled; and the eyes of the lofty shall be humbled;

5:16 But the Lord of hosts shall be exalted in judgment, and God that is holy shall be sanctified in righteousness.

5:17 Then shall the lambs feed after their manner, and the waste places of the fat ones shall strangers eat.

5:18 Woe unto them that draw iniquity with cords of vanity, and sin as it were with a cart rope,

15:13Therefore, my people are gone into captivity, because they have no knowledge; and their honorable men are famished, and their multitude dried up with thirst.

15:14Therefore, hell hath enlarged herself, and opened her mouth without measure; and their glory, and their multitude, and their pomp, and he that rejoiceth, shall descend into it.

15:15And the mean man shall be brought down, and the mighty man shall be humbled, and the eyes of the lofty shall be humbled.

15:16But the Lord of Hosts shall be exalted in judgment, and God that is holy shall be sanctified in righteousness.

15:17Then shall the lambs feed after their manner, and the waste places of the fat ones shall strangers eat.

15:18Wo unto them that draw iniquity with cords of vanity, and sin as it were with a cart rope;

[19] That say, Let him make speed, and hasten his work, that we may see it: and let the counsel of the Holy One of Israel draw nigh and come, that we may know it!

[20] Woe unto them that call evil good, and good evil; that put darkness for light, and light for darkness; that put bitter for sweet, and sweet for bitter!

[21] Woe unto them that are wise in their own eyes, and prudent in their own sight!

[22] Woe unto them that are mighty to drink wine, and men of strength to mingle strong drink:

[23] Which justify the wicked for reward, and take away the righteousness of the righteous from him!

[24] Therefore as the fire devoureth the stubble, and the flame consumeth the chaff, so their root shall be as rottenness, and their blossom shall go up as dust: because they have cast away the law of the LORD of hosts, and despised the word of the Holy One of Israel.

5:19 That say, Let him make speed and hasten his work, that we may see it; and let the counsel of the Holy One of Israel draw nigh and come, that we may know it!

5:20 Woe unto them that call evil good, and good evil; that put darkness for light, and light for darkness; that put bitter for sweet, and sweet for bitter!

5:21 Woe unto the wise in their own eyes, and prudent in their own sight!

5:22 Woe unto the mighty to drink wine, and men of strength to mingle strong drink,

5:23 Which justify the wicked for reward and take away the righteousness of the righteous from him!

5:24 Therefore, as the fire devoureth the stubble and the flame consumeth the chaff, so their root shall be as rottenness, and their blossom shall go up as dust because they have cast away the law of the Lord of hosts and despised the word of the Holy One of Israel.

15:19that say: Let him make speed, hasten his work, that we may see it; and let the counsel of the Holy One of Israel draw nigh and come, that we may know it.

15:20Wo unto them that call evil good, and good evil, that put darkness for light, and light for darkness, that put bitter for sweet, and sweet for bitter!

15:21Wo unto the wise in their own eyes and prudent in their own sight!

15:22Wo unto the mighty to drink wine, and men of strength to mingle strong drink;

15:23who justify the wicked for reward, and take away the righteousness of the righteous from him!

15:24Therefore, as the fire devoureth the stubble, and the flame consumeth the chaff, their root shall be rottenness, and their blossoms shall go up as dust; because they have cast away the law of the Lord of Hosts, and despised the word of the Holy One of Israel.

[25] Therefore is the anger of the LORD kindled against his people, and he hath stretched forth his hand against them, and hath smitten them: and the hills did tremble, and their carcases were torn in the midst of the streets. For all this his anger is not turned away, but his hand is stretched out still.

[26] And he will lift up an ensign to the nations from far, and will hiss unto them from the end of the earth: and, behold, they shall come with speed swiftly:

[27] None shall be weary nor stumble among them; none shall slumber nor sleep; neither shall the girdle of their loins be loosed, nor the latchet of their shoes be broken:

[28] Whose arrows are sharp, and all their bows bent, their horses' hoofs shall be counted like flint, and their wheels like a whirlwind:

29 Their roaring shall be like a lion, they shall roar like young lions: yea, they shall roar, and lay hold of the prey, and shall carry it away safe, and none shall deliver it.

5:25 Therefore is the anger of the Lord kindled against his people, and he hath stretched forth his hand against them and hath smitten them; and the hills did tremble, and their carcasses were torn in the midst of the streets. For all this, his anger is not turned away, but his hand is stretched out still.

5:26 And he will lift up an ensign to the nations from far and will hiss unto them from the end of the earth; and behold, they shall come with speed swiftly;

5:27 None shall be weary nor stumble among them; none shall slumber nor sleep; neither shall the girdle of their loins be loosed nor the latchet of their shoes be broken,

5:28 Whose arrows shall be sharp, and all their bows bent, and their horses' hooves shall be counted like flint, and their wheels like a whirlwind; their roaring shall be like a lion.

5:29 They shall roar like young lions; yea, they shall roar, and lay hold of the prey, and shall carry away safe, and none shall deliver.

15:25Therefore, is the anger of the Lord kindled against his people, and he hath stretched forth his hand against them, and hath smitten them; and the hills did tremble, and their carcasses were torn in the midst of the streets. For all this his anger is not turned away, but his hand is stretched out still.

15:26And he will lift up an ensign to the nations from far, and will hiss unto them from the end of the earth; and behold, they shall come with speed swiftly; none shall be weary nor stumble among them.

15:27None shall slumber nor sleep; neither shall the girdle of their loins be loosed, nor the latchet of their shoes be broken;

15:28whose arrows shall be sharp, and all their bows bent, and their horses' hoofs shall be counted like flint, and their wheels like a whirlwind, their roaring like a lion.

15:29They shall roar like young lions; yea, they shall roar, and lay hold of the prey, and shall carry away safe, and none shall deliver.

[30] And in that day they shall roar against them like the roaring of the sea: and if one look unto the land, behold darkness and sorrow, and the light is darkened in the heavens thereof.

6

[1] In the year that king Uzziah died I saw also the Lord sitting upon a throne, high and lifted up, and his train filled the temple.

[2] Above it stood the seraphims: each one had six wings; with twain he covered his face, and with twain he covered his feet, and with twain he did fly.

[3] And one cried unto another, and said, Holy, holy, holy, is the LORD of hosts: the whole earth is full of his glory.

[4] And the posts of the door moved at the voice of him that cried, and the house was filled with smoke.

[5] Then said I, Woe is me! for I am undone; because I am a man of unclean lips, and I dwell in the midst of a people of unclean lips: for mine eyes have seen the King, the LORD of hosts.

5:30 And in that day they shall roar against them like the roaring of the sea; and if they look unto the land, behold darkness and sorrow; and the light is darkened in the heavens thereof.

Chapter 6

6:1 In the year that king Uzziah died, I saw also the Lord sitting upon a throne, high and lifted up; and his train filled the temple.

6:2 Above it stood the seraphim; each one had six wings; with twain he covered his face, and with twain he covered his feet, and with twain he did fly.

6:3 And one cried unto another and said, Holy, holy, holy is the Lord of hosts; the whole earth is full of his glory.

6:4 And the posts of the door moved at the voice of him that cried, and the house was filled with smoke.

6:5 Then said I, Woe is me! For I am undone because I am a man of unclean lips, and I dwell in the midst of a people of unclean lips; for mine eyes have seen the King, the Lord of hosts.

15:30And in that day they shall roar against them like the roaring of the sea; and if they look unto the land, behold, darkness and sorrow, and the light is darkened in the heavens thereof.

<IX>

16:1In the year that king Uzziah died, I saw also the Lord sitting upon a throne, high and lifted up, and his train filled the temple.

16:2Above it stood the seraphim; each one had six wings; with twain he covered his face, and with twain he covered his feet, and with twain he did fly.

16:3And one cried unto another, and said: Holy, holy, holy, is the Lord of Hosts; the whole earth is full of his glory.

16:4And the posts of the door moved at the voice of him that cried, and the house was filled with smoke.

16:5Then said I: Wo is unto me! for I am undone; because I am a man of unclean lips; and I dwell in the midst of a people of unclean lips; for mine eyes have seen the King, the Lord of Hosts.

[6] Then flew one of the seraphims unto me, having a live coal in his hand, which he had taken with the tongs from off the altar:

[7] And he laid it upon my mouth, and said, Lo, this hath touched thy lips; and thine iniquity is taken away, and thy sin purged.

[8] Also I heard the voice of the Lord, saying, Whom shall I send, and who will go for us? Then said I, Here am I; send me.

[9] And he said, Go, and tell this people, Hear ye indeed, but understand not; and see ye indeed, but perceive not.

[10] Make the heart of this people fat, and make their ears heavy, and shut their eyes; lest they see with their eyes, and hear with their ears, and understand with their heart, and convert, and be healed.

6:6 Then flew one of the seraphim unto me, having a live coal in his hand, which he had taken with the tongs from off the altar;

6:7 And he laid it upon my mouth and said, Lo, this has touched thy lips; and thine iniquity is taken away, and thy sin purged.

6:8 Also, I heard the voice of the Lord, saying, Whom shall I send, and who will go for us? Then said I, Here am I; send me.

6:9 And he said, Go, and tell this people, Hear ye indeed, but they understood not; and see ye indeed, but they perceived not.

6:10 Make the heart of this people fat, and make their ears heavy, and shut their eyes, lest they see with their eyes, and hear with their ears, and understand with their hearts, and convert, and be healed.

16:6Then flew one of the seraphim unto me, having a live coal in his hand, which he had taken with the tongs from off the altar;

16:7and he laid it upon my mouth, and said: Lo, this has touched thy lips; and thine iniquity is taken away, and thy sin purged.

16:8Also I heard the voice of the Lord, saying: Whom shall I send, and who will go for us? Then I said: Here am I; send me.

16:9And he said: Go and tell this people— Hear ye indeed, but they understood not; and see ye indeed, but they perceived not.

16:10Make the heart of this people fat, and make their ears heavy, and shut their eyes—lest they see with their eyes, and hear with their ears, and understand with their heart, and be converted and be healed.

[11] Then said I, Lord, how long? And he answered, Until the cities be wasted without inhabitant, and the houses without man, and the land be utterly desolate,	6:11 Then said I, Lord, how long? And he said, Until the cities be wasted without inhabitant, and the houses without man, and the land be utterly desolate,	16:11Then said I: Lord, how long? And he said: Until the cities be wasted without inhabitant, and the houses without man, and the land be utterly desolate;
[12] And the LORD have removed men far away, and there be a great forsaking in the midst of the land.	6:12 And the Lord have removed men far away; for there shall be a great forsaking in the midst of the land.	16:12and the Lord have removed men far away, for there shall be a great forsaking in the midst of the land.
[13] But yet in it shall be a tenth, and it shall return, and shall be eaten: as a teil tree, and as an oak, whose substance is in them, when they cast their leaves: so the holy seed shall be the substance thereof.	6:13 But yet in it there shall be a tenth, and they shall return and shall be eaten-- as a teil tree and as an oak, whose substance is in them when they cast their leaves, so the holy seed shall be the substance thereof.	16:13But yet there shall be a tenth, and they shall return, and shall be eaten, as a teil-tree, and as an oak whose substance is in them when they cast their leaves; so the holy seed shall be the substance thereof.
7	Chapter 7	
[1] And it came to pass in the days of Ahaz the son of Jotham, the son of Uzziah, king of Judah, that Rezin the king of Syria, and Pekah the son of Remaliah, king of Israel, went up toward Jerusalem to war against it, but could not prevail against it.	7:1 And it came to pass in the days of Ahaz, the son of Jotham, the son of Uzziah, king of Judah, that Rezin, the king of Syria, and Pekah, the son of Remaliah, king of Israel, went up toward Jerusalem to war against it but could not prevail against it.	17:1And it came to pass in the days of Ahaz the son of Jotham, the son of Uzziah, king of Judah, that Rezin, king of Syria, and Pekah the son of Remaliah, king of Israel, went up toward Jerusalem to war against it, but could not prevail against it.

[2] And it was told the house of David, saying, Syria is confederate with Ephraim. And his heart was moved, and the heart of his people, as the trees of the wood are moved with the wind.

[3] Then said the LORD unto Isaiah, Go forth now to meet Ahaz, thou, and Shear-jashub thy son, at the end of the conduit of the upper pool in the highway of the fuller's field;

[4] And say unto him, Take heed, and be quiet; fear not, neither be fainthearted for the two tails of these smoking firebrands, for the fierce anger of Rezin with Syria, and of the son of Remaliah.

[5] Because Syria, Ephraim, and the son of Remaliah, have taken evil counsel against thee, saying,
[
6] Let us go up against Judah, and vex it, and let us make a breach therein for us, and set a king in the midst of it, even the son of Tabeal:

[7] Thus saith the Lord GOD, It shall not stand, neither shall it come to pass.

7:2 And it was told the house of David, saying, Syria is confederate with Ephraim. And his heart was moved and the heart of his people, as the trees of the wood are moved with the wind.

7:3 Then said the Lord unto Isaiah, Go forth now to meet Ahaz, thou and Shear-jashub, thy son, at the end of the conduit of the upper pool, in the highway of the fuller's field,

7:4 And say unto him, Take heed, and be quiet; fear not; neither be faint-hearted for the two tails of these smoking firebrands, for the fierce anger of Rezin with Syria and of the son of Remaliah.

7:5 Because Syria, Ephraim, and the son of Remaliah have taken evil counsel against thee, saying,

7:6 Let us go up against Judah and vex it, and let us make a breach therein for us and set a king in the midst of it, yea, even the son of Tabeal,

7:7 Thus saith the Lord God, It shall not stand; neither shall it come to pass.

17:2And it was told the house of David, saying: Syria is confederate with Ephraim. And his heart was moved, and the heart of his people, as the trees of the wood are moved with the wind.

17:3Then said the Lord unto Isaiah: Go forth now to meet Ahaz, thou and Shearjashub thy son, at the end of the conduit of the upper pool in the highway of the fuller's field;

17:4and say unto him: Take heed, and be quiet; fear not, neither be faint-hearted for the two tails of these smoking firebrands, for the fierce anger of Rezin with Syria, and of the son of Remaliah.

17:5Because Syria, Ephraim, and the son of Remaliah, have taken evil counsel against thee, saying:

17:6Let us go up against Judah and vex it, and let us make a breach therein for us, and set a king in the midst of it, yea, the son of Tabeal.

17:7Thus saith the Lord God: It shall not stand, neither shall it come to pass.

[8] For the head of Syria is Damascus, and the head of Damascus is Rezin; and within threescore and five years shall Ephraim be broken, that it be not a people.	7:8 For the head of Syria is Damascus, and the head of Damascus is Rezin; and within threescore and five years shall Ephraim be broken, that it be not a people.	17:8For the head of Syria is Damascus, and the head of Damascus, Rezin; and within three score and five years shall Ephraim be broken that it be not a people.
[9] And the head of Ephraim is Samaria, and the head of Samaria is Remaliah's son. If ye will not believe, surely ye shall not be established.	7:9 And the head of Ephraim is Samaria, and the head of Samaria is Remaliah's son. If ye will not believe, surely ye shall not be established.	17:9And the head of Ephraim is Samaria, and the head of Samaria is Remaliah's son. If ye will not believe surely ye shall not be established.
[10] Moreover the LORD spake again unto Ahaz, saying,	7:10 Moreover, the Lord spake again unto Ahaz, saying,	17:10Moreover, the Lord spake again unto Ahaz, saying:
[11] Ask thee a sign of the LORD thy God; ask it either in the depth, or in the height above.	7:11 Ask thee a sign of the Lord, thy God; ask it either in the depth or in the height above.	17:11Ask thee a sign of the Lord thy God; ask it either in the depths, or in the heights above.
[12] But Ahaz said, I will not ask, neither will I tempt the LORD.	7:12 But Ahaz said, I will not ask; neither will I tempt the Lord.	17:12But Ahaz said: I will not ask, neither will I tempt the Lord.
[13] And he said, Hear ye now, O house of David; Is it a small thing for you to weary men, but will ye weary my God also?	7:13 And he said, Hear ye now, O house of David. Is it a small thing for you to weary men, but will ye weary my God also?	17:13And he said: Hear ye now, O house of David; is it a small thing for you to weary men, but will ye weary my God also?
[14] Therefore the Lord himself shall give you a sign; Behold, a virgin shall conceive, and bear a son, and shall call his name Immanuel.	7:14 Therefore, the Lord himself shall give you a sign: Behold, a virgin shall conceive, and shall bear a son, and shall call his name Immanuel.	17:14Therefore, the Lord himself shall give you a sign—Behold, a virgin shall conceive, and shall bear a son, and shall call his name Immanuel.

[15] Butter and honey shall he eat, that he may know to refuse the evil, and choose the good.

[16] For before the child shall know to refuse the evil, and choose the good, the land that thou abhorrest shall be forsaken of both her kings.

[17] The LORD shall bring upon thee, and upon thy people, and upon thy father's house, days that have not come, from the day that Ephraim departed from Judah; even the king of Assyria.

[18] And it shall come to pass in that day, that the LORD shall hiss for the fly that is in the uttermost part of the rivers of Egypt, and for the bee that is in the land of Assyria.

[19] And they shall come, and shall rest all of them in the desolate valleys, and in the holes of the rocks, and upon all thorns, and upon all bushes.

[20] In the same day shall the Lord shave with a rasor that is hired, namely, by them beyond the river, by the king of Assyria, the head, and the hair of the feet: and it shall also consume the beard.

7:15 Butter and honey shall he eat, that he may know to refuse the evil and to choose the good.

7:16 For before the child shall know to refuse the evil and choose the good, the land that thou abhorrest shall be forsaken of both her kings.

7:17 The Lord shall bring upon thee, and upon thy people, and upon thy father's house days that have not come, from the day that Ephraim departed from Judah-- even the king of Assyria.

7:18 And it shall come to pass in that day, that the Lord shall hiss for the fly that is in the uttermost part of Egypt and for the bee that is in the land of Assyria.

7:19 And they shall come and shall rest, all of them in the desolate valleys, and in the holes of the rocks, and upon all thorns, and upon all bushes.

7:20 In the same day shall the Lord shave with a razor that is hired, namely, by them beyond the river, by the king of Assyria, the head and the hair of the feet; and it shall also consume the beard.

17:15 Butter and honey shall he eat, that he may know to refuse the evil and to choose the good.

17:16 For before the child shall know to refuse the evil and choose the good, the land that thou abhorrest shall be forsaken of both her kings.

17:17 The Lord shall bring upon thee, and upon thy people, and upon thy father's house, days that have not come from the day that Ephraim departed from Judah, the king of Assyria.

17:18 And it shall come to pass in that day that the Lord shall hiss for the fly that is in the uttermost part of Egypt, and for the bee that is in the land of Assyria.

17:19 And they shall come, and shall rest all of them in the desolate valleys, and in the holes of the rocks, and upon all thorns, and upon all bushes.

17:20 In the same day shall the Lord shave with a razor that is hired, by them beyond the river, by the king of Assyria, the head, and the hair of the feet; and it shall also consume the beard.

[21] And it shall come to pass in that day, that a man shall nourish a young cow, and two sheep;

[22] And it shall come to pass, for the abundance of milk that they shall give he shall eat butter: for butter and honey shall every one eat that is left in the land.

[23] And it shall come to pass in that day, that every place shall be, where there were a thousand vines at a thousand silverlings, it shall even be for briers and thorns.

[24] With arrows and with bows shall men come thither; because all the land shall become briers and thorns.

[25] And on all hills that shall be digged with the mattock, there shall not come thither the fear of briers and thorns: but it shall be for the sending forth of oxen, and for the treading of lesser cattle.

8
[1] Moreover the LORD said unto me, Take thee a great roll, and write in it with a man's pen concerning Maher-shalal-hash-baz.

7:21 And it shall come to pass in that day that a man shall nourish a young cow and two sheep.

7:22 And it shall come to pass, for the abundance of milk that they shall give, he shall eat butter; for butter and honey shall everyone eat that is left in the land.

7:23 And it shall come to pass in that day, that every place shall be, where there were a thousand vines at a thousand silverlings, which shall even be for briers and thorns.

7:24 With arrows and with bows shall men come thither because all the land shall become briers and thorns.

7:25 And on all hills that shall be digged with the mattock, there shall not come thither the fear of briers and thorns; but it shall be for the sending forth of oxen and for the treading of lesser cattle.

Chapter 8
8:1 Moreover, the word of the Lord said unto me, Take thee a great roll, and write in it with a man's pen concerning Maher-shalal-hash-baz.

17:21And it shall come to pass in that day, a man shall nourish a young cow and two sheep;

17:22and it shall come to pass, for the abundance of milk they shall give he shall eat butter; for butter and honey shall every one eat that is left in the land.

17:23And it shall come to pass in that day, every place shall be, where there were a thousand vines at a thousand silverlings, which shall be for briers and thorns.

17:24With arrows and with bows shall men come thither, because all the land shall become briers and thorns.

17:25And all hills that shall be digged with the mattock, there shall not come thither the fear of briers and thorns; but it shall be for the sending forth of oxen, and the treading of lesser cattle.

18:1Moreover, the word of the Lord said unto me: Take thee a great roll, and write in it with a man's pen, concerning Maher-shalal-hash-baz.

[2] And I took unto me faithful witnesses to record, Uriah the priest, and Zechariah the son of Jeberechiah.

[3] And I went unto the prophetess; and she conceived, and bare a son. Then said the LORD to me, Call his name Maher-shalal-hash-baz.

[4] For before the child shall have knowledge to cry, My father, and my mother, the riches of Damascus and the spoil of Samaria shall be taken away before the king of Assyria.

[5] The LORD spake also unto me again, saying,

[6] Forasmuch as this people refuseth the waters of Shiloah that go softly, and rejoice in Rezin and Remaliah's son;

[7] Now therefore, behold, the Lord bringeth up upon them the waters of the river, strong and many, even the king of Assyria, and all his glory: and he shall come up over all his channels, and go over all his banks:

8:2 And I took unto me faithful witnesses to record, Uriah, the priest, and Zechariah, the son of Jeberechiah.

8:3 And I went unto the prophetess; and she conceived and bare a son. Then said the Lord to me, Call his name Maher-shalal-hash-baz.

8:4 For behold, the child shall not have knowledge to cry, My father and my mother, before the riches of Damascus and the spoil of Samaria shall be taken away before the king of Assyria.

8:5 The Lord spake also unto me again, saying,

8:6 Forasmuch as this people refuseth the waters of Shiloah that go softly and rejoice in Rezin and Remaliah's son,

8:7 Now, therefore, behold, the Lord bringeth up upon them the waters of the river, strong and many, even the king of Assyria and all his glory; and he shall come up over all his channels and go over all his banks;

18:2And I took unto me faithful witnesses to record, Uriah the priest, and Zechariah the son of Jeberechiah.

18:3And I went unto the prophetess; and she conceived and bare a son. Then said the Lord to me: Call his name, Maher-shalal-hash-baz.

18:4For behold, the child shall not have knowledge to cry, My father, and my mother, before the riches of Damascus and the spoil of Samaria shall be taken away before the king of Assyria.

18:5The Lord spake also unto me again, saying:

18:6Forasmuch as this people refuseth the waters of Shiloah that go softly, and rejoice in Rezin and Remaliah's son;

18:7now therefore, behold, the Lord bringeth up upon them the waters of the river, strong and many, even the king of Assyria and all his glory; and he shall come up over all his channels, and go over all his banks.

[8] And he shall pass through Judah; he shall overflow and go over, he shall reach even to the neck; and the stretching out of his wings shall fill the breadth of thy land, O Immanuel.

[9] Associate yourselves, O ye people, and ye shall be broken in pieces; and give ear, all ye of far countries: gird yourselves, and ye shall be broken in pieces; gird yourselves, and ye shall be broken in pieces.

[10] Take counsel together, and it shall come to nought; speak the word, and it shall not stand: for God is with us.

[11] For the LORD spake thus to me with a strong hand, and instructed me that I should not walk in the way of this people, saying,

[12] Say ye not, A confederacy, to all them to whom this people shall say, A confederacy; neither fear ye their fear, nor be afraid.

[13] Sanctify the LORD of hosts himself; and let him be your fear, and let him be your dread.

8:8 And he shall pass through Judah; he shall overflow and go over; he shall reach even to the neck; and the stretching out of his wings shall fill the breadth of thy land, O Immanuel.

8:9 Associate yourselves, O ye people, and ye shall be broken in pieces; and give ear, all ye of far countries; gird yourselves, and ye shall be broken in pieces; gird yourselves, and ye shall be broken in pieces.

8:10 Take counsel together, and it shall come to naught; speak the word, and it shall not stand; for God is with us.

8:11 For the Lord spake thus to me with a strong hand and instructed me that I should not walk in the way of this people, saying,

8:12 Say ye not, A confederacy, to all them to whom this people shall say, A confederacy; neither fear ye their fear nor be afraid.

8:13 Sanctify the Lord of hosts himself; and let him be your fear, and let him be your dread.

18:8And he shall pass through Judah; he shall overflow and go over, he shall reach even to the neck; and the stretching out of his wings shall fill the breadth of thy land, O Immanuel.

18:9Associate yourselves, O ye people, and ye shall be broken in pieces; and give ear all ye of far countries; gird yourselves, and ye shall be broken in pieces; gird yourselves, and ye shall be broken in pieces.

18:10Take counsel together, and it shall come to naught; speak the word, and it shall not stand; for God is with us.

18:11For the Lord spake thus to me with a strong hand, and instructed me that I should not walk in the way of this people, saying:

18:12Say ye not, A confederacy, to all to whom this people shall say, A confederacy; neither fear ye their fear, nor be afraid.

18:13Sanctify the Lord of Hosts himself, and let him be your fear, and let him be your dread.

[14] And he shall be for a sanctuary; but for a stone of stumbling and for a rock of offence to both the houses of Israel, for a gin and for a snare to the inhabitants of Jerusalem.

[15] And many among them shall stumble, and fall, and be broken, and be snared, and be taken.

[16] Bind up the testimony, seal the law among my disciples.

[17] And I will wait upon the LORD, that hideth his face from the house of Jacob, and I will look for him.

[18] Behold, I and the children whom the LORD hath given me are for signs and for wonders in Israel from the LORD of hosts, which dwelleth in mount Zion.

[19] And when they shall say unto you, Seek unto them that have familiar spirits, and unto wizards that peep, and that mutter: should not a people seek unto their God? for the living to the dead?

8:14 And he shall be for a sanctuary--but for a stone of stumbling and for a rock of offense to both the houses of Israel, for a gin and for a snare to the inhabitants of Jerusalem.

8:15 And many among them shall stumble, and fall, and be broken, and be snared, and be taken.

8:16 Bind up the testimony; seal the law among my disciples.

8:17 And I will wait upon the Lord, that hideth his face from the house of Jacob; and I will look for him.

8:18 Behold, I and the children whom the Lord hath given me are for signs and for wonders in Israel from the Lord of hosts, which dwelleth in Mount Zion.

8:19 And when they shall say unto you, Seek unto them that have familiar spirits and unto wizards that peep and that mutter, should not a people seek unto their God? For the living to hear from the dead?

18:14 And he shall be for a sanctuary; but for a stone of stumbling, and for a rock of offense to both the houses of Israel, for a gin and a snare to the inhabitants of Jerusalem.

18:15 And many among them shall stumble and fall, and be broken, and be snared, and be taken.

18:16 Bind up the testimony, seal the law among my disciples.

18:17 And I will wait upon the Lord, that hideth his face from the house of Jacob, and I will look for him.

18:18 Behold, I and the children whom the Lord hath given me are for signs and for wonders in Israel from the Lord of Hosts, which dwelleth in Mount Zion.

18:19 And when they shall say unto you: Seek unto them that have familiar spirits, and unto wizards that peep and mutter— should not a people seek unto their God for the living to hear from the dead?

[20] To the law and to the testimony: if they speak not according to this word, it is because there is no light in them.

[21] And they shall pass through it, hardly bestead and hungry: and it shall come to pass, that when they shall be hungry, they shall fret themselves, and curse their king and their God, and look upward.

[22] And they shall look unto the earth; and behold trouble and darkness, dimness of anguish; and they shall be driven to darkness.

9

[1] Nevertheless the dimness shall not be such as was in her vexation, when at the first he lightly afflicted the land of Zebulun and the land of Naphtali, and afterward did more grievously afflict her by the way of the sea, beyond Jordan, in Galilee of the nations.

[2] The people that walked in darkness have seen a great light: they that dwell in the land of the shadow of death, upon them hath the light shined.

8:20 To the law and to the testimony-- and if they speak not according to this word, it is because there is no light in them.

8:21 And they shall pass through it, hardly bestead and hungry; and it shall come to pass that when they shall be hungry, they shall fret themselves, and curse their king and their God, and look upward.

8:22 And they shall look unto the earth and behold trouble and darkness, dimness of anguish; and they shall be driven to darkness.

Chapter 9

9:1 Nevertheless, the dimness shall not be such as was in her vexation, when at the first he lightly afflicted the land of Zebulun and the land of Naphtali and afterward did more grievously afflict her by the way of the Red Sea, beyond Jordan, in Galilee of the nations.

9:2 The people that walked in darkness have seen a great light; they that dwell in the land of the shadow of death, upon them hath the light shined.

[18:20]To the law and to the testimony; and if they speak not according to this word, it is because there is no light in them.

[18:21]And they shall pass through it hardly bestead and hungry; and it shall come to pass that when they shall be hungry, they shall fret themselves, and curse their king and their God, and look upward.

[18:22]And they shall look unto the earth and behold trouble, and darkness, dimness of anguish, and shall be driven to darkness.

[19:1]Nevertheless, the dimness shall not be such as was in her vexation, when at first he lightly afflicted the land of Zebulun, and the land of Naphtali, and afterwards did more grievously afflict by the way of the Red Sea beyond Jordan in Galilee of the nations.

[19:2]The people that walked in darkness have seen a great light; they that dwell in the land of the shadow of death, upon them hath the light shined.

[3] Thou hast multiplied the nation, and not increased the joy: they joy before thee according to the joy in harvest, and as men rejoice when they divide the spoil.

[4] For thou hast broken the yoke of his burden, and the staff of his shoulder, the rod of his oppressor, as in the day of Midian.

[5] For every battle of the warrior is with confused noise, and garments rolled in blood; but this shall be with burning and fuel of fire.

[6] For unto us a child is born, unto us a son is given: and the government shall be upon his shoulder: and his name shall be called Wonderful, Counseller, The mighty God, The everlasting Father, The Prince of Peace.

[7] Of the increase of his government and peace there shall be no end, upon the throne of David, and upon his kingdom, to order it, and to establish it with judgment and with justice from henceforth even for ever. The zeal of the LORD of hosts will perform this.

9:3 Thou hast multiplied the nation and increased the joy; and they joy before thee according to the joy in harvest and as men rejoice when they divide the spoil.

9:4 For thou hast broken the yoke of his burden and the staff of his shoulder, the rod of his oppressor, as in the day of Midian.

9:5 For every battle of the warrior is with confused noise and garments rolled in blood; but this shall be with burning and fuel of fire.

9:6 For unto us a child is born; unto us a son is given; and the government shall be upon his shoulder; and his name shall be called Wonderful, Counselor, the mighty God, the everlasting Father, the Prince of Peace.

9:7 Of the increase of his government and peace there is no end, upon the throne of David and upon his kingdom, to order it and to establish it with judgment and with justice from henceforth, even forever. The zeal of the Lord of hosts will perform this.

19:3Thou hast multiplied the nation, and increased the joy—they joy before thee according to the joy in harvest, and as men rejoice when they divide the spoil.

19:4For thou hast broken the yoke of his burden, and the staff of his shoulder, the rod of his oppressor.

19:5For every battle of the warrior is with confused noise, and garments rolled in blood; but this shall be with burning and fuel of fire.

19:6For unto us a child is born, unto us a son is given; and the government shall be upon his shoulder; and his name shall be called, Wonderful, Counselor, The Mighty God, The Everlasting Father, The Prince of Peace.

19:7Of the increase of government and peace there is no end, upon the throne of David, and upon his kingdom to order it, and to establish it with judgment and with justice from henceforth, even forever. The zeal of the Lord of Hosts will perform this.

[8] The Lord sent a word into Jacob, and it hath lighted upon Israel.	9:8 The Lord sent his word unto Jacob, and it hath lighted upon Israel.	19:8The Lord sent his word unto Jacob and it hath lighted upon Israel.
[9] And all the people shall know, even Ephraim and the inhabitant of Samaria, that say in the pride and stoutness of heart,	9:9 And all the people shall know, even Ephraim and the inhabitant of Samaria, that say in the pride and stoutness of heart,	19:9And all the people shall know, even Ephraim and the inhabitants of Samaria, that say in the pride and stoutness of heart:
[10] The bricks are fallen down, but we will build with hewn stones: the sycomores are cut down, but we will change them into cedars.	9:10 The bricks are fallen down, but we will build with hewn stones; the sycamores are cut down, but we will change them into cedars.	19:10The bricks are fallen down, but we will build with hewn stones; the sycamores are cut down, but we will change them into cedars.
[11] Therefore the LORD shall set up the adversaries of Rezin against him, and join his enemies together;	9:11 Therefore, the Lord shall set up the adversaries of Rezin against him and join his enemies together:	19:11Therefore the Lord shall set up the adversaries of Rezin against him, and join his enemies together;
[12] The Syrians before, and the Philistines behind; and they shall devour Israel with open mouth. For all this his anger is not turned away, but his hand is stretched out still.	9:12 The Syrians before and the Philistines behind; and they shall devour Israel with open mouth. For all this, his anger is not turned away, but his hand is stretched out still.	19:12the Syrians before and the Philistines behind; and they shall devour Israel with open mouth. For all this his anger is not turned away, but his hand is stretched out still.
[13] For the people turneth not unto him that smiteth them, neither do they seek the LORD of hosts.	9:13 For the people turneth not unto him that smiteth them; neither do they seek the Lord of hosts.	19:13For the people turneth not unto him that smiteth them, neither do they seek the Lord of Hosts.
[14] Therefore the LORD will cut off from Israel head and tail, branch and rush, in one day.	9:14 Therefore, the Lord will cut off from Israel head and tail, branch and rush, in one day.	19:14Therefore will the Lord cut off from Israel head and tail, branch and rush in one day.

[15] The ancient and honourable, he is the head; and the prophet that teacheth lies, he is the tail.

[16] For the leaders of this people cause them to err; and they that are led of them are destroyed.

[17] Therefore the Lord shall have no joy in their young men, neither shall have mercy on their fatherless and widows: for every one is an hypocrite and an evildoer, and every mouth speaketh folly. For all this his anger is not turned away, but his hand is stretched out still.

[18] For wickedness burneth as the fire: it shall devour the briers and thorns, and shall kindle in the thickets of the forest, and they shall mount up like the lifting up of smoke.

[19] Through the wrath of the LORD of hosts is the land darkened, and the people shall be as the fuel of the fire: no man shall spare his brother.

9:15 The ancient and honorable, he is the head; and the prophet that teacheth lies, he is the tail.

9:16 For the leaders of this people cause them to err; and they that are led of them are destroyed.

9:17 Therefore, the Lord shall have no joy in their young men, neither shall have mercy on their fatherless and widows; for every one of them is a hypocrite and an evildoer, and every mouth speaketh folly. For all this, his anger is not turned away, but his hand is stretched out still.

9:18 For wickedness burneth as the fire; it shall devour the briers and thorns and shall kindle in the thickets of the forest; and they shall mount up like the lifting up of smoke.

9:19 Through the wrath of the Lord of hosts is the land darkened, and the people shall be as the fuel of the fire; no man shall spare his brother.

19:15The ancient, he is the head; and the prophet that teacheth lies, he is the tail.

19:16For the leaders of this people cause them to err; and they that are led of them are destroyed.

19:17Therefore the Lord shall have no joy in their young men, neither shall have mercy on their fatherless and widows; for every one of them is a hypocrite and an evildoer, and every mouth speaketh folly. For all this his anger is not turned away, but his hand is stretched out still.

19:18For wickedness burneth as the fire; it shall devour the briers and thorns, and shall kindle in the thickets of the forests, and they shall mount up like the lifting up of smoke.

19:19Through the wrath of the Lord of Hosts is the land darkened, and the people shall be as the fuel of the fire; no man shall spare his brother.

[20] And he shall snatch on the right hand, and be hungry; and he shall eat on the left hand, and they shall not be satisfied: they shall eat every man the flesh of his own arm:

[21] Manasseh, Ephraim; and Ephraim, Manasseh: and they together shall be against Judah. For all this his anger is not turned away, but his hand is stretched out still.

10

[1] Woe unto them that decree unrighteous decrees, and that write grievousness which they have prescribed;

[2] To turn aside the needy from judgment, and to take away the right from the poor of my people, that widows may be their prey, and that they may rob the fatherless!

[3] And what will ye do in the day of visitation, and in the desolation which shall come from far? to whom will ye flee for help? and where will ye leave your glory?

9:20 And he shall snatch on the right hand and be hungry; and he shall eat on the left hand, and they shall not be satisfied; they shall eat, every man, the flesh of his own arm--

9:21 Manasseh, Ephraim; and Ephraim, Manasseh; and they together shall be against Judah. For all this, his anger is not turned away, but his hand is stretched out still.

Chapter 10

10:1 Woe unto them that decree unrighteous decrees and that write grievousness which they have prescribed,

10:2 To turn aside the needy from judgment and to take away the right from the poor of my people, that widows may be their prey and that they may rob the fatherless!

10:3 And what will ye do in the day of visitation and in the desolation which shall come from far? To whom will ye flee for help? And where will ye leave your glory?

[19:20]And he shall snatch on the right hand and be hungry; and he shall eat on the left hand and they shall not be satisfied; they shall eat every man the flesh of his own arm—

[19:21]Manasseh, Ephraim; and Ephraim, Manasseh; they together shall be against Judah. For all this his anger is not turned away, but his hand is stretched out still.

[20:1]Wo unto them that decree unrighteous decrees, and that write grievousness which they have prescribed;

[20:2]to turn away the needy from judgment, and to take away the right from the poor of my people, that widows may be their prey, and that they may rob the fatherless!

[20:3]And what will ye do in the day of visitation, and in the desolation which shall come from far? to whom will ye flee for help? and where will ye leave your glory?

[4] Without me they shall bow down under the prisoners, and they shall fall under the slain. For all this his anger is not turned away, but his hand is stretched out still.

[5] O Assyrian, the rod of mine anger, and the staff in their hand is mine indignation.

[6] I will send him against an hypocritical nation, and against the people of my wrath will I give him a charge, to take the spoil, and to take the prey, and to tread them down like the mire of the streets.

[7] Howbeit he meaneth not so, neither doth his heart think so; but it is in his heart to destroy and cut off nations not a few.

[8] For he saith, Are not my princes altogether kings?

[9] Is not Calno as Carchemish? is not Hamath as Arpad? is not Samaria as Damascus?

10:4 Without me they shall bow down under the prisoners, and they shall fall under the slain. For all this, his anger is not turned away, but his hand is stretched out still.

10:5 O Assyrian, the rod of mine anger, and the staff in their hand is mine indignation.

10:6 I will send him against a hypocritical nation; and against the people of my wrath will I give him a charge: to take the spoil, and to take the prey, and to tread them down like the mire of the streets.

10:7 Howbeit he meaneth not so; neither doth his heart think so; but in his heart it is to destroy and cut off nations not a few.

10:8 For he saith, Are not my princes altogether kings?

10:9 Is not Calno as Carchemish? Is not Hamath as Arpad? Is not Samaria as Damascus?

20:4Without me they shall bow down under the prisoners, and they shall fall under the slain. For all this his anger is not turned away, but his hand is stretched out still.

20:5O Assyrian, the rod of mine anger, and the staff in their hand is their indignation.

20:6I will send him against a hypocritical nation, and against the people of my wrath will I give him a charge to take the spoil, and to take the prey, and to tread them down like the mire of the streets.

20:7Howbeit he meaneth not so, neither doth his heart think so; but in his heart it is to destroy and cut off nations not a few.

20:8For he saith: Are not my princes altogether kings?

20:9Is not Calno as Carchemish? Is not Hamath as Arpad? Is not Samaria as Damascus?

[10] As my hand hath found the kingdoms of the idols, and whose graven images did excel them of Jerusalem and of Samaria;

[11] Shall I not, as I have done unto Samaria and her idols, so do to Jerusalem and her idols?

[12] Wherefore it shall come to pass, that when the Lord hath performed his whole work upon mount Zion and on Jerusalem, I will punish the fruit of the stout heart of the king of Assyria, and the glory of his high looks.

[13] For he saith, By the strength of my hand I have done it, and by my wisdom; for I am prudent: and I have removed the bounds of the people, and have robbed their treasures, and I have put down the inhabitants like a valiant man:

[14] And my hand hath found as a nest the riches of the people: and as one gathereth eggs that are left, have I gathered all the earth; and there was none that moved the wing, or opened the mouth, or peeped.

10:10 As my hand hath founded the kingdoms of the idols, and whose graven images did excel them of Jerusalem and of Samaria,

10:11 Shall I not, as I have done unto Samaria and her idols, so do to Jerusalem and to her idols?

10:12 Wherefore, it shall come to pass that when the Lord hath performed his whole work upon Mount Zion and upon Jerusalem, I will punish the fruit of the stout heart of the king of Assyria and the glory of his high looks.

10:13 For he saith, By the strength of my hand and by my wisdom I have done these things; for I am prudent, and I have moved the borders of the people and have robbed their treasures; and I have put down the inhabitants like a valiant man.

10:14 And my hand hath found as a nest the riches of the people; and as one gathereth eggs that are left, have I gathered all the earth; and there was none that moved the wing, or opened the mouth, or peeped.

20:10As my hand hath founded the kingdoms of the idols, and whose graven images did excel them of Jerusalem and of Samaria;

20:11shall I not, as I have done unto Samaria and her idols, so do to Jerusalem and to her idols?

20:12Wherefore it shall come to pass that when the Lord hath performed his whole work upon Mount Zion and upon Jerusalem, I will punish the fruit of the stout heart of the king of Assyria, and the glory of his high looks.

20:13For he saith: By the strength of my hand and by my wisdom I have done these things; for I am prudent; and I have moved the borders of the people, and have robbed their treasures, and I have put down the inhabitants like a valiant man;

20:14and my hand hath found as a nest the riches of the people; and as one gathereth eggs that are left have I gathered all the earth; and there was none that moved the wing, or opened the mouth, or peeped.

[15] Shall the axe boast itself against him that heweth therewith? or shall the saw magnify itself against him that shaketh it? as if the rod should shake itself against them that lift it up, or as if the staff should lift up itself, as if it were no wood.

[16] Therefore shall the Lord, the Lord of hosts, send among his fat ones leanness; and under his glory he shall kindle a burning like the burning of a fire.

[17] And the light of Israel shall be for a fire, and his Holy One for a flame: and it shall burn and devour his thorns and his briers in one day;

[18] And shall consume the glory of his forest, and of his fruitful field, both soul and body: and they shall be as when a standardbearer fainteth.

[19] And the rest of the trees of his forest shall be few, that a child may write them.

10:15 Shall the axe boast itself against him that heweth therewith? Or shall the saw magnify itself against him that shaketh it? As if the rod should shake itself against them that lift it up, or as if the staff should lift up itself, as if it were no wood.

10:16 Therefore shall the Lord, the Lord of hosts, send among his fat ones leanness; and under his glory he shall kindle a burning like the burning of a fire.

10:17 And the light of Israel shall be for a fire, and his Holy One for a flame; and it shall burn and devour his thorns and his briers in one day,

10:18 And shall consume the glory of his forest and of his fruitful field, both soul and body; and they shall be as when a standard-bearer fainteth.

10:19 And the rest of the trees of his forest shall be few, that a child may write them.

20:15Shall the ax boast itself against him that heweth therewith? Shall the saw magnify itself against him that shaketh it? As if the rod should shake itself against them that lift it up, or as if the staff should lift up itself as if it were no wood!

20:16Therefore shall the Lord, the Lord of Hosts, send among his fat ones, leanness; and under his glory he shall kindle a burning like the burning of a fire.

20:17And the light of Israel shall be for a fire, and his Holy One for a flame, and shall burn and shall devour his thorns and his briers in one day;

20:18and shall consume the glory of his forest, and of his fruitful field, both soul and body; and they shall be as when a standard-bearer fainteth.

20:19And the rest of the trees of his forest shall be few, that a child may write them.

[20] And it shall come to pass in that day, that the remnant of Israel, and such as are escaped of the house of Jacob, shall no more again stay upon him that smote them; but shall stay upon the LORD, the Holy One of Israel, in truth.

[21] The remnant shall return, even the remnant of Jacob, unto the mighty God.

[22] For though thy people Israel be as the sand of the sea, yet a remnant of them shall return: the consumption decreed shall overflow with righteousness.

[23] For the Lord GOD of hosts shall make a consumption, even determined, in the midst of all the land.

[24] Therefore thus saith the Lord GOD of hosts, O my people that dwellest in Zion, be not afraid of the Assyrian: he shall smite thee with a rod, and shall lift up his staff against thee, after the manner of Egypt.

[25] For yet a very little while, and the indignation shall cease, and mine anger in their destruction.

10:20 And it shall come to pass in that day, that the remnant of Israel and such as are escaped of the house of Jacob shall no more again stay upon him that smote them, but shall stay upon the Lord, the Holy One of Israel, in truth.

10:21 The remnant shall return, yea, even the remnant of Jacob, unto the mighty God.

10:22 For though thy people Israel be as the sand of the sea, yet a remnant of them shall return; the consumption decreed shall overflow with righteousness.

10:23 For the Lord God of hosts shall make a consumption, even determined, in all the land.

10:24 Therefore, thus saith the Lord God of hosts, O my people that dwellest in Zion, be not afraid of the Assyrian; he shall smite thee with a rod and shall lift up his staff against thee after the manner of Egypt.

10:25 For yet a very little while, and the indignation shall cease, and mine anger in their destruction.

20:20 And it shall come to pass in that day, that the remnant of Israel, and such as are escaped of the house of Jacob, shall no more again stay upon him that smote them, but shall stay upon the Lord, the Holy One of Israel, in truth.

20:21 The remnant shall return, yea, even the remnant of Jacob, unto the mighty God.

20:22 For though thy people Israel be as the sand of the sea, yet a remnant of them shall return; the consumption decreed shall overflow with righteousness.

20:23 For the Lord God of Hosts shall make a consumption, even determined in all the land.

20:24 Therefore, thus saith the Lord God of Hosts: O my people that dwellest in Zion, be not afraid of the Assyrian; he shall smite thee with a rod, and shall lift up his staff against thee, after the manner of Egypt.

20:25 For yet a very little while, and the indignation shall cease, and mine anger in their destruction.

[26] And the LORD of hosts shall stir up a scourge for him according to the slaughter of Midian at the rock of Oreb: and as his rod was upon the sea, so shall he lift it up after the manner of Egypt.

[27] And it shall come to pass in that day, that his burden shall be taken away from off thy shoulder, and his yoke from off thy neck, and the yoke shall be destroyed because of the anointing.

[28] He is come to Aiath, he is passed to Migron; at Michmash he hath laid up his carriages:

[29] They are gone over the passage: they have taken up their lodging at Geba; Ramah is afraid; Gibeah of Saul is fled.

[30] Lift up thy voice, O daughter of Gallim: cause it to be heard unto Laish, O poor Anathoth.

[31] Madmenah is removed; the inhabitants of Gebim gather themselves to flee.

10:26 And the Lord of hosts shall stir up a scourge for him according to the slaughter of Midian at the rock of Oreb; and as his rod was upon the sea, so shall he lift it up after the manner of Egypt.

10:27 And it shall come to pass in that day, that his burden shall be taken away from off thy shoulder and his yoke from off thy neck; and the yoke shall be destroyed because of the anointing.

10:28 He is come to Aiath; he is passed to Migron; at Michmash he hath laid up his carriages;

10:29 They are gone over the passage; they have taken up their lodging at Geba; Ramah is afraid; Gibeah of Saul is fled.

10:30 Lift up thy voice, O daughter of Gallim; cause it to be heard unto Laish, O poor Anathoth.

10:31 Madmenah is removed; the inhabitants of Gebim gather themselves to flee.

20:26 And the Lord of Hosts shall stir up a scourge for him according to the slaughter of Midian at the rock of Oreb; and as his rod was upon the sea so shall he lift it up after the manner of Egypt.

20:27 And it shall come to pass in that day that his burden shall be taken away from off thy shoulder, and his yoke from off thy neck, and the yoke shall be destroyed because of the anointing.

20:28 He is come to Aiath, he is passed to Migron; at Michmash he hath laid up his carriages.

20:29 They are gone over the passage; they have taken up their lodging at Geba; Ramath is afraid; Gibeah of Saul is fled.

20:30 Lift up the voice, O daughter of Gallim; cause it to be heard unto Laish, O poor Anathoth.

20:31 Madmenah is removed; the inhabitants of Gebim gather themselves to flee.

[32] As yet shall he remain at Nob that day: he shall shake his hand against the mount of the daughter of Zion, the hill of Jerusalem.	10:32 As yet shall he remain at Nob that day; he shall shake his hand against the mount of the daughter of Zion, the hill of Jerusalem.	20:32As yet shall he remain at Nob that day; he shall shake his hand against the mount of the daughter of Zion, the hill of Jerusalem.
[33] Behold, the Lord, the LORD of hosts, shall lop the bough with terror: and the high ones of stature shall be hewn down, and the haughty shall be humbled.	10:33 Behold, the Lord, the Lord of hosts, shall lop the bough with terror; and the high ones of stature shall be hewn down, and the haughty shall be humbled.	20:33Behold, the Lord, the Lord of Hosts shall lop the bough with terror; and the high ones of stature shall be hewn down; and the haughty shall be humbled.
[34] And he shall cut down the thickets of the forest with iron, and Lebanon shall fall by a mighty one.	10:34 And he shall cut down the thickets of the forest with iron, and Lebanon shall fall by a mighty one.	20:34And he shall cut down the thickets of the forests with iron, and Lebanon shall fall by a mighty one.
11	Chapter 11	
[1] And there shall come forth a rod out of the stem of Jesse, and a Branch shall grow out of his roots:	11:1 And there shall come forth a rod out of the stem of Jesse, and a Branch shall grow out of his roots;	21:1And there shall come forth a rod out of the stem of Jesse, and a branch shall grow out of his roots.
[2] And the spirit of the LORD shall rest upon him, the spirit of wisdom and understanding, the spirit of counsel and might, the spirit of knowledge and of the fear of the LORD;	11:2 And the Spirit of the Lord shall rest upon him, the spirit of wisdom and understanding, the spirit of counsel and might, the spirit of knowledge and of the fear of the Lord,	21:2And the Spirit of the Lord shall rest upon him, the spirit of wisdom and understanding, the spirit of counsel and might, the spirit of knowledge and of the fear of the Lord;
[3] And shall make him of quick understanding in the fear of the LORD: and he shall not judge after the sight of his eyes, neither reprove after the hearing of his ears:	11:3 And shall make him of quick understanding in the fear of the Lord; and he shall not judge after the sight of his eyes, neither reprove after the hearing of his ears;	21:3and shall make him of quick understanding in the fear of the Lord; and he shall not judge after the sight of his eyes, neither reprove after the hearing of his ears.

[4] But with righteousness shall he judge the poor and reprove with equity for the meek of the earth: and he shall smite the earth with the rod of his mouth, and with the breath of his lips shall he slay the wicked.

[5] And righteousness shall be the girdle of his loins, and faithfulness the girdle of his reins.

[6] The wolf also shall dwell with the lamb, and the leopard shall lie down with the kid; and the calf and the young lion and the fatling together; and a little child shall lead them.

[7] And the cow and the bear shall feed; their young ones shall lie down together: and the lion shall eat straw like the ox.

[8] And the sucking child shall play on the hole of the asp, and the weaned child shall put his hand on the cockatrice' den.

[9] They shall not hurt nor destroy in all my holy mountain: for the earth shall be full of the knowledge of the LORD, as the waters cover the sea.

11:4 But with righteousness shall he judge the poor and reprove with equity for the meek of the earth; and he shall smite the earth with the rod of his mouth, and with the breath of his lips shall he slay the wicked.

11:5 And righteousness shall be the girdle of his loins, and faithfulness the girdle of his reins.

11:6 The wolf also shall dwell with the lamb, and the leopard shall lie down with the kid, and the calf, and the young lion, and the fatling together; and a little child shall lead them.

11:7 And the cow and the bear shall feed; their young ones shall lie down together; and the lion shall eat straw like the ox.

11:8 And the sucking child shall play on the hole of the asp, and the weaned child shall put his hand on the cockatrice den.

11:9 They shall not hurt nor destroy in all my holy mountain; for the earth shall be full of the knowledge of the Lord, as the waters cover the sea.

21:4But with righteousness shall he judge the poor, and reprove with equity for the meek of the earth; and he shall smite the earth with the rod of his mouth, and with the breath of his lips shall he slay the wicked.

21:5And righteousness shall be the girdle of his loins, and faithfulness the girdle of his reins.

21:6The wolf also shall dwell with the lamb, and the leopard shall lie down with the kid, and the calf and the young lion and fatling together; and a little child shall lead them.

21:7And the cow and the bear shall feed; their young ones shall lie down together; and the lion shall eat straw like the ox.

21:8And the sucking child shall play on the hole of the asp, and the weaned child shall put his hand on the cockatrice's den.

21:9They shall not hurt nor destroy in all my holy mountain, for the earth shall be full of the knowledge of the Lord, as the waters cover the sea.

[10] And in that day there shall be a root of Jesse, which shall stand for an ensign of the people; to it shall the Gentiles seek: and his rest shall be glorious.

[11] And it shall come to pass in that day, that the Lord shall set his hand again the second time to recover the remnant of his people, which shall be left, from Assyria, and from Egypt, and from Pathros, and from Cush, and from Elam, and from Shinar, and from Hamath, and from the islands of the sea.

[12] And he shall set up an ensign for the nations, and shall assemble the outcasts of Israel, and gather together the dispersed of Judah from the four corners of the earth.

[13] The envy also of Ephraim shall depart, and the adversaries of Judah shall be cut off: Ephraim shall not envy Judah, and Judah shall not vex Ephraim.

11:10 And in that day there shall be a root of Jesse, which shall stand for an ensign of the people; to it shall the Gentiles seek; and his rest shall be glorious.

11:11 And it shall come to pass in that day, that the Lord shall set his hand again the second time to recover the remnant of his people, which shall be left, from Assyria, and from Egypt, and from Pathros, and from Cush, and from Elam, and from Shinar, and from Hamath, and from the islands of the sea.

11:12 And he shall set up an ensign for the nations, and shall assemble the outcasts of Israel, and gather together the dispersed of Judah from the four corners of the earth.

11:13 The envy also of Ephraim shall depart, and the adversaries of Judah shall be cut off; Ephraim shall not envy Judah, and Judah shall not vex Ephraim.

21:10 And in that day there shall be a root of Jesse, which shall stand for an ensign of the people; to it shall the Gentiles seek; and his rest shall be glorious.

21:11 And it shall come to pass in that day that the Lord shall set his hand again the second time to recover the remnant of his people which shall be left, from Assyria, and from Egypt, and from Pathros, and from Cush, and from Elam, and from Shinar, and from Hamath, and from the islands of the sea.

21:12 And he shall set up an ensign for the nations, and shall assemble the outcasts of Israel, and gather together the dispersed of Judah from the four corners of the earth.

21:13 The envy of Ephraim also shall depart, and the adversaries of Judah shall be cut off; Ephraim shall not envy Judah, and Judah shall not vex Ephraim.

[14] But they shall fly upon the shoulders of the Philistines toward the west; they shall spoil them of the east together: they shall lay their hand upon Edom and Moab; and the children of Ammon shall obey them.

[15] And the LORD shall utterly destroy the tongue of the Egyptian sea; and with his mighty wind shall he shake his hand over the river, and shall smite it in the seven streams, and make men go over dryshod.

[16] And there shall be an highway for the remnant of his people, which shall be left, from Assyria; like as it was to Israel in the day that he came up out of the land of Egypt.

12

[1] And in that day thou shalt say, O LORD, I will praise thee: though thou wast angry with me, thine anger is turned away, and thou comfortedst me.

[2] Behold, God is my salvation; I will trust, and not be afraid: for the LORD JEHOVAH is my strength and my song; he also is become my salvation.

11:14 But they shall fly upon the shoulders of the Philistines toward the west; they shall spoil them of the east together; they shall lay their hand upon Edom and Moab; and the children of Ammon shall obey them.

11:15 And the Lord shall utterly destroy the tongue of the Egyptian sea; and with his mighty wind shall he shake his hand over the river, and shall smite it in the seven streams, and make men go over dry-shod.

11:16 And there shall be a highway for the remnant of his people, which shall be left from Assyria, like as it was to Israel in the day that he came up out of the land of Egypt.

Chapter 12

12:1 And in that day thou shalt say, O Lord, I will praise thee; though thou wast angry with me, thine anger is turned away, and thou comfortedst me.

12:2 Behold, God is my salvation; I will trust and not be afraid; for the Lord JEHOVAH is my strength and my song; he also is become my salvation.

21:14But they shall fly upon the shoulders of the Philistines towards the west; they shall spoil them of the east together; they shall lay their hand upon Edom and Moab; and the children of Ammon shall obey them.

21:15And the Lord shall utterly destroy the tongue of the Egyptian sea; and with his mighty wind he shall shake his hand over the river, and shall smite it in the seven streams, and make men go over dry shod.

21:16And there shall be a highway for the remnant of his people which shall be left, from Assyria, like as it was to Israel in the day that he came up out of the land of Egypt.

22:1And in that day thou shalt say: O Lord, I will praise thee; though thou wast angry with me thine anger is turned away, and thou comfortedest me.

22:2Behold, God is my salvation; I will trust, and not be afraid; for the Lord Jehovah is my strength and my song; he also has become my salvation.

[3] Therefore with joy shall ye draw water out of the wells of salvation.	12:3 Therefore, with joy shall ye draw water out of the wells of salvation.	22:3Therefore, with joy shall ye draw water out of the wells of salvation.
[4] And in that day shall ye say, Praise the LORD, call upon his name, declare his doings among the people, make mention that his name is exalted.	12:4 And in that day shall ye say, Praise the Lord, call upon his name, declare his doings among the people, make mention that his name is exalted.	22:4And in that day shall ye say: Praise the Lord, call upon his name, declare his doings among the people, make mention that his name is exalted.
[5] Sing unto the LORD; for he hath done excellent things: this is known in all the earth.	12:5 Sing unto the Lord, for he hath done excellent things; this is known in all the earth.	22:5Sing unto the Lord; for he hath done excellent things; this is known in all the earth.
[6] Cry out and shout, thou inhabitant of Zion: for great is the Holy One of Israel in the midst of thee.	12:6 Cry out and shout, thou inhabitant of Zion; for great is the Holy One of Israel in the midst of thee.	22:6Cry out and shout, thou inhabitant of Zion; for great is the Holy One of Israel in the midst of thee.
13	Chapter 13	<X>
[1] The burden of Babylon, which Isaiah the son of Amoz did see.	13:1 The burden of Babylon, which Isaiah, the son of Amoz, did see:	23:1The burden of Babylon, which Isaiah the son of Amoz did see.
[2] Lift ye up a banner upon the high mountain, exalt the voice unto them, shake the hand, that they may go into the gates of the nobles.	13:2 Lift ye up my banner upon the high mountain; exalt the voice unto them; shake the hand, that they may go into the gates of the nobles.	23:2Lift ye up a banner upon the high mountain, exalt the voice unto them, shake the hand, that they may go into the gates of the nobles.
[3] I have commanded my sanctified ones, I have also called my mighty ones for mine anger, even them that rejoice in my highness.	13:3 I have commanded my sanctified ones; I have also called my mighty ones, for mine anger is not upon them that rejoice in my highness.	23:3I have commanded my sanctified ones, I have also called my mighty ones, for mine anger is not upon them that rejoice in my highness.

[4] The noise of a multitude in the mountains, like as of a great people; a tumultuous noise of the kingdoms of nations gathered together: the LORD of hosts mustereth the host of the battle.

[5] They come from a far country, from the end of heaven, even the LORD, and the weapons of his indignation, to destroy the whole land.

[6] Howl ye; for the day of the LORD is at hand; it shall come as a destruction from the Almighty.

[7] Therefore shall all hands be faint, and every man's heart shall melt:

[8] And they shall be afraid: pangs and sorrows shall take hold of them; they shall be in pain as a woman that travaileth: they shall be amazed one at another; their faces shall be as flames.

[9] Behold, the day of the LORD cometh, cruel both with wrath and fierce anger, to lay the land desolate: and he shall destroy the sinners thereof out of it.

13:4 The noise of the multitude in the mountains like as of a great people, a tumultuous noise of the kingdoms of nations gathered together--the Lord of hosts mustereth the hosts of the battle.

13:5 They come from a far country, from the end of heaven, yea, the Lord and the weapons of his indignation, to destroy the whole land.

13:6 Howl ye; for the day of the Lord is at hand; it shall come as a destruction from the Almighty.

13:7 Therefore shall all hands be faint, and every man's heart shall melt;

13:8 And they shall be afraid; pangs and sorrows shall take hold of them; they shall be in pain as a woman that travaileth; they shall be amazed one at another; their faces shall be as flames.

13:9 Behold, the day of the Lord cometh, cruel both with wrath and fierce anger, to lay the land desolate; and he shall destroy the sinners thereof out of it.

23:4The noise of the multitude in the mountains like as of a great people, a tumultuous noise of the kingdoms of nations gathered together, the Lord of Hosts mustereth the hosts of the battle.

23:5They come from a far country, from the end of heaven, yea, the Lord, and the weapons of his indignation, to destroy the whole land.

23:6Howl ye, for the day of the Lord is at hand; it shall come as a destruction from the Almighty.

23:7Therefore shall all hands be faint, every man's heart shall melt;

23:8and they shall be afraid; pangs and sorrows shall take hold of them; they shall be amazed one at another; their faces shall be as flames.

23:9Behold, the day of the Lord cometh, cruel both with wrath and fierce anger, to lay the land desolate; and he shall destroy the sinners thereof out of it.

[10] For the stars of heaven and the constellations thereof shall not give their light: the sun shall be darkened in his going forth, and the moon shall not cause her light to shine.

[11] And I will punish the world for their evil, and the wicked for their iniquity; and I will cause the arrogancy of the proud to cease, and will lay low the haughtiness of the terrible.

[12] I will make a man more precious than fine gold; even a man than the golden wedge of Ophir.

[13] Therefore I will shake the heavens, and the earth shall remove out of her place, in the wrath of the LORD of hosts, and in the day of his fierce anger.

[14] And it shall be as the chased roe, and as a sheep that no man taketh up: they shall every man turn to his own people, and flee every one into his own land.

[15] Every one that is found shall be thrust through; and every one that is joined unto them shall fall by the sword.

13:10 For the stars of heaven and the constellations thereof shall not give their light; the sun shall be darkened in his going forth, and the moon shall not cause her light to shine.

13:11 And I will punish the world for their evil and the wicked for their iniquity; and I will cause the arrogancy of the proud to cease and will lay low the haughtiness of the terrible.

13:12 I will make a man more precious than fine gold, even a man than the golden wedge of Ophir.

13:13 Therefore, I will shake the heavens, and the earth shall remove out of her place in the wrath of the Lord of hosts and in the day of his fierce anger.

13:14 And it shall be as the chased roe and as a sheep that no man taketh up; they shall, every man, turn to his own people and flee, everyone into his own land.

13:15 Everyone that is proud shall be thrust through; and everyone that is joined to the wicked shall fall by the sword.

23:10For the stars of heaven and the constellations thereof shall not give their light; the sun shall be darkened in his going forth, and the moon shall not cause her light to shine.

23:11And I will punish the world for evil, and the wicked for their iniquity; I will cause the arrogancy of the proud to cease, and will lay down the haughtiness of the terrible.

23:12I will make a man more precious than fine gold; even a man than the golden wedge of Ophir.

23:13Therefore, I will shake the heavens, and the earth shall remove out of her place, in the wrath of the Lord of Hosts, and in the day of his fierce anger.

23:14And it shall be as the chased roe, and as a sheep that no man taketh up; and they shall every man turn to his own people, and flee every one into his own land.

23:15Every one that is proud shall be thrust through; yea, and every one that is joined to the wicked shall fall by the sword.

[16] Their children also shall be dashed to pieces before their eyes; their houses shall be spoiled, and their wives ravished.

[17] Behold, I will stir up the Medes against them, which shall not regard silver; and as for gold, they shall not delight in it.

[18] Their bows also shall dash the young men to pieces; and they shall have no pity on the fruit of the womb; their eye shall not spare children.

[19] And Babylon, the glory of kingdoms, the beauty of the Chaldees' excellency, shall be as when God overthrew Sodom and Gomorrah.

[20] It shall never be inhabited, neither shall it be dwelt in from generation to generation: neither shall the Arabian pitch tent there; neither shall the shepherds make their fold there.

[21] But wild beasts of the desert shall lie there; and their houses shall be full of doleful creatures; and owls shall dwell there, and satyrs shall dance there.

13:16 Their children also shall be dashed to pieces before their eyes; their houses shall be spoiled and their wives ravished.

13:17 Behold, I will stir up the Medes against them, which shall not regard silver; and as for gold, they shall not delight in it.

13:18 Their bows also shall dash the young men to pieces; and they shall have no pity on the fruit of the womb; their eye shall not spare children.

13:19 And Babylon, the glory of kingdoms, the beauty of the Chaldees' excellency, shall be as when God overthrew Sodom and Gomorrah.

13:20 It shall never be inhabited; neither shall it be dwelt in from generation to generation; neither shall the Arabian pitch tent there; neither shall the shepherds make their fold there.

13:21 But wild beasts of the desert shall lie there; and their houses shall be full of doleful creatures; and owls shall dwell there, and satyrs shall dance there.

23:16 Their children also shall be dashed to pieces before their eyes; their houses shall be spoiled and their wives ravished.

23:17 Behold, I will stir up the Medes against them, which shall not regard silver and gold, nor shall they delight in it.

23:18 Their bows shall also dash the young men to pieces; and they shall have no pity on the fruit of the womb; their eyes shall not spare children.

23:19 And Babylon, the glory of kingdoms, the beauty of the Chaldees' excellency, shall be as when God overthrew Sodom and Gomorrah.

23:20 It shall never be inhabited, neither shall it be dwelt in from generation to generation: neither shall the Arabian pitch tent there; neither shall the shepherds make their fold there.

23:21 But wild beasts of the desert shall lie there; and their houses shall be full of doleful creatures; and owls shall dwell there, and satyrs shall dance there.

[22] And the wild beasts of the islands shall cry in their desolate houses, and dragons in their pleasant palaces: and her time is near to come, and her days shall not be prolonged.	13:22 And the wild beasts of the islands shall cry in their desolate houses, and dragons in their pleasant palaces; and her time is near to come, and her days shall not be prolonged; for I will destroy her speedily; yea, for I will be merciful unto my people, but the wicked shall perish.	23:22And the wild beasts of the islands shall cry in their desolate houses, and dragons in their pleasant palaces; and her time is near to come, and her day shall not be prolonged. For I will destroy her speedily; yea, for I will be merciful unto my people, but the wicked shall perish.

14

Chapter 14

[1] For the LORD will have mercy on Jacob, and will yet choose Israel, and set them in their own land: and the strangers shall be joined with them, and they shall cleave to the house of Jacob.

14:1 For the Lord will have mercy on Jacob, and will yet choose Israel, and set them in their own land; and the strangers shall be joined with them, and they shall cleave to the house of Jacob.

24:1For the Lord will have mercy on Jacob, and will yet choose Israel, and set them in their own land; and the strangers shall be joined with them, and they shall cleave to the house of Jacob.

[2] And the people shall take them, and bring them to their place: and the house of Israel shall possess them in the land of the LORD for servants and handmaids: and they shall take them captives, whose captives they were; and they shall rule over their oppressors.

14:2 And the people shall take them and bring them to their place, yea, from far, unto the end of the earth; and they shall return to their land of promise. And the house of Israel shall possess them in the land of the Lord for servants and handmaids; and they shall take them captives, whose captives they were; and they shall rule over their oppressors.

24:2And the people shall take them and bring them to their place; yea, from far unto the ends of the earth; and they shall return to their lands of promise. And the house of Israel shall possess them, and the land of the Lord shall be for servants and handmaids; and they shall take them captives unto whom they were captives; and they shall rule over their oppressors.

[3] And it shall come to pass in the day that the LORD shall give thee rest from thy sorrow, and from thy fear, and from the hard bondage wherein thou wast made to serve,

14:3 And it shall come to pass in that day that the Lord shall give thee rest from thy sorrow, and from thy fear, and from the hard bondage wherein thou wast made to serve.

24:3And it shall come to pass in that day that the Lord shall give thee rest, from thy sorrow, and from thy fear, and from the hard bondage wherein thou wast made to serve.

[4] That thou shalt take up this proverb against the king of Babylon, and say, How hath the oppressor ceased! the golden city ceased!	14:4 And it shall come to pass in that day that thou shalt take up this proverb against the king of Babylon and say, How hath the oppressor ceased, the golden city ceased!	24:4And it shall come to pass in that day, that thou shalt take up this proverb against the king of Babylon, and say: How hath the oppressor ceased, the golden city ceased!
[5] The LORD hath broken the staff of the wicked, and the sceptre of the rulers.	14:5 The Lord hath broken the staff of the wicked and the scepters of the rulers.	24:5The Lord hath broken the staff of the wicked, the scepters of the rulers.
[6] He who smote the people in wrath with a continual stroke, he that ruled the nations in anger, is persecuted, and none hindereth.	14:6 He who smote the people in wrath with a continual stroke, he that ruled the nations in anger, is persecuted, and none hindereth.	24:6He who smote the people in wrath with a continual stroke, he that ruled the nations in anger, is persecuted, and none hindereth.
[7] The whole earth is at rest, and is quiet: they break forth into singing.	14:7 The whole earth is at rest and is quiet; they break forth into singing.	24:7The whole earth is at rest, and is quiet; they break forth into singing.
[8] Yea, the fir trees rejoice at thee, and the cedars of Lebanon, saying, Since thou art laid down, no feller is come up against us.	14:8 Yea, the fir trees rejoice at thee, and also the cedars of Lebanon, saying, Since thou art laid down, no feller is come up against us.	24:8Yea, the fir-trees rejoice at thee, and also the cedars of Lebanon, saying: Since thou art laid down no feller is come up against us.
[9] Hell from beneath is moved for thee to meet thee at thy coming: it stirreth up the dead for thee, even all the chief ones of the earth; it hath raised up from their thrones all the kings of the nations.	14:9 Hell from beneath is moved for thee to meet thee at thy coming; it stirreth up the dead for thee, even all the chief ones of the earth; it hath raised up from their thrones all the kings of the nations.	24:9Hell from beneath is moved for thee to meet thee at thy coming; it stirreth up the dead for thee, even all the chief ones of the earth; it hath raised up from their thrones all the kings of the nations.
[10] All they shall speak and say unto thee, Art thou also become weak as we? art thou become like unto us?	14:10 All they shall speak and say unto thee, Art thou also become weak as we? Art thou become like unto us?	24:10All they shall speak and say unto thee: Art thou also become weak as we? Art thou become like unto us?

[11] Thy pomp is brought down to the grave, and the noise of thy viols: the worm is spread under thee, and the worms cover thee.

[12] How art thou fallen from heaven, O Lucifer, son of the morning! how art thou cut down to the ground, which didst weaken the nations!

[13] For thou hast said in thine heart, I will ascend into heaven, I will exalt my throne above the stars of God: I will sit also upon the mount of the congregation, in the sides of the north:

[14] I will ascend above the heights of the clouds; I will be like the most High.

[15] Yet thou shalt be brought down to hell, to the sides of the pit.

[16] They that see thee shall narrowly look upon thee, and consider thee, saying, Is this the man that made the earth to tremble, that did shake kingdoms;

14:11 Thy pomp is brought down to the grave, and the noise of thy viols; the worm is spread under thee, and the worms cover thee.

14:12 How art thou fallen from heaven, O Lucifer, son of the morning! How art thou cut down to the ground, which didst weaken the nations!

14:13 For thou hast said in thine heart, I will ascend into heaven; I will exalt my throne above the stars of God; I will sit also upon the mount of the congregation in the sides of the north;

14:14 I will ascend above the heights of the clouds; I will be like the Most High.

14:15 Yet thou shalt be brought down to hell, to the sides of the pit.

14:16 They that see thee shall narrowly look upon thee, and shall consider thee, and shall say, Is this the man that made the earth to tremble, that did shake kingdoms,

24:11Thy pomp is brought down to the grave; the noise of thy viols is not heard; the worm is spread under thee, and the worms cover thee.

24:12How art thou fallen from heaven, O Lucifer, son of the morning! Art thou cut down to the ground, which did weaken the nations!

24:13For thou hast said in thy heart: I will ascend into heaven, I will exalt my throne above the stars of God; I will sit also upon the mount of the congregation, in the sides of the north;

24:14I will ascend above the heights of the clouds; I will be like the Most High.

24:15Yet thou shalt be brought down to hell, to the sides of the pit.

24:16They that see thee shall narrowly look upon thee, and shall consider thee, and shall say: Is this the man that made the earth to tremble, that did shake kingdoms?

[17] That made the world as a wilderness, and destroyed the cities thereof; that opened not the house of his prisoners?

[18] All the kings of the nations, even all of them, lie in glory, every one in his own house.

[19] But thou art cast out of thy grave like an abominable branch, and as the raiment of those that are slain, thrust through with a sword, that go down to the stones of the pit; as a carcase trodden under feet.

[20] Thou shalt not be joined with them in burial, because thou hast destroyed thy land, and slain thy people: the seed of evildoers shall never be renowned.

[21] Prepare slaughter for his children for the iniquity of their fathers; that they do not rise, nor possess the land, nor fill the face of the world with cities.

[22] For I will rise up against them, saith the LORD of hosts, and cut off from Babylon the name, and remnant, and son, and nephew, saith the LORD.

14:17 And made the world as a wilderness, and destroyed the cities thereof, and opened not the house of his prisoners?

14:18 All the kings of the nations, yea, all of them, lie in glory, every one of them in his own house.

14:19 But thou art cast out of thy grave like an abominable branch and the remnant of those that are slain, thrust through with a sword, that go down to the stones of the pit as a carcass trodden under feet.

14:20 Thou shalt not be joined with them in burial because thou hast destroyed thy land and slain thy people; the seed of evildoers shall never be renowned.

14:21 Prepare slaughter for his children, for the iniquities of their fathers, that they do not rise, nor possess the land, nor fill the face of the world with cities.

14:22 For I will rise up against them, saith the Lord of hosts, and cut off from Babylon the name, and remnant, and son, and nephew, saith the Lord.

24:17And made the world as a wilderness, and destroyed the cities thereof, and opened not the house of his prisoners?

24:18All the kings of the nations, yea, all of them, lie in glory, every one of them in his own house.

24:19But thou art cast out of thy grave like an abominable branch, and the remnant of those that are slain, thrust through with a sword, that go down to the stones of the pit; as a carcass trodden under feet.

24:20Thou shalt not be joined with them in burial, because thou hast destroyed thy land and slain thy people; the seed of evil-doers shall never be renowned.

24:21Prepare slaughter for his children for the iniquities of their fathers, that they do not rise, nor possess the land, nor fill the face of the world with cities.

24:22For I will rise up against them, saith the Lord of Hosts, and cut off from Babylon the name, and remnant, and son, and nephew, saith the Lord.

[23] I will also make it a possession for the bittern, and pools of water: and I will sweep it with the besom of destruction, saith the LORD of hosts.

[24] The LORD of hosts hath sworn, saying, Surely as I have thought, so shall it come to pass; and as I have purposed, so shall it stand:

[25] That I will break the Assyrian in my land, and upon my mountains tread him under foot: then shall his yoke depart from off them, and his burden depart from off their shoulders.

[26] This is the purpose that is purposed upon the whole earth: and this is the hand that is stretched out upon all the nations.

[27] For the LORD of hosts hath purposed, and who shall disannul it? and his hand is stretched out, and who shall turn it back?

[28] In the year that king Ahaz died was this burden.

14:23 I will also make it a possession for the bittern and pools of water; and I will sweep it with the besom of destruction, saith the Lord of hosts.

14:24 The Lord of hosts hath sworn, saying, Surely as I have thought, so shall it come to pass; and as I have purposed, so shall it stand,

14:25 That I will break the Assyrian in my land and upon my mountains tread him underfoot; then shall his yoke depart from off them, and his burden depart from off their shoulders.

14:26 This is the purpose that is purposed upon the whole earth; and this is the hand that is stretched out upon all the nations.

14:27 For the Lord of hosts hath purposed. And who shall disannul it? And his hand is stretched out. And who shall turn it back?

14:28 In the year that King Ahaz died was this burden.

24:23 I will also make it a possession for the bittern, and pools of water; and I will sweep it with the besom of destruction, saith the Lord of Hosts.

24:24 The Lord of Hosts hath sworn, saying: Surely as I have thought, so shall it come to pass; and as I have purposed, so shall it stand—

24:25 that I will bring the Assyrian in my land, and upon my mountains tread him under foot; then shall his yoke depart from off them, and his burden depart from off their shoulders.

24:26 This is the purpose that is purposed upon the whole earth; and this is the hand that is stretched out upon all nations.

24:27 For the Lord of Hosts hath purposed, and who shall disannul? And his hand is stretched out, and who shall turn it back?

24:28 In the year that king Ahaz died was this burden.

[29] Rejoice not thou, whole Palestina, because the rod of him that smote thee is broken: for out of the serpent's root shall come forth a cockatrice, and his fruit shall be a fiery flying serpent.

[30] And the firstborn of the poor shall feed, and the needy shall lie down in safety: and I will kill thy root with famine, and he shall slay thy remnant.

[31] Howl, O gate; cry, O city; thou, whole Palestina, art dissolved: for there shall come from the north a smoke, and none shall be alone in his appointed times.

[32] What shall one then answer the messengers of the nation? That the LORD hath founded Zion, and the poor of his people shall trust in it.

15

[1] The burden of Moab. Because in the night Ar of Moab is laid waste, and brought to silence; because in the night Kir of Moab is laid waste, and brought to silence;

14:29 Rejoice not thou, whole Palestina, because the rod of him that smote thee is broken; for out of the serpent's root shall come forth a cockatrice, and his fruit shall be a fiery flying serpent.

14:30 And the firstborn of the poor shall feed, and the needy shall lie down in safety; and I will kill thy root with famine, and he shall slay thy remnant.

14:31 Howl, O gate; cry, O city; thou, whole Palestina, art dissolved; for there shall come from the north a smoke, and none shall be alone in his appointed times.

14:32 What shall then answer the messengers of the nation? That the Lord hath founded Zion, and the poor of his people shall trust in it.

Chapter 15

15:1 The burden of Moab: Because in the night Ar of Moab is laid waste and brought to silence; because in the night Kir of Moab is laid waste, and brought to silence;

24:29Rejoice not thou, whole Palestina, because the rod of him that smote thee is broken; for out of the serpent's root shall come forth a cockatrice, and his fruit shall be a fiery flying serpent.

24:30And the first-born of the poor shall feed, and the needy shall lie down in safety; and I will kill thy root with famine, and he shall slay thy remnant.

24:31Howl, O gate; cry, O city; thou, whole Palestina, art dissolved; for there shall come from the north a smoke, and none shall be alone in his appointed times.

24:32What shall then answer the messengers of the nations? That the Lord hath founded Zion, and the poor of his people shall trust in it.

[2] He is gone up to Bajith, and to Dibon, the high places, to weep: Moab shall howl over Nebo, and over Medeba: on all their heads shall be baldness, and every beard cut off.

[3] In their streets they shall gird themselves with sackcloth: on the tops of their houses, and in their streets, every one shall howl, weeping abundantly.

[4] And Heshbon shall cry, and Elealeh: their voice shall be heard even unto Jahaz: therefore the armed soldiers of Moab shall cry out; his life shall be grievous unto him.

[5] My heart shall cry out for Moab; his fugitives shall flee unto Zoar, an heifer of three years old: for by the mounting up of Luhith with weeping shall they go it up; for in the way of Horonaim they shall raise up a cry of destruction.

[6] For the waters of Nimrim shall be desolate: for the hay is withered away, the grass faileth, there is no green thing.

15:2 He is gone up to Bajith and to Dibon, the high places, to weep; Moab shall howl over Nebo and over Medeba; on all their heads shall be baldness, and every beard cut off.

15:3 In their streets they shall gird themselves with sackcloth; on the tops of their houses and in their streets everyone shall howl, weeping abundantly.

15:4 And Heshbon shall cry and Elealeh; their voice shall be heard even unto Jahaz; therefore, the armed soldiers of Moab shall cry out; his life shall be grievous unto him.

15:5 My heart shall cry out for Moab; his fugitives shall flee unto Zoar, a heifer of three years old; for by the mounting up of Luhith, with weeping shall they go it up; for in the way of Horonaim they shall raise up a cry of destruction.

15:6 For the waters of Nimrim shall be desolate; for the hay is withered away; the grass faileth; there is no green thing.

[7] Therefore the abundance they have gotten, and that which they have laid up, shall they carry away to the brook of the willows.

[8] For the cry is gone round about the borders of Moab; the howling thereof unto Eglaim, and the howling thereof unto Beer-elim.

[9] For the waters of Dimon shall be full of blood: for I will bring more upon Dimon, lions upon him that escapeth of Moab, and upon the remnant of the land.

.16

[1] Send ye the lamb to the ruler of the land from Sela to the wilderness, unto the mount of the daughter of Zion.

[2] For it shall be, that, as a wandering bird cast out of the nest, so the daughters of Moab shall be at the fords of Arnon.

[3] Take counsel, execute judgment; make thy shadow as the night in the midst of the noonday; hide the outcasts; bewray not him that wandereth.

15:7 Therefore, the abundance they have gotten and that which they have laid up shall they carry away to the brook of the willows.

15:8 For the cry is gone round about the borders of Moab--the howling thereof unto Eglaim, and the howling thereof unto Beer-elim.

15:9 For the waters of Dimon shall be full of blood; for I will bring more upon Dimon, lions upon him that escapeth of Moab and upon the remnant of the land.

Chapter 16

16:1 Send ye the lamb to the ruler of the land, from Sela to the wilderness, unto the mount of the daughter of Zion.

16:2 For it shall be that, as a wandering bird cast out of the nest, so the daughters of Moab shall be at the fords of Arnon.

16:3 Take counsel; execute judgment; make thy shadow as the night in the midst of the noonday; hide the outcasts; bewray not him that wandereth.

[4] Let mine outcasts dwell with thee, Moab; be thou a covert to them from the face of the spoiler: for the extortioner is at an end, the spoiler ceaseth, the oppressors are consumed out of the land.

[5] And in mercy shall the throne be established: and he shall sit upon it in truth in the tabernacle of David, judging, and seeking judgment, and hasting righteousness.

[6] We have heard of the pride of Moab; he is very proud: even of his haughtiness, and his pride, and his wrath: but his lies shall not be so.

[7] Therefore shall Moab howl for Moab, every one shall howl: for the foundations of Kir-hareseth shall ye mourn; surely they are stricken.

[8] For the fields of Heshbon languish, and the vine of Sibmah: the lords of the heathen have broken down the principal plants thereof, they are come even unto Jazer, they wandered through the wilderness: her branches are stretched out, they are gone over the sea.

16:4 Let mine outcasts dwell with thee, Moab; be thou a covert to them from the face of the spoiler; for the extortioner is at an end; the spoiler ceaseth; the oppressors are consumed out of the land.

16:5 And in mercy shall the throne be established; and he shall sit upon it in truth in the tabernacle of David, judging, and seeking judgment, and hasting righteousness.

16:6 We have heard of the pride of Moab--of his haughtiness and his pride, for he is very proud--and his wrath, his lies, and all his evil works.

16:7 Therefore shall Moab howl for Moab; everyone shall howl; for the foundations of Kir-hareseth shall ye mourn; surely they are stricken.

16:8 For the fields of Heshbon languish, and the vine of Sibmah; the lords of the heathen have broken down the principal plants thereof; they are come even unto Jazer; they wandered through the wilderness; her branches are stretched out; they are gone over the sea.

[9] Therefore I will bewail with the weeping of Jazer the vine of Sibmah: I will water thee with my tears, O Heshbon, and Elealeh: for the shouting for thy summer fruits and for thy harvest is fallen.

[10] And gladness is taken away, and joy out of the plentiful field; and in the vineyards there shall be no singing, neither shall there be shouting: the treaders shall tread out no wine in their presses; I have made their vintage shouting to cease.

[11] Wherefore my bowels shall sound like an harp for Moab, and mine inward parts for Kir-haresh.

[12] And it shall come to pass, when it is seen that Moab is weary on the high place, that he shall come to his sanctuary to pray; but he shall not prevail.

[13] This is the word that the LORD hath spoken concerning Moab since that time.

16:9 Therefore, I will bewail with the weeping of Jazer, the vine of Sibmah; I will water thee with my tears, O Heshbon and Elealeh; for the shouting for thy summer fruits and for thy harvest is fallen.

16:10 And gladness is taken away, and joy out of the plentiful field; and in the vineyards there shall be no singing; neither shall there be shouting; the treaders shall tread out no wine in their presses; I have made their vintage shouting to cease.

16:11 Wherefore, my bowels shall sound like a harp for Moab, and mine inward parts for Kir-haresh.

16:12 And it shall come to pass, when it is seen that Moab is weary on the high place, that he shall come to his sanctuary to pray; but he shall not prevail.

16:13 This is the word that the Lord hath spoken concerning Moab since that time.

[14] But now the LORD hath spoken, saying, Within three years, as the years of an hireling, and the glory of Moab shall be contemned, with all that great multitude; and the remnant shall be very small and feeble.

.17

[1] The burden of Damascus. Behold, Damascus is taken away from being a city, and it shall be a ruinous heap.

[2] The cities of Aroer are forsaken: they shall be for flocks, which shall lie down, and none shall make them afraid.

[3] The fortress also shall cease from Ephraim, and the kingdom from Damascus, and the remnant of Syria: they shall be as the glory of the children of Israel, saith the LORD of hosts.

[4] And in that day it shall come to pass, that the glory of Jacob shall be made thin, and the fatness of his flesh shall wax lean.

16:14 But now the Lord hath spoken, saying, Within three years, as the years of a hireling, and the glory of Moab shall be contemned with all that great multitude; and the remnant shall be very small and feeble.

Chapter 17

17:1 The burden of Damascus: Behold, Damascus is taken away from being a city, and it shall be a ruinous heap.

17:2 The cities of Aroer are forsaken; they shall be for flocks, which shall lie down, and none shall make them afraid.

17:3 The fortress also shall cease from Ephraim, and the kingdom from Damascus, and the remnant of Syria; they shall be as the glory of the children of Israel, saith the Lord of hosts.

17:4 And in that day it shall come to pass that the glory of Jacob shall be made thin, and the fatness of his flesh shall wax lean.

[5] And it shall be as when the harvestman gathereth the corn, and reapeth the ears with his arm; and it shall be as he that gathereth ears in the valley of Rephaim.

[6] Yet gleaning grapes shall be left in it, as the shaking of an olive tree, two or three berries in the top of the uppermost bough, four or five in the outmost fruitful branches thereof, saith the LORD God of Israel.

[7] At that day shall a man look to his Maker, and his eyes shall have respect to the Holy One of Israel.

[8] And he shall not look to the altars, the work of his hands, neither shall respect that which his fingers have made, either the groves, or the images.

[9] In that day shall his strong cities be as a forsaken bough, and an uppermost branch, which they left because of the children of Israel: and there shall be desolation.

17:5 And it shall be as when the harvestman gathereth the corn and reapeth the ears with his arm; and it shall be as he that gathereth ears in the valley of Rephaim.

17:6 Yet gleaning grapes shall be left in it, as the shaking of an olive tree, two or three berries in the top of the uppermost bough, four or five in the outmost fruitful branches thereof, saith the Lord God of Israel.

17:7 At that day shall a man look to his Maker, and his eyes shall have respect to the Holy One of Israel.

17:8 And he shall not look to the altars, the work of his hands, neither shall respect that which his fingers have made, either the groves or the images.

17:9 In that day shall his strong cities be as a forsaken bough and an uppermost branch, which they left because of the children of Israel; and there shall be desolation.

[10] Because thou hast forgotten the God of thy salvation, and hast not been mindful of the rock of thy strength, therefore shalt thou plant pleasant plants, and shalt set it with strange slips:

[11] In the day shalt thou make thy plant to grow, and in the morning shalt thou make thy seed to flourish: but the harvest shall be a heap in the day of grief and of desperate sorrow.

[12] Woe to the multitude of many people, which make a noise like the noise of the seas; and to the rushing of nations, that make a rushing like the rushing of mighty waters!

[13] The nations shall rush like the rushing of many waters: but God shall rebuke them, and they shall flee far off, and shall be chased as the chaff of the mountains before the wind, and like a rolling thing before the whirlwind.

[14] And behold at eveningtide trouble; and before the morning he is not. This is the portion of them that spoil us, and the lot of them that rob us.

17:10 Because thou hast forgotten the God of thy salvation and hast not been mindful of the Rock of thy strength, therefore shalt thou plant pleasant plants and shalt set it with strange slips;

17:11 In the day shalt thou make thy plant to grow, and in the morning shalt thou make thy seed to flourish; but the harvest shall be a heap in the day of grief and of desperate sorrow.

17:12 Woe to the multitude of many people, which make a noise like the noise of the seas, and to the rushing of nations, that make a rushing like the rushing of mighty waters!

17:13 The nations shall rush like the rushing of many waters; but God shall rebuke them, and they shall flee far off and shall be chased as the chaff of the mountains before the wind and like a rolling thing before the whirlwind.

17:14 And behold, at eventide trouble; and before the morning he is not. This is the portion of them that spoil us and the lot of them that rob us.

[1] Woe to the land shadowing with wings, which is beyond the rivers of Ethiopia:

[2] That sendeth ambassadors by the sea, even in vessels of bulrushes upon the waters, saying, Go, ye swift messengers, to a nation scattered and peeled, to a people terrible from their beginning hitherto; a nation meted out and trodden down, whose land the rivers have spoiled!

[3] All ye inhabitants of the world, and dwellers on the earth, see ye, when he lifteth up an ensign on the mountains; and when he bloweth a trumpet, hear ye.

[4] For so the LORD said unto me, I will take my rest, and I will consider in my dwelling place like a clear heat upon herbs, and like a cloud of dew in the heat of harvest.

[5] For afore the harvest, when the bud is perfect, and the sour grape is ripening in the flower, he shall both cut off the sprigs with pruning hooks, and take away and cut down the branches.

Chapter 18

18:1 Woe to the land shadowing with wings, which is beyond the rivers of Ethiopia,

18:2 That sendeth ambassadors by the sea, even in vessels of bulrushes upon the waters, saying, Go, ye swift messengers, to a nation scattered and peeled, to a people terrible from their beginning hitherto--a nation meted out and trodden down, whose land the rivers have spoiled!

18:3 All ye inhabitants of the world and dwellers on the earth, see ye, when he lifteth up an ensign on the mountains; and when he bloweth a trumpet, hear ye.

18:4 For so the Lord said unto me, I will take my rest, and I will consider in my dwelling place like a clear heat upon herbs and like a cloud of dew in the heat of harvest.

18:5 For afore the harvest, when the bud is perfect and the sour grape is ripening in the flower, he shall both cut off the sprigs with pruning hooks and take away and cut down the branches.

[6] They shall be left together unto the fowls of the mountains, and to the beasts of the earth: and the fowls shall summer upon them, and all the beasts of the earth shall winter upon them.

[7] In that time shall the present be brought unto the LORD of hosts of a people scattered and peeled, and from a people terrible from their beginning hitherto; a nation meted out and trodden under foot, whose land the rivers have spoiled, to the place of the name of the LORD of hosts, the mount Zion.

.19

[1] The burden of Egypt. Behold, the LORD rideth upon a swift cloud, and shall come into Egypt: and the idols of Egypt shall be moved at his presence, and the heart of Egypt shall melt in the midst of it.

[2] And I will set the Egyptians against the Egyptians: and they shall fight every one against his brother, and every one against his neighbour; city against city, and kingdom against kingdom.

18:6 They shall be left together unto the fowls of the mountains and to the beasts of the earth; and the fowls shall summer upon them, and all the beasts of the earth shall winter upon them.

18:7 In that time shall the present be brought unto the Lord of hosts of a people scattered and peeled, and from a people terrible from their beginning hitherto--a nation meted out and trodden underfoot, whose land the rivers have spoiled, to the place of the name of the Lord of hosts, the Mount Zion.

Chapter 19

19:1 The burden of Egypt: Behold, the Lord rideth upon a swift cloud and shall come into Egypt; and the idols of Egypt shall be moved at his presence, and the heart of Egypt shall melt in the midst of it.

19:2 And I will set the Egyptians against the Egyptians; and they shall fight, everyone against his brother and everyone against his neighbor, city against city and kingdom against kingdom.

[3] And the spirit of Egypt shall fail in the midst thereof; and I will destroy the counsel thereof: and they shall seek to the idols, and to the charmers, and to them that have familiar spirits, and to the wizards.

[4] And the Egyptians will I give over into the hand of a cruel lord; and a fierce king shall rule over them, saith the Lord, the LORD of hosts.

[5] And the waters shall fail from the sea, and the river shall be wasted and dried up.

[6] And they shall turn the rivers far away; and the brooks of defence shall be emptied and dried up: the reeds and flags shall wither.

[7] The paper reeds by the brooks, by the mouth of the brooks, and every thing sown by the brooks, shall wither, be driven away, and be no more.

[8] The fishers also shall mourn, and all they that cast angle into the brooks shall lament, and they that spread nets upon the waters shall languish.

19:3 And the spirit of Egypt shall fail in the midst thereof; and I will destroy the counsel thereof; and they shall seek to the idols, and to the charmers, and to them that have familiar spirits, and to the wizards.

19:4 And the Egyptians will I give over into the hand of a cruel lord; and a fierce king shall rule over them, saith the Lord, the Lord of hosts.

19:5 And the waters shall fail from the sea, and the river shall be wasted and dried up.

19:6 And they shall turn the rivers far away; and the brooks of defense shall be emptied and dried up; the reeds and flags shall wither.

19:7 The paper reeds by the brooks, by the mouth of the brooks, and everything sown by the brooks shall wither, be driven away, and be no more.

19:8 The fishers also shall mourn; and all they that cast angle into the brooks shall lament; and they that spread nets upon the waters shall languish.

[**9**] Moreover they that work in fine flax, and they that weave networks, shall be confounded.

[**10**] And they shall be broken in the purposes thereof, all that make sluices and ponds for fish.

[**11**] Surely the princes of Zoan are fools, the counsel of the wise counsellers of Pharaoh is become brutish: how say ye unto Pharaoh, I am the son of the wise, the son of ancient kings?

[**12**] Where are they? where are thy wise men? and let them tell thee now, and let them know what the LORD of hosts hath purposed upon Egypt.

[**13**] The princes of Zoan are become fools, the princes of Noph are deceived; they have also seduced Egypt, even they that are the stay of the tribes thereof.

[**14**] The LORD hath mingled a perverse spirit in the midst thereof: and they have caused Egypt to err in every work thereof, as a drunken man staggereth in his vomit.

19:9 Moreover, they that work in fine flax and they that weave networks shall be confounded.

19:10 And they shall be broken in the purposes thereof, all that make sluices and ponds for fish.

19:11 Surely the princes of Zoan are fools; the counsel of the wise counselors of Pharaoh is become brutish. How say ye unto Pharaoh, I am the son of the wise, the son of ancient kings?

19:12 Where are they? Where are thy wise men? And let them tell thee now, and let them know what the Lord of hosts hath purposed upon Egypt.

19:13 The princes of Zoan are become fools; the princes of Noph are deceived; they have also seduced Egypt, even they that are the stay of the tribes thereof.

19:14 The Lord hath mingled a perverse spirit in the midst thereof; and they have caused Egypt to err in every work thereof, as a drunken man staggereth in his vomit.

[15] Neither shall there be any work for Egypt, which the head or tail, branch or rush, may do.

[16] In that day shall Egypt be like unto women: and it shall be afraid and fear because of the shaking of the hand of the LORD of hosts, which he shaketh over it.

[17] And the land of Judah shall be a terror unto Egypt, every one that maketh mention thereof shall be afraid in himself, because of the counsel of the LORD of hosts, which he hath determined against it.

[18] In that day shall five cities in the land of Egypt speak the language of Canaan, and swear to the LORD of hosts; one shall be called, The city of destruction.

[19] In that day shall there be an altar to the LORD in the midst of the land of Egypt, and a pillar at the border thereof to the LORD.

19:15 Neither shall there be any work for Egypt, which the head or tail, branch or rush, may do.

19:16 In that day shall Egypt be like unto women; and it shall be afraid and fear because of the shaking of the hand of the Lord of hosts, which he shaketh over it.

19:17 And the land of Judah shall be a terror unto Egypt, everyone that maketh mention thereof shall be afraid in himself because of the counsel of the Lord of hosts which he hath determined against it.

19:18 In that day shall five cities in the land of Egypt speak the language of Canaan and swear to the Lord of hosts; one shall be called the city of destruction.

19:19 In that day shall there be an altar to the Lord in the midst of the land of Egypt and a pillar at the border thereof to the Lord.

[20] And it shall be for a sign and for a witness unto the LORD of hosts in the land of Egypt: for they shall cry unto the LORD because of the oppressors, and he shall send them a saviour, and a great one, and he shall deliver them.

[21] And the LORD shall be known to Egypt, and the Egyptians shall know the LORD in that day, and shall do sacrifice and oblation; yea, they shall vow a vow unto the LORD, and perform it.

[22] And the LORD shall smite Egypt: he shall smite and heal it: and they shall return even to the LORD, and he shall be intreated of them, and shall heal them.

[23] In that day shall there be a highway out of Egypt to Assyria, and the Assyrian shall come into Egypt, and the Egyptian into Assyria, and the Egyptians shall serve with the Assyrians.

[24] In that day shall Israel be the third with Egypt and with Assyria, even a blessing in the midst of the land:

19:20 And it shall be for a sign and for a witness unto the Lord of hosts in the land of Egypt; for they shall cry unto the Lord because of the oppressors; and he shall send them a savior, and a great one, and he shall deliver them.

19:21 And the Lord shall be known to Egypt, and the Egyptians shall know the Lord in that day and shall do sacrifice and oblation; yea, they shall vow a vow unto the Lord and perform it.

19:22 And the Lord shall smite Egypt; he shall smite and heal it; and they shall return even to the Lord; and he shall be entreated of them and shall heal them.

19:23 In that day shall there be a highway out of Egypt to Assyria, and the Assyrian shall come into Egypt, and the Egyptian into Assyria; and the Egyptians shall serve with the Assyrians.

19:24 In that day shall Israel be the third with Egypt and with Assyria, even a blessing in the midst of the land,

[25] Whom the LORD of hosts shall bless, saying, Blessed be Egypt my people, and Assyria the work of my hands, and Israel mine inheritance.

.20

[1] In the year that Tartan came unto Ashdod, (when Sargon the king of Assyria sent him,) and fought against Ashdod, and took it;

[2] At the same time spake the LORD by Isaiah the son of Amoz, saying, Go and loose the sackcloth from off thy loins, and put off thy shoe from thy foot. And he did so, walking naked and barefoot.

[3] And the LORD said, Like as my servant Isaiah hath walked naked and barefoot three years for a sign and wonder upon Egypt and upon Ethiopia;

[4] So shall the king of Assyria lead away the Egyptians prisoners, and the Ethiopians captives, young and old, naked and barefoot, even with their buttocks uncovered, to the shame of Egypt.

19:25 Whom the Lord of hosts shall bless, saying, Blessed be Egypt, my people, and Assyria, the work of my hands, and Israel, mine inheritance.

Chapter 20

20:1 In the year that Tartan came unto Ashdod (when Sargon, the king of Assyria, sent him), and fought against Ashdod, and took it,

20:2 At the same time spake the Lord by Isaiah, the son of Amoz, saying, Go, and loose the sackcloth from off thy loins, and put off thy shoe from thy foot. And he did so, walking naked and barefoot.

20:3 And the Lord said, Like as my servant Isaiah hath walked naked and barefoot three years for a sign and wonder upon Egypt and upon Ethiopia,

20:4 So shall the king of Assyria lead away the Egyptians prisoners and the Ethiopians captives, young and old, naked and barefoot, even with their buttocks uncovered, to the shame of Egypt.

[5] And they shall be afraid and ashamed of Ethiopia their expectation, and of Egypt their glory.

[6] And the inhabitant of this isle shall say in that day, Behold, such is our expectation, whither we flee for help to be delivered from the king of Assyria: and how shall we escape?

.21

[1] The burden of the desert of the sea. As whirlwinds in the south pass through; so it cometh from the desert, from a terrible land.

[2] A grievous vision is declared unto me; the treacherous dealer dealeth treacherously, and the spoiler spoileth. Go up, O Elam: besiege, O Media; all the sighing thereof have I made to cease.

[3] Therefore are my loins filled with pain: pangs have taken hold upon me, as the pangs of a woman that travaileth: I was bowed down at the hearing of it; I was dismayed at the seeing of it.

20:5 And they shall be afraid and ashamed of Ethiopia, their expectation, and of Egypt, their glory.

20:6 And the inhabitant of this isle shall say in that day, Behold, such is our expectation--whither we flee for help to be delivered from the king of Assyria. And how shall we escape?

Chapter 21

21:1 The burden of the desert of the sea: As whirlwinds in the south pass through, so it cometh from the desert, from the terrible land.

21:2 A grievous vision is declared unto me: The treacherous dealer dealeth treacherously, and the spoiler spoileth. Go up, O Elam; besiege, O Media; all the sighing thereof have I made to cease.

21:3 Therefore are my loins filled with pain; pangs have taken hold upon me as the pangs of a woman that travaileth; I was bowed down at the hearing of it; I was dismayed at the seeing of it.

[4] My heart panted, fearfulness affrighted me: the night of my pleasure hath he turned into fear unto me.

[5] Prepare the table, watch in the watchtower, eat, drink: arise, ye princes, and anoint the shield.

[6] For thus hath the Lord said unto me, Go, set a watchman, let him declare what he seeth.

[7] And he saw a chariot with a couple of horsemen, a chariot of asses, and a chariot of camels; and he hearkened diligently with much heed:

[8] And he cried, A lion: My lord, I stand continually upon the watchtower in the daytime, and I am set in my ward whole nights:

[9] And, behold, here cometh a chariot of men, with a couple of horsemen. And he answered and said, Babylon is fallen, is fallen; and all the graven images of her gods he hath broken unto the ground.

21:4 My heart panted; fearfulness affrighted me; the night of my pleasure hath he turned into fear unto me.

21:5 Prepare the table; watch in the watchtower; eat; drink; arise, ye princes, and anoint the shield.

21:6 For thus hath the Lord said unto me, Go; set a watchman; let him declare what he seeth.

21:7 And he saw a chariot with a couple of horsemen, a chariot of asses, and a chariot of camels; and he hearkened diligently with much heed.

21:8 And he cried, A lion! My lord, I stand continually upon the watchtower in the daytime, and I am set in my ward whole nights;

21:9 And behold, here cometh a chariot of men with a couple of horsemen. And he answered and said, Babylon is fallen, is fallen; and all the graven images of her gods he hath broken unto the ground.

[10] O my threshing, and the corn of my floor: that which I have heard of the LORD of hosts, the God of Israel, have I declared unto you.

[11] The burden of Dumah. He calleth to me out of Seir, Watchman, what of the night? Watchman, what of the night?

[12] The watchman said, The morning cometh, and also the night: if ye will inquire, inquire ye: return, come.

[13] The burden upon Arabia. In the forest in Arabia shall ye lodge, O ye travelling companies of Dedanim.

[14] The inhabitants of the land of Tema brought water to him that was thirsty, they prevented with their bread him that fled.

[15] For they fled from the swords, from the drawn sword, and from the bent bow, and from the grievousness of war.

[16] For thus hath the Lord said unto me, Within a year, according to the years of an hireling, and all the glory of Kedar shall fail:

21:10 O my threshing and the corn of my floor; that which I have heard of the Lord of hosts, the God of Israel, have I declared unto you.

21:11 The burden of Dumah: He calleth to me out of Seir, Watchman, what of the night? Watchman, what of the night?

21:12 The watchman said, The morning cometh, and also the night; if ye will inquire, inquire ye; return; come.

21:13 The burden upon Arabia: In the forest in Arabia shall ye lodge, O ye traveling companies of Dedanim.

21:14 The inhabitants of the land of Tema brought water to him that was thirsty; they prevented with their bread him that fled.

21:15 For they fled from the swords, from the drawn sword, and from the bent bow, and from the grievousness of war.

21:16 For thus hath the Lord said unto me, Within a year, according to the years of a hireling, and all the glory of Kedar shall fail;

[17] And the residue of the number of archers, the mighty men of the children of Kedar, shall be diminished: for the LORD God of Israel hath spoken it.

.22

[1] The burden of the valley of vision. What aileth thee now, that thou art wholly gone up to the housetops?

[2] Thou that art full of stirs, a tumultuous city, a joyous city: thy slain men are not slain with the sword, nor dead in battle.

[3] All thy rulers are fled together, they are bound by the archers: all that are found in thee are bound together, which have fled from far.

[4] Therefore said I, Look away from me; I will weep bitterly, labour not to comfort me, because of the spoiling of the daughter of my people.

[5] For it is a day of trouble, and of treading down, and of perplexity by the Lord GOD of hosts in the valley of vision, breaking down the walls, and of crying to the mountains.

21:17 And the residue of the number of archers, the mighty men of the children of Kedar, shall be diminished; for the Lord God of Israel hath spoken it.

Chapter 22

22:1 The burden of the valley of vision: What aileth thee now, that thou art wholly gone up to the housetops?

22:2 Thou that art full of stirs, a tumultuous city, a joyous city; thy slain men are not slain with the sword nor dead in battle.

22:3 All thy rulers are fled together; they are bound by the archers; all that are found in thee are bound together which have fled from far.

22:4 Therefore said I, Look away from me; I will weep bitterly; labor not to comfort me because of the spoiling of the daughter of my people.

22:5 For it is a day of trouble, and of treading down, and of perplexity by the Lord God of hosts in the valley of vision, breaking down the walls, and of crying to the mountains.

[6] And Elam bare the quiver with chariots of men and horsemen, and Kir uncovered the shield.

[7] And it shall come to pass, that thy choicest valleys shall be full of chariots, and the horsemen shall set themselves in array at the gate.

[8] And he discovered the covering of Judah, and thou didst look in that day to the armour of the house of the forest.

[9] Ye have seen also the breaches of the city of David, that they are many: and ye gathered together the waters of the lower pool.

[10] And ye have numbered the houses of Jerusalem, and the houses have ye broken down to fortify the wall.

[11] Ye made also a ditch between the two walls for the water of the old pool: but ye have not looked unto the maker thereof, neither had respect unto him that fashioned it long ago.

22:6 And Elam bare the quiver with chariots of men and horsemen, and Kir uncovered the shield.

22:7 And it shall come to pass that thy choicest valleys shall be full of chariots, and the horsemen shall set themselves in array at the gate.

22:8 And he discovered the covering of Judah, and thou didst look in that day to the armor of the house of the forest.

22:9 Ye have seen also the breaches of the city of David, that they are many; and ye gathered together the waters of the lower pool.

22:10 And ye have numbered the houses of Jerusalem, and the houses have ye broken down to fortify the wall.

22:11 Ye made also a ditch between the two walls for the water of the old pool; but ye have not looked unto the maker thereof, neither had respect unto him that fashioned it long ago.

[12] And in that day did the Lord GOD of hosts call to weeping, and to mourning, and to baldness, and to girding with sackcloth:

[13] And behold joy and gladness, slaying oxen, and killing sheep, eating flesh, and drinking wine: let us eat and drink; for to morrow we shall die.

[14] And it was revealed in mine ears by the LORD of hosts, Surely this iniquity shall not be purged from you till ye die, saith the Lord GOD of hosts.

[15] Thus saith the Lord GOD of hosts, Go, get thee unto this treasurer, even unto Shebna, which is over the house, and say,

[16] What hast thou here? and whom hast thou here, that thou hast hewed thee out a sepulchre here, as he that heweth him out a sepulchre on high, and that graveth an habitation for himself in a rock?

[17] Behold, the LORD will carry thee away with a mighty captivity, and will surely cover thee.

22:12 And in that day did the Lord God of hosts call to weeping, and to mourning, and to baldness, and to girding with sackcloth;

22:13 And behold joy and gladness, slaying oxen, and killing sheep, eating flesh, and drinking wine; let us eat and drink, for tomorrow we shall die.

22:14 And it was revealed in mine ears by the Lord of hosts, Surely this iniquity shall not be purged from you till ye die, saith the Lord God of hosts.

22:15 Thus saith the Lord God of hosts, Go, get thee unto this treasurer, even unto Shebna, which is over the house, and say,

22:16 What hast thou here, and whom hast thou here, that thou hast hewed thee out a sepulcher here, as he that heweth him out a sepulcher on high and that graveth a habitation for himself in a rock?

22:17 Behold, the Lord will carry thee away with a mighty captivity and will surely cover thee.

[18] He will surely violently turn and toss thee like a ball into a large country: there shalt thou die, and there the chariots of thy glory shall be the shame of thy lord's house.

[19] And I will drive thee from thy station, and from thy state shall he pull thee down.

[20] And it shall come to pass in that day, that I will call my servant Eliakim the son of Hilkiah:

[21] And I will clothe him with thy robe, and strengthen him with thy girdle, and I will commit thy government into his hand: and he shall be a father to the inhabitants of Jerusalem, and to the house of Judah.

[22] And the key of the house of David will I lay upon his shoulder; so he shall open, and none shall shut; and he shall shut, and none shall open.

[23] And I will fasten him as a nail in a sure place; and he shall be for a glorious throne to his father's house.

22:18 He will surely violently turn and toss thee like a ball into a large country; there shalt thou die, and there the chariots of thy glory shall be the shame of thy lord's house.

22:19 And I will drive thee from thy station, and from thy state shall he pull thee down.

22:20 And it shall come to pass in that day, that I will call my servant Eliakim, the son of Hilkiah;

22:21 And I will clothe him with thy robe and strengthen him with thy girdle, and I will commit thy government into his hand; and he shall be a father to the inhabitants of Jerusalem and to the house of Judah.

22:22 And the key of the house of David will I lay upon his shoulder; so he shall open, and none shall shut; and he shall shut, and none shall open.

22:23 And I will fasten him as a nail in a sure place; and he shall be for a glorious throne to his father's house.

[24] And they shall hang upon him all the glory of his father's house, the offspring and the issue, all vessels of small quantity, from the vessels of cups, even to all the vessels of flagons.

[25] In that day, saith the LORD of hosts, shall the nail that is fastened in the sure place be removed, and be cut down, and fall; and the burden that was upon it shall be cut off: for the LORD hath spoken it.

.23

[1] The burden of Tyre. Howl, ye ships of Tarshish; for it is laid waste, so that there is no house, no entering in: from the land of Chittim it is revealed to them.

[2] Be still, ye inhabitants of the isle; thou whom the merchants of Zidon, that pass over the sea, have replenished.

[3] And by great waters the seed of Sihor, the harvest of the river, is her revenue; and she is a mart of nations.

22:24 And they shall hang upon him all the glory of his father's house, the offspring and the issue, all vessels of small quantity, from the vessels of cups, even to all the vessels of flagons.

22:25 In that day, saith the Lord of hosts, shall the nail that is fastened in the sure place be removed, and be cut down, and fall; and the burden that was upon it shall be cut off; for the Lord hath spoken it.

Chapter 23

23:1 The burden of Tyre: Howl, ye ships of Tarshish; for it is laid waste so that there is no house, no entering in; from the land of Chittim it is revealed to them.

23:2 Be still, ye inhabitants of the isle, thou whom the merchants of Zidon, that pass over the sea, have replenished.

23:3 And by great waters the seed of Sihor, the harvest of the river, is her revenue; and she is a mart of nations.

[4] Be thou ashamed, O Zidon: for the sea hath spoken, even the strength of the sea, saying, I travail not, nor bring forth children, neither do I nourish up young men, nor bring up virgins.

[5] As at the report concerning Egypt, so shall they be sorely pained at the report of Tyre.

[6] Pass ye over to Tarshish; howl, ye inhabitants of the isle.

[7] Is this your joyous city, whose antiquity is of ancient days? her own feet shall carry her afar off to sojourn.

[8] Who hath taken this counsel against Tyre, the crowning city, whose merchants are princes, whose traffickers are the honourable of the earth?

[9] The LORD of hosts hath purposed it, to stain the pride of all glory, and to bring into contempt all the honourable of the earth.

[10] Pass through thy land as a river, O daughter of Tarshish: there is no more strength.

23:4 Be thou ashamed, O Zidon; for the sea hath spoken, even the strength of the sea, saying, I travail not nor bring forth children; neither do I nourish up young men nor bring up virgins.

23:5 As at the report concerning Egypt, so shall they be sorely pained at the report of Tyre.

23:6 Pass ye over to Tarshish; howl, ye inhabitants of the isle.

23:7 Is this your joyous city, whose antiquity is of ancient days? Her own feet shall carry her afar off to sojourn.

23:8 Who hath taken this counsel against Tyre, the crowning city, whose merchants are princes, whose traffickers are the honorable of the earth?

23:9 The Lord of hosts hath purposed it, to stain the pride of all glory and to bring into contempt all the honorable of the earth.

23:10 Pass through thy land as a river, O daughter of Tarshish; there is no more strength in thee.

[11] He stretched out his hand over the sea, he shook the kingdoms: the LORD hath given a commandment against the merchant city, to destroy the strong holds thereof.

[12] And he said, Thou shalt no more rejoice, O thou oppressed virgin, daughter of Zidon: arise, pass over to Chittim; there also shalt thou have no rest.

[13] Behold the land of the Chaldeans; this people was not, till the Assyrian founded it for them that dwell in the wilderness: they set up the towers thereof, they raised up the palaces thereof; and he brought it to ruin.

[14] Howl, ye ships of Tarshish: for your strength is laid waste.

[15] And it shall come to pass in that day, that Tyre shall be forgotten seventy years, according to the days of one king: after the end of seventy years shall Tyre sing as an harlot.

23:11 He stretched out his hand over the sea; he shook the kingdoms; the Lord hath given a commandment against the merchant city to destroy the strongholds thereof.

23:12 And he said, Thou shalt no more rejoice, O thou oppressed virgin, daughter of Zidon; arise; pass over to Chittim; there also shalt thou have no rest.

23:13 Behold the land of the Chaldeans; this people was not, till the Assyrian founded it for them that dwell in the wilderness; they set up the towers thereof; they raised up the palaces thereof; and he brought it to ruin.

23:14 Howl, ye ships of Tarshish; for your strength is laid waste.

23:15 And it shall come to pass in that day, that Tyre shall be forgotten seventy years, according to the days of one king; after the end of seventy years shall Tyre sing as a harlot.

[16] Take an harp, go about the city, thou harlot that hast been forgotten; make sweet melody, sing many songs, that thou mayest be remembered.

[17] And it shall come to pass after the end of seventy years, that the LORD will visit Tyre, and she shall turn to her hire, and shall commit fornication with all the kingdoms of the world upon the face of the earth.

[18] And her merchandise and her hire shall be holiness to the LORD: it shall not be treasured nor laid up; for her merchandise shall be for them that dwell before the LORD, to eat sufficiently, and for durable clothing.

.24

[1] Behold, the LORD maketh the earth empty, and maketh it waste, and turneth it upside down, and scattereth abroad the inhabitants thereof.

23:16 Take a harp; go about the city, thou harlot that hast been forgotten; make sweet melody; sing many songs, that thou mayest be remembered.

23:17 And it shall come to pass, after the end of seventy years, that the Lord will visit Tyre; and she shall turn to her hire and shall commit fornication with all the kingdoms of the world upon the face of the earth.

23:18 And her merchandise and her hire shall be holiness to the Lord; it shall not be treasured nor laid up; for her merchandise shall be for them that dwell before the Lord, to eat sufficiently and for durable clothing.

Chapter 24

24:1 Behold, the Lord maketh the earth empty, and maketh it waste, and turneth it upside down, and scattereth abroad the inhabitants thereof.

[2] And it shall be, as with the people, so with the priest; as with the servant, so with his master; as with the maid, so with her mistress; as with the buyer, so with the seller; as with the lender, so with the borrower; as with the taker of usury, so with the giver of usury to him.

[3] The land shall be utterly emptied, and utterly spoiled: for the LORD hath spoken this word.

[4] The earth mourneth and fadeth away, the world languisheth and fadeth away, the haughty people of the earth do languish.

[5] The earth also is defiled under the inhabitants thereof; because they have transgressed the laws, changed the ordinance, broken the everlasting covenant.

[6] Therefore hath the curse devoured the earth, and they that dwell therein are desolate: therefore the inhabitants of the earth are burned, and few men left.

[7] The new wine mourneth, the vine languisheth, all the merryhearted do sigh.

24:2 And it shall be, as with the people, so with the priest; as with the servant, so with his master; as with the maid, so with her mistress; as with the buyer, so with the seller; as with the lender, so with the borrower; as with the taker of usury, so with the giver of usury to him.

24:3 The land shall be utterly emptied and utterly spoiled; for the Lord hath spoken this word.

24:4 The earth mourneth and fadeth away; the world languisheth and fadeth away; the haughty people of the earth do languish.

24:5 The earth also is defiled under the inhabitants thereof because they have transgressed the laws, changed the ordinance, broken the everlasting covenant.

24:6 Therefore hath the curse devoured the earth, and they that dwell therein are desolate; therefore, the inhabitants of the earth are burned and few men left.

24:7 The new wine mourneth; the vine languisheth; all the merry-hearted do sigh.

[8] The mirth of tabrets ceaseth, the noise of them that rejoice endeth, the joy of the harp ceaseth.

[9] They shall not drink wine with a song; strong drink shall be bitter to them that drink it.

[10] The city of confusion is broken down: every house is shut up, that no man may come in.

[11] There is a crying for wine in the streets; all joy is darkened, the mirth of the land is gone.

[12] In the city is left desolation, and the gate is smitten with destruction.

[13] When thus it shall be in the midst of the land among the people, there shall be as the shaking of an olive tree, and as the gleaning grapes when the vintage is done.

[14] They shall lift up their voice, they shall sing for the majesty of the LORD, they shall cry aloud from the sea.

[15] Wherefore glorify ye the LORD in the fires, even the name of the LORD God of Israel in the isles of the sea.

24:8 The mirth of tabrets ceaseth; the noise of them that rejoice endeth; the joy of the harp ceaseth.

24:9 They shall not drink wine with a song; strong drink shall be bitter to them that drink it.

24:10 The city of confusion is broken down; every house is shut up, that no man may come in.

24:11 There is a crying for wine in the streets; all joy is darkened; the mirth of the land is gone.

24:12 In the city is left desolation, and the gate is smitten with destruction.

13 When thus it shall be in the midst of the land among the people, there shall be as the shaking of an olive tree and as the gleaning grapes when the vintage is done.

24:14 They shall lift up their voice; they shall sing for the majesty of the Lord; they shall cry aloud from the sea.

24:15 Wherefore, glorify ye the Lord in the fires, even the name of the Lord God of Israel in the isles of the sea.

[16] From the uttermost part of the earth have we heard songs, even glory to the righteous. But I said, My leanness, my leanness, woe unto me! the treacherous dealers have dealt treacherously; yea, the treacherous dealers have dealt very treacherously.

[17] Fear, and the pit, and the snare, are upon thee, O inhabitant of the earth.

[18] And it shall come to pass, that he who fleeth from the noise of the fear shall fall into the pit; and he that cometh up out of the midst of the pit shall be taken in the snare: for the windows from on high are open, and the foundations of the earth do shake.

[19] The earth is utterly broken down, the earth is clean dissolved, the earth is moved exceedingly.

[20] The earth shall reel to and fro like a drunkard, and shall be removed like a cottage; and the transgression thereof shall be heavy upon it; and it shall fall, and not rise again.

24:16 From the uttermost part of the earth have we heard songs, even glory to the righteous. But I said, My leanness, my leanness, woe unto me! The treacherous dealers have dealt treacherously; yea, the treacherous dealers have dealt very treacherously.

24:17 Fear, and the pit, and the snare are upon thee, O inhabitant of the earth.

24:18 And it shall come to pass that he who fleeth from the noise of the fear shall fall into the pit; and he that cometh up out of the midst of the pit shall be taken in the snare; for the windows from on high are open, and the foundations of the earth do shake.

24:19 The earth is utterly broken down; the earth is clean dissolved; the earth is moved exceedingly.

24:20 The earth shall reel to and fro like a drunkard and shall be removed like a cottage; and the transgression thereof shall be heavy upon it; and it shall fall and not rise again.

[21] And it shall come to pass in that day, that the LORD shall punish the host of the high ones that are on high, and the kings of the earth upon the earth.

[22] And they shall be gathered together, as prisoners are gathered in the pit, and shall be shut up in the prison, and after many days shall they be visited.

[23] Then the moon shall be confounded, and the sun ashamed, when the LORD of hosts shall reign in mount Zion, and in Jerusalem, and before his ancients gloriously.

.25

[1] O LORD, thou art my God; I will exalt thee, I will praise thy name; for thou hast done wonderful things; thy counsels of old are faithfulness and truth.

[2] For thou hast made of a city an heap; of a defenced city a ruin: a palace of strangers to be no city; it shall never be built.

[3] Therefore shall the strong people glorify thee, the city of the terrible nations shall fear thee.

24:21 And it shall come to pass in that day, that the Lord shall punish the host of the high ones that are on high and the kings of the earth upon the earth.

24:22 And they shall be gathered together, as prisoners are gathered in the pit, and shall be shut up in the prison; and after many days shall they be visited.

24:23 Then the moon shall be confounded and the sun ashamed when the Lord of hosts shall reign in Mount Zion, and in Jerusalem, and before his ancients gloriously.

Chapter 25

25:1 O Lord, thou art my God; I will exalt thee; I will praise thy name, for thou hast done wonderful things; thy counsels of old are faithfulness and truth.

25:2 For thou hast made of a city, a heap; of a defensed city, a ruin; a palace of strangers to be no city; it shall never be built.

25:3 Therefore shall the strong people glorify thee; the city of the terrible nations shall fear thee.

[4] For thou hast been a strength to the poor, a strength to the needy in his distress, a refuge from the storm, a shadow from the heat, when the blast of the terrible ones is as a storm against the wall.

[5] Thou shalt bring down the noise of strangers, as the heat in a dry place; even the heat with the shadow of a cloud: the branch of the terrible ones shall be brought low.

[6] And in this mountain shall the LORD of hosts make unto all people a feast of fat things, a feast of wines on the lees, of fat things full of marrow, of wines on the lees well refined.

[7] And he will destroy in this mountain the face of the covering cast over all people, and the vail that is spread over all nations.

[8] He will swallow up death in victory; and the Lord GOD will wipe away tears from off all faces; and the rebuke of his people shall he take away from off all the earth: for the LORD hath spoken it.

25:4 For thou hast been a strength to the poor, a strength to the needy in his distress, a refuge from the storm, a shadow from the heat when the blast of the terrible ones is as a storm against the wall.

25:5 Thou shalt bring down the noise of strangers as the heat in a dry place, even the heat with the shadow of a cloud; the branch of the terrible ones shall be brought low.

25:6 And in this mountain shall the Lord of hosts make unto all people a feast of fat things, a feast of wines on the lees, of fat things full of marrow, of wines on the lees well refined.

25:7 And he will destroy in this mountain the face of the covering cast over all people and the veil that is spread over all nations.

25:8 He will swallow up death in victory; and the Lord God will wipe away tears from off all faces; and the rebuke of his people shall he take away from off all the earth; for the Lord hath spoken it.

[9] And it shall be said in that day, Lo, this is our God; we have waited for him, and he will save us: this is the LORD; we have waited for him, we will be glad and rejoice in his salvation.

[10] For in this mountain shall the hand of the LORD rest, and Moab shall be trodden down under him, even as straw is trodden down for the dunghill.

[11] And he shall spread forth his hands in the midst of them, as he that swimmeth spreadeth forth his hands to swim: and he shall bring down their pride together with the spoils of their hands.

[12] And the fortress of the high fort of thy walls shall he bring down, lay low, and bring to the ground, even to the dust.

.26

[1] In that day shall this song be sung in the land of Judah; We have a strong city; salvation will God appoint for walls and bulwarks.

[2] Open ye the gates, that the righteous nation which keepeth the truth may enter in.

25:9 And it shall be said in that day, Lo, this is our God; we have waited for him, and he will save us; this is the Lord; we have waited for him; we will be glad and rejoice in his salvation.

25:10 For in this mountain shall the hand of the Lord rest; and Moab shall be trodden down under him, even as straw is trodden down for the dunghill.

25:11 And he shall spread forth his hands in the midst of them as he that swimmeth spreadeth forth his hands to swim; and he shall bring down their pride together with the spoils of their hands.

25:12 And the fortress of the high fort of thy walls shall he bring down, lay low, and bring to the ground, even to the dust.

Chapter 26

26:1 In that day shall this song be sung in the land of Judah: We have a strong city; salvation will God appoint for walls and bulwarks.

26:2 Open ye the gates, that the righteous nation which keepeth the truth may enter in.

[3] Thou wilt keep him in perfect peace, whose mind is stayed on thee: because he trusteth in thee.

[4] Trust ye in the LORD for ever: for in the Lord JEHOVAH is everlasting strength:

[5] For he bringeth down them that dwell on high; the lofty city, he layeth it low; he layeth it low, even to the ground; he bringeth it even to the dust.

[6] The foot shall tread it down, even the feet of the poor, and the steps of the needy.

[7] The way of the just is uprightness: thou, most upright, dost weigh the path of the just.

[8] Yea, in the way of thy judgments, O LORD, have we waited for thee; the desire of our soul is to thy name, and to the remembrance of thee.

[9] With my soul have I desired thee in the night; yea, with my spirit within me will I seek thee early: for when thy judgments are in the earth, the inhabitants of the world will learn righteousness.

26:3 Thou wilt keep him in perfect peace whose mind is stayed on thee because he trusteth in thee.

26:4 Trust ye in the Lord forever; for in the Lord JEHOVAH is everlasting strength.

26:5 For he bringeth down them that dwell on high; the lofty city, he layeth it low; he layeth it low, even to the ground; he bringeth it even to the dust.

26:6 The foot shall tread it down, even the feet of the poor and the steps of the needy.

26:7 The way of the just is uprightness; thou, most upright, dost weigh the path of the just.

26:8 Yea, in the way of thy judgments, O Lord, have we waited for thee; the desire of our soul is to thy name and to the remembrance of thee.

26:9 With my soul have I desired thee in the night; yea, with my spirit within me will I seek thee early; for when thy judgments are in the earth, the inhabitants of the world will learn righteousness.

[10] Let favour be shewed to the wicked, yet will he not learn righteousness: in the land of uprightness will he deal unjustly, and will not behold the majesty of the LORD.

[11] LORD, when thy hand is lifted up, they will not see: but they shall see, and be ashamed for their envy at the people; yea, the fire of thine enemies shall devour them.

[12] LORD, thou wilt ordain peace for us: for thou also hast wrought all our works in us.

[13] O LORD our God, other lords beside thee have had dominion over us: but by thee only will we make mention of thy name.

[14] They are dead, they shall not live; they are deceased, they shall not rise: therefore hast thou visited and destroyed them, and made all their memory to perish.

[15] Thou hast increased the nation, O LORD, thou hast increased the nation: thou art glorified: thou hadst removed it far unto all the ends of the earth.

26:10 Let favor be showed to the wicked; yet will he not learn righteousness; in the land of uprightness will he deal unjustly and will not behold the majesty of the Lord.

26:11 Lord, when thy hand is lifted up, they will not see; but they shall see and be ashamed for their envy at the people; yea, the fire of thine enemies shall devour them.

26:12 Lord, thou wilt ordain peace for us; for thou also hast wrought all our works in us.

26:13 O Lord, our God, other lords besides thee have had dominion over us; but by thee only will we make mention of thy name.

26:14 They are dead; they shall not live; they are deceased; they shall not rise; therefore hast thou visited, and destroyed them, and made all their memory to perish.

26:15 Thou hast increased the nation, O Lord; thou hast increased the nation; thou art glorified; thou hadst removed it far unto all the ends of the earth.

[16] LORD, in trouble have they visited thee, they poured out a prayer when thy chastening was upon them.

[17] Like as a woman with child, that draweth near the time of her delivery, is in pain, and crieth out in her pangs; so have we been in thy sight, O LORD.

[18] We have been with child, we have been in pain, we have as it were brought forth wind; we have not wrought any deliverance in the earth; neither have the inhabitants of the world fallen.

[19] Thy dead men shall live, together with my dead body shall they arise. Awake and sing, ye that dwell in dust: for thy dew is as the dew of herbs, and the earth shall cast out the dead.

[20] Come, my people, enter thou into thy chambers, and shut thy doors about thee: hide thyself as it were for a little moment, until the indignation be overpast.

26:16 Lord, in trouble have they visited thee; they poured out a prayer when thy chastening was upon them.

26:17 Like as a woman with child, that draweth near the time of her delivery, is in pain and crieth out in her pangs, so have we been in thy sight, O Lord.

26:18 We have been with child; we have been in pain; we have, as it were, brought forth wind; we have not wrought any deliverance in the earth; neither have the inhabitants of the world fallen.

26:19 Thy dead men shall live; together with my dead body shall they arise. Awake and sing, ye that dwell in dust; for thy dew is as the dew of herbs, and the earth shall cast out the dead.

26:20 Come, my people; enter thou into thy chambers, and shut thy doors about thee; hide thyself, as it were, for a little moment until the indignation be overpast.

[21] For, behold, the LORD cometh out of his place to punish the inhabitants of the earth for their iniquity: the earth also shall disclose her blood, and shall no more cover her slain.

.27

[1] In that day the LORD with his sore and great and strong sword shall punish leviathan the piercing serpent, even leviathan that crooked serpent; and he shall slay the dragon that is in the sea.

[2] In that day sing ye unto her, A vineyard of red wine.

[3] I the LORD do keep it; I will water it every moment: lest any hurt it, I will keep it night and day.

[4] Fury is not in me: who would set the briers and thorns against me in battle? I would go through them, I would burn them together.

[5] Or let him take hold of my strength, that he may make peace with me; and he shall make peace with me.

26:21 For behold, the Lord cometh out of his place to punish the inhabitants of the earth for their iniquity; the earth also shall disclose her blood and shall no more cover her slain.

Chapter 27

27:1 In that day the Lord with his sore, and great, and strong sword shall punish leviathan, the piercing serpent, even leviathan, that crooked serpent; and he shall slay the dragon that is in the sea.

27:2 In that day sing ye unto her, A vineyard of red wine.

27:3 I, the Lord, do keep it; I will water it every moment; lest any hurt it, I will keep it night and day.

27:4 Fury is not in me; who would set the briers and thorns against me in battle, I would go through them; I would burn them together.

27:5 Or let him take hold of my strength, that he may make peace with me; and he shall make peace with me.

[6] He shall cause them that come of Jacob to take root: Israel shall blossom and bud, and fill the face of the world with fruit.

[7] Hath he smitten him, as he smote those that smote him? or is he slain according to the slaughter of them that are slain by him?

[8] In measure, when it shooteth forth, thou wilt debate with it: he stayeth his rough wind in the day of the east wind.

[9] By this therefore shall the iniquity of Jacob be purged; and this is all the fruit to take away his sin; when he maketh all the stones of the altar as chalkstones that are beaten in sunder, the groves and images shall not stand up.

[10] Yet the defenced city shall be desolate, and the habitation forsaken, and left like a wilderness: there shall the calf feed, and there shall he lie down, and consume the branches thereof.

27:6 He shall cause them that come of Jacob to take root; Israel shall blossom, and bud, and fill the face of the world with fruit.

27:7 Hath he smitten him, as he smote those that smote him? Or is he slain according to the slaughter of them that are slain by him?

27:8 In measure, when it shooteth forth, thou wilt debate with it; he stayeth his rough wind in the day of the east wind.

27:9 By this, therefore, shall the iniquity of Jacob be purged; and this is all the fruit to take away his sin; when he maketh all the stones of the altar as chalkstones that are beaten in sunder, the groves and images shall not stand up.

27:10 Yet the defensed city shall be desolate and the habitation forsaken and left like a wilderness; there shall the calf feed, and there shall he lie down and consume the branches thereof.

[11] When the boughs thereof are withered, they shall be broken off: the women come, and set them on fire: for it is a people of no understanding: therefore he that made them will not have mercy on them, and he that formed them will shew them no favour.

[12] And it shall come to pass in that day, that the LORD shall beat off from the channel of the river unto the stream of Egypt, and ye shall be gathered one by one, O ye children of Israel.

[13] And it shall come to pass in that day, that the great trumpet shall be blown, and they shall come which were ready to perish in the land of Assyria, and the outcasts in the land of Egypt, and shall worship the LORD in the holy mount at Jerusalem.

.28

[1] Woe to the crown of pride, to the drunkards of Ephraim, whose glorious beauty is a fading flower, which are on the head of the fat valleys of them that are overcome with wine!

27:11 When the boughs thereof are withered, they shall be broken off; the women come and set them on fire; for it is a people of no understanding; therefore, he that made them will not have mercy on them, and he that formed them will show them no favor.

27:12 And it shall come to pass in that day, that the Lord shall beat off from the channel of the river unto the stream of Egypt; and ye shall be gathered one by one, O ye children of Israel.

27:13 And it shall come to pass in that day, that the great trumpet shall be blown; and they shall come, which were ready to perish in the land of Assyria and the outcasts in the land of Egypt, and shall worship the Lord in the holy mount at Jerusalem.

Chapter 28

28:1 Woe to the crown of pride, to the drunkards of Ephraim, whose glorious beauty is a fading flower, which are on the head of the fat valleys of them that are overcome with wine!

[2] Behold, the Lord hath a mighty and strong one, which as a tempest of hail and a destroying storm, as a flood of mighty waters overflowing, shall cast down to the earth with the hand.

[3] The crown of pride, the drunkards of Ephraim, shall be trodden under feet:

[4] And the glorious beauty, which is on the head of the fat valley, shall be a fading flower, and as the hasty fruit before the summer; which when he that looketh upon it seeth, while it is yet in his hand he eateth it up.

[5] In that day shall the LORD of hosts be for a crown of glory, and for a diadem of beauty, unto the residue of his people,

[6] And for a spirit of judgment to him that sitteth in judgment, and for strength to them that turn the battle to the gate.

[7] But they also have erred through wine, and through strong drink are out of the way; the priest and the prophet have erred through strong drink, they are swallowed up of wine, they are out of the way through strong drink; they err in vision, they stumble in judgment.

28:2 Behold, the Lord hath a mighty and strong one, which, as a tempest of hail and a destroying storm, as a flood of mighty waters overflowing, shall cast down to the earth with the hand.

28:3 The crown of pride, the drunkards of Ephraim, shall be trodden underfoot;

28:4 And the glorious beauty, which is on the head of the fat valley, shall be a fading flower; and as the hasty fruit before the summer, which, when he that looketh upon it seeth, while it is yet in his hand, he eateth it up.

28:5 In that day shall the Lord of hosts be for a crown of glory, and for a diadem of beauty unto the residue of his people,

28:6 And for a spirit of judgment to him that sitteth in judgment, and for strength to them that turn the battle to the gate.

28:7 But they also have erred through wine, and through strong drink are out of the way; the priest and the prophet have erred through strong drink; they are swallowed up of wine; they are out of the way through strong drink; they err in vision; they stumble in judgment.

[8] For all tables are full of vomit and filthiness, so that there is no place clean.

[9] Whom shall he teach knowledge? and whom shall he make to understand doctrine? them that are weaned from the milk, and drawn from the breasts.

[10] For precept must be upon precept, precept upon precept; line upon line, line upon line; here a little, and there a little:

[11] For with stammering lips and another tongue will he speak to this people.

[12] To whom he said, This is the rest wherewith ye may cause the weary to rest; and this is the refreshing: yet they would not hear.

[13] But the word of the LORD was unto them precept upon precept, precept upon precept; line upon line, line upon line; here a little, and there a little; that they might go, and fall backward, and be broken, and snared, and taken.

[14] Wherefore hear the word of the LORD, ye scornful men, that rule this people which is in Jerusalem.

28:8 For all tables are full of vomit and filthiness so that there is no place clean.

28:9 Whom shall he teach knowledge? And whom shall he make to understand doctrine? Them that are weaned from the milk and drawn from the breasts.

28:10 For precept must be upon precept, precept upon precept; line upon line, line upon line; here a little, and there a little;

28:11 For with stammering lips and another tongue will he speak to this people,

28:12 To whom he said, This is the rest wherewith ye may cause the weary to rest; and this is the refreshing. Yet they would not hear.

28:13 But the word of the Lord was unto them--precept upon precept, precept upon precept; line upon line, line upon line; here a little, and there a little--that they might go, and fall backward, and be broken, and snared, and taken.

28:14 Wherefore hear the word of the Lord, ye scornful men that rule this people which is in Jerusalem.

(2 Ne 28:30 - Paraphrasing)
10 & 13 For behold, thus saith the Lord God: I will give unto the children of men line upon line, ^aprecept upon precept, here a little and there a little; and blessed are those who hearken unto my precepts, and lend an ear unto my counsel, for they shall learn ^bwisdom; for unto him that ^creceiveth I will give ^dmore; and from them that shall say, We have enough, from them shall be taken away even that which they have.

[15] Because ye have said, We have made a covenant with death, and with hell are we at agreement; when the overflowing scourge shall pass through, it shall not come unto us: for we have made lies our refuge, and under falsehood have we hid ourselves:

[16] Therefore thus saith the Lord GOD, Behold, I lay in Zion for a foundation a stone, a tried stone, a precious corner stone, a sure foundation: he that believeth shall not make haste.

[17] Judgment also will I lay to the line, and righteousness to the plummet: and the hail shall sweep away the refuge of lies, and the waters shall overflow the hiding place.

[18] And your covenant with death shall be disannulled, and your agreement with hell shall not stand; when the overflowing scourge shall pass through, then ye shall be trodden down by it.

[19] From the time that it goeth forth it shall take you: for morning by morning shall it pass over, by day and by night: and it shall be a vexation only to understand the report.

28:15 Because ye have said, We have made a covenant with death, and with hell are we at agreement, when the overflowing scourge shall pass through, it shall not come unto us; for we have made lies our refuge, and under falsehood have we hid ourselves.

28:16 Therefore, thus saith the Lord God, Behold, I lay in Zion for a foundation a stone, a tried stone, a precious cornerstone, a sure foundation; he that believeth shall not make haste.

28:17 Judgment also will I lay to the line, and righteousness to the plummet; and the hail shall sweep away the refuge of lies, and the waters shall overflow the hiding place.

28:18 And your covenant with death shall be disannulled, and your agreement with hell shall not stand; when the overflowing scourge shall pass through, then ye shall be trodden down by it.

28:19 From the time that it goeth forth, it shall take you; for morning by morning shall it pass over, by day and by night; and it shall be a vexation only to understand the report.

[20] For the bed is shorter than that a man can stretch himself on it: and the covering narrower than that he can wrap himself in it.

[21] For the LORD shall rise up as in mount Perazim, he shall be wroth as in the valley of Gibeon, that he may do his work, his strange work; and bring to pass his act, his strange act.

[22] Now therefore be ye not mockers, lest your bands be made strong: for I have heard from the Lord GOD of hosts a consumption, even determined upon the whole earth.

[23] Give ye ear, and hear my voice; hearken, and hear my speech.

[24] Doth the plowman plow all day to sow? doth he open and break the clods of his ground?

[25] When he hath made plain the face thereof, doth he not cast abroad the fitches, and scatter the cummin, and cast in the principal wheat and the appointed barley and rie in their place?

28:20 For the bed is shorter than that a man can stretch himself on it; and the covering narrower than that he can wrap himself in it.

28:21 For the Lord shall rise up as in Mount Perazim; he shall be wroth as in the valley of Gibeon, that he may do his work, his strange work, and bring to pass his act, his strange act.

28:22 Now, therefore, be ye not mockers, lest your bands be made strong; for I have heard from the Lord God of hosts a consumption, even determined upon the whole earth.

28:23 Give ye ear, and hear my voice; hearken, and hear my speech.

28:24 Doth the plowman plow all day to sow? Doth he open and break the clods of his ground?

28:25 When he hath made plain the face thereof, doth he not cast abroad the fitches, and scatter the cummin, and cast in the principal wheat, and the appointed barley, and the rye in their place?

[26] For his God doth instruct him to discretion, and doth teach him.

[27] For the fitches are not threshed with a threshing instrument, neither is a cart wheel turned about upon the cummin; but the fitches are beaten out with a staff, and the cummin with a rod.

[28] Bread corn is bruised; because he will not ever be threshing it, nor break it with the wheel of his cart, nor bruise it with his horsemen.

[29] This also cometh forth from the LORD of hosts, which is wonderful in counsel, and excellent in working.

.29

[1] Woe to Ariel, to Ariel, the city where David dwelt! add ye year to year; let them kill sacrifices.

[2] Yet I will distress Ariel, and there shall be heaviness and sorrow: and it shall be unto me as Ariel.

28:26 For his God doth instruct him to discretion and doth teach him.

28:27 For the fitches are not threshed with a threshing instrument; neither is a cartwheel turned about upon the cummin; but the fitches are beaten out with a staff, and the cummin with a rod.

28:28 Bread corn is bruised because he will not ever be threshing it, nor break it with the wheel of his cart, nor bruise it with his horsemen.

28:29 This also cometh forth from the Lord of hosts, which is wonderful in counsel and excellent in working.

Chapter 29

29:1 Woe to Ariel, to Ariel, the city where David dwelt! Add ye year to year; let them kill sacrifices.

29:2 Yet I will distress Ariel, and there shall be heaviness and sorrow; for thus hath the Lord said unto me, It shall be unto Ariel,

[3] And I will camp against thee round about, and will lay siege against thee with a mount, and I will raise forts against thee.	29:3 That I, the Lord, will camp against her round about and will lay siege against her with a mount; and I will raise forts against her.	
[4] And thou shalt be brought down, and shalt speak out of the ground, and thy speech shall be low out of the dust, and thy voice shall be, as of one that hath a familiar spirit, out of the ground, and thy speech shall whisper out of the dust.	29:4 And she shall be brought down and shall speak out of the ground, and her speech shall be low out of the dust; and her voice shall be as of one that hath a familiar spirit, out of the ground, and her speech shall whisper out of the dust.	
[5] Moreover the multitude of thy strangers shall be like small dust, and the multitude of the terrible ones shall be as chaff that passeth away: yea, it shall be at an instant suddenly.	29:5 Moreover, the multitude of her strangers shall be like small dust, and the multitude of the terrible ones shall be as chaff that passeth away; yea, it shall be at an instant suddenly.	**(2 Ne 26:18)** 18 Wherefore, as those who have been destroyed have been destroyed speedily; and the multitude of their [a]terrible ones shall be as [b]chaff that passeth away—yea, thus saith the Lord God: It shall be at an instant, suddenly
[6] Thou shalt be visited of the LORD of hosts with thunder, and with earthquake, and great noise, with storm and tempest, and the flame of devouring fire.	29:6 For they shall be visited of the Lord of hosts with thunder, and with earthquake, and great noise, with storm, and tempest, and the flame of devouring fire.	**(2 Ne 27:2-5)** 2 And when that day shall come they shall be [a]visited of the Lord of Hosts, with thunder and with earthquake, and with a great noise, and with storm, and with tempest, and with the [b]flame of devouring fire.

[7] And the multitude of all the nations that fight against Ariel, even all that fight against her and her munition, and that distress her, shall be as a dream of a night vision.

[8] It shall even be as when an hungry man dreameth, and, behold, he eateth; but he awaketh, and his soul is empty: or as when a thirsty man dreameth, and, behold, he drinketh; but he awaketh, and, behold, he is faint, and his soul hath appetite: so shall the multitude of all the nations be, that fight against mount Zion.

[9] Stay yourselves, and wonder; cry ye out, and cry: they are drunken, but not with wine; they stagger, but not with strong drink.

[10] For the LORD hath poured out upon you the spirit of deep sleep, and hath closed your eyes: the prophets and your rulers, the seers hath he covered.

29:7 And the multitude of all the nations that fight against Ariel, even all that fight against her and her munition, and that distress her, shall be as a dream of a night vision.

29:8 Yea, it shall be unto them even as unto a hungry man who dreameth; and behold, he eateth, but he awaketh, and his soul is empty--or like unto a thirsty man who dreameth; and behold, he drinketh, but he awaketh, and behold, he is faint; and his soul hath appetite. Yea, even so shall the multitude of all the nations be that fight against Mount Zion.

29:9 For behold, all ye that do iniquity, stay yourselves and wonder; for ye shall cry out and cry; yea, ye shall be drunken, but not with wine; ye shall stagger, but not with strong drink.

29:10 For behold, the Lord hath poured out upon you the spirit of deep sleep. For behold, ye have closed your eyes, and ye have rejected the prophets and your rulers; and the seers hath he covered because of your iniquities.

3 And all the [a]nations that [b]fight against Zion, and that distress her, shall be as a dream of a night vision;

(3) yea, it shall be unto them, even as unto a hungry man which dreameth, and behold he eateth but he awaketh and his soul is empty; or like unto a thirsty man which dreameth, and behold he drinketh but he awaketh and behold he is faint, and his soul hath appetite; yea, even so shall the multitude of all the nations be that fight against Mount Zion.

4 For behold, all ye that doeth iniquity, stay yourselves and wonder, for ye shall cry out, and cry; yea, ye shall be [a]drunken but not with wine, ye shall stagger but not with strong drink.

5 For behold, the Lord hath poured out upon you the spirit of deep sleep. For behold, ye have closed your [a]eyes, and ye have [b]rejected the prophets; and your rulers, and the seers hath he covered because of your iniquity.

[11] And the vision of all is become unto you as the words of a book that is sealed, which men deliver to one that is learned, saying, Read this, I pray thee: and he saith, I cannot; for it is sealed:

[12] And the book is delivered to him that is not learned, saying, Read this, I pray thee: and he saith, I am not learned.

29:11 And it shall come to pass that the Lord God shall bring forth unto you the words of a book; and they shall be the words of them which have slumbered.

29:12 And behold, the book shall be sealed; and in the book shall be a revelation from God, from the beginning of the world to the ending thereof.

29:13 Wherefore, because of the things which are sealed up, the things which are sealed shall not be delivered in the day of the wickedness and abominations of the people. Wherefore, the book shall be kept from them.

29:14 But the book shall be delivered unto a man, and he shall deliver the words of the book, which are the words of those who have slumbered in the dust; and he shall deliver these words unto another, but the words that are sealed he shall not deliver; neither shall he deliver the book.

29:15 For the book shall be sealed by the power of God, and the revelation which was sealed shall be kept in the book until the own due time of the Lord, that they may come forth; for behold, they reveal all things from the foundation of the world unto the end thereof.

29:16 And the day cometh that the words of the book which were sealed shall be read upon the housetops; and they shall be read by the power of Christ; and all things shall be revealed unto the children of men, which ever have been among the children of men and which ever will be, even unto the end of the earth.

29:17 Wherefore, at that day when the book shall be delivered unto the man of whom I have spoken, the book shall be hid from the eyes of the world, that the eyes of none shall behold it, save it be that three witnesses shall behold it by the power of God, besides him to whom the book shall be delivered; and they shall testify to the truth of the book and the things therein.

29:18 And there is none other which shall view it, save it be a few according to the will of God, to bear testimony of his word unto the children of men; for the Lord God hath said that the words of the faithful should speak, as it were, from the dead.

29:19 Wherefore, the Lord God will proceed to bring forth the words of the book; and in the mouth of as many witnesses as seemeth him good will he establish his word; and woe be unto him that rejecteth the word of God.

29:20 But behold, it shall come to pass that the Lord God shall say unto him to whom he shall deliver the book, Take these words which are not sealed and deliver them to another, that he may show them unto the learned, saying, Read this, I pray thee.

29:21 And the learned shall say, Bring hither the book, and I will read them; and now because of the glory of the world and to get gain will they say this, and not for the glory of God. And the man shall say, I cannot bring the book for it is sealed. Then shall the learned say, I cannot read it.

(2 Ne 27: 15-23)
15 But behold, it shall come to pass that the Lord God shall say unto him to whom he shall deliver the book: Take these words which are not sealed and deliver them to another, that he may show them unto the learned, saying: *a*Read this, I pray thee.

(15) And the learned shall say: Bring hither the book, and I will read them.
16 And now, because of the glory of the world and to get *a*gain will they say this, and not for the glory of God.
17 And the man shall say: I cannot bring the book, for it is sealed.
18 Then shall the learned say: I cannot read it.

29:22 Wherefore, it shall come to pass that the Lord God will deliver again the book and the words thereof to him that is not learned; and the man that is not learned shall say, I am not learned. Then shall the Lord God say unto him, The learned shall not read them, for they have rejected them; and I am able to do mine own work; wherefore, thou shalt read the words which I shall give unto thee.

29:23 Touch not the things which are sealed, for I will bring them forth in mine own due time; for I will show unto the children of men that I am able to do mine own work.

29:24 Wherefore, when thou hast read the words which I have commanded thee and obtained the witnesses which I have promised unto thee, then shalt thou seal up the book again and hide it up unto me, that I may preserve the words which thou hast not read until I shall see fit in mine own wisdom to reveal all things unto the children of men.

19 Wherefore it shall come to pass, that the Lord God will *ᵃ*deliver again the book and the words thereof to him that is not learned; and the man that is not learned shall say: I am not learned.
20 Then shall the Lord God say unto him: The learned shall not read them, for they have rejected them, and I am *ᵃ*able to do mine own work; wherefore thou shalt read the words which I shall give unto thee.

21 *ᵃ*Touch not the things which are sealed, for I will bring them forth in mine own due time; for I will show unto the children of men that I am able to do mine own work.

22 Wherefore, when thou hast read the words which I have commanded thee, and obtained the *ᵃ*witnesses which I have promised unto thee, then shalt thou seal up the book again, and hide it up unto me, that I may preserve the words which thou hast not read, until I shall see fit in mine own *ᵇ*wisdom to *ᶜ*reveal all things unto the children of men.

29:25 For behold, I am God; and I am a God of miracles; and I will show unto the world that I am the same yesterday, today, and forever; and I work not among the children of men, save it be according to their faith.

23 For behold, I am God; and I am a God of *a*miracles; and I will show unto the *b*world that I am the same yesterday, today, and forever; and I *c*work not among the children of men save it be *d*according to their faith.

(2 Ne 27:25-35)

[13] Wherefore the Lord said, Forasmuch as this people draw near me with their mouth, and with their lips do honour me, but have removed their heart far from me, and their fear toward me is taught by the precept of men:

29:26 And again it shall come to pass that the Lord shall say unto him that shall read the words that shall be delivered him, Forasmuch as this people draw near unto me with their mouth, and with their lips do honor me, but have removed their hearts far from me, and their fear toward me is taught by the precepts of men, therefore, I will proceed to do a marvelous work among this people, yea, a marvelous work and a wonder; for the wisdom of their wise and learned shall perish, and the understanding of their prudent shall be hid.

25 *a*Forasmuch as this people draw near unto me with their mouth, and with their lips do *b*honor me, but have removed their *c*hearts far from me, and their fear towards me is taught by the *d*precepts of men—

[14] Therefore, behold, I will proceed to do a marvellous work among this people, even a marvellous work and a wonder: for the wisdom of their wise men shall perish, and the understanding of their prudent men shall be hid.

26 Therefore, I will proceed to do a *a*marvelous work among this people, yea, a *b*marvelous work and a wonder, for the *c*wisdom of their wise and *d*learned shall perish, and the *e*understanding of their *f*prudent shall be hid.

[15] Woe unto them that seek deep to hide their counsel from the LORD, and their works are in the dark, and they say, Who seeth us? and who knoweth us?

[16] Surely your turning of things upside down shall be esteemed as the potter's clay: for shall the work say of him that made it, He made me not? or shall the thing framed say of him that framed it, He had no understanding?

[17] Is it not yet a very little while, and Lebanon shall be turned into a fruitful field, and the fruitful field shall be esteemed as a forest?

[18] And in that day shall the deaf hear the words of the book, and the eyes of the blind shall see out of obscurity, and out of darkness.

[19] The meek also shall increase their joy in the LORD, and the poor among men shall rejoice in the Holy One of Israel.

29:27 And woe unto them that seek deep to hide their counsel from the Lord. And their works are in the dark. And they say, Who seeth us and who knoweth us? And they also say, Surely, your turning of things upside down shall be esteemed as the potter's clay.

29:28 But behold, I will show unto them, saith the Lord of hosts, that I know all their works. For shall the work say of him that made it, He made me not? Or shall the thing framed say of him that framed it, He had no understanding?

29:29 But behold, saith the Lord of hosts, I will show unto the children of men that it is not yet a very little while and Lebanon shall be turned into a fruitful field; and the fruitful field shall be esteemed as a forest.

29:30 And in that day shall the deaf hear the words of the book; and the eyes of the blind shall see out of obscurity and out of darkness; and the meek also shall increase, and their joy shall be in the Lord; and the poor among men shall rejoice in the Holy One of Israel.

---

27 And ªwo unto them that seek deep to hide their ᵇcounsel from the Lord! And their works are in the ᶜdark; and they say: Who seeth us, and who knoweth us? And they also say: Surely, your turning of things upside down shall be esteemed as the ᵈpotter's clay. But behold, I will show unto them, saith the Lord of Hosts, that I ᵉknow all their works. For shall the work say of him that made it, he made me not? Or shall the thing framed say of him that framed it, he had no understanding?

28 But behold, saith the Lord of Hosts: I will show unto the children of men that it is yet a very little while and Lebanon shall be turned into a fruitful field; and the ªfruitful field shall be esteemed as a forest.

29 ªAnd in that day shall the ᵇdeaf hear the words of the book, and the eyes of the blind shall see out of obscurity and out of darkness.

30 And the ªmeek also shall increase, and their ᵇjoy shall be in the Lord, and the poor among men shall rejoice in the Holy One of Israel.

[20] For the terrible one is brought to nought, and the scorner is consumed, and all that watch for iniquity are cut off:

[21] That make a man an offender for a word, and lay a snare for him that reproveth in the gate, and turn aside the just for a thing of nought.

[22] Therefore thus saith the LORD, who redeemed Abraham, concerning the house of Jacob, Jacob shall not now be ashamed, neither shall his face now wax pale.

[23] But when he seeth his children, the work of mine hands, in the midst of him, they shall sanctify my name, and sanctify the Holy One of Jacob, and shall fear the God of Israel.

[24] They also that erred in spirit shall come to understanding, and they that murmured shall learn doctrine.

29:31 For assuredly as the Lord liveth, they shall see that the terrible one is brought to naught, and the scorner is consumed, and all that watch for iniquity are cut off, and they that make a man an offender for a word, and lay a snare for him that reproveth in the gate, and turn aside the just for a thing of naught.

29:32 Therefore, thus saith the Lord who redeemed Abraham concerning the house of Jacob, Jacob shall not now be ashamed; neither shall his face now wax pale; but when he seeth his children, the work of my hands, in the midst of him, they shall sanctify my name, and sanctify the Holy One of Jacob, and shall fear the God of Israel. They also that erred in spirit shall come to understanding, and they that murmured shall learn doctrine.

31 For assuredly as the Lord liveth they shall see that the *a*terrible one is brought to naught, and the scorner is consumed, and all that watch for iniquity are cut off; 32 And they that make a man an *a*offender for a word, and lay a snare for him that reproveth in the *b*gate, and *c*turn aside the just for a thing of naught.

33 Therefore, thus saith the Lord, who redeemed Abraham, concerning the house of Jacob: Jacob shall *a*not now be ashamed, neither shall his face now wax pale.

34 But when he *a*seeth his children, the work of my hands, in the midst of him, they shall sanctify my name, and sanctify the Holy One of Jacob, and shall fear the God of Israel.

35 They also that *a*erred in spirit shall come to understanding, and they that murmured shall *b*learn doctrine.

.30

[1] Woe to the rebellious children, saith the LORD, that take counsel, but not of me; and that cover with a covering, but not of my spirit, that they may add sin to sin:

[2] That walk to go down into Egypt, and have not asked at my mouth; to strengthen themselves in the strength of Pharaoh, and to trust in the shadow of Egypt!

[3] Therefore shall the strength of Pharaoh be your shame, and the trust in the shadow of Egypt your confusion.

[4] For his princes were at Zoan, and his ambassadors came to Hanes.

[5] They were all ashamed of a people that could not profit them, nor be an help nor profit, but a shame, and also a reproach.

Chapter 30

30:1 Woe to the rebellious children, saith the Lord, that take counsel, but not of me, and that cover with a covering, but not of my Spirit, that they may add sin to sin,

30:2 That walk to go down into Egypt, and have not asked at my mouth, to strengthen themselves in the strength of Pharaoh, and to trust in the shadow of Egypt!

30:3 Therefore shall the strength of Pharaoh be your shame, and the trust in the shadow of Egypt your confusion.

30:4 For his princes were at Zoan, and his ambassadors came to Hanes.

30:5 They were all ashamed of a people that could not profit them, nor be a help nor profit, but a shame and also a reproach.

[6] The burden of the beasts of the south: into the land of trouble and anguish, from whence come the young and old lion, the viper and fiery flying serpent, they will carry their riches upon the shoulders of young asses, and their treasures upon the bunches of camels, to a people that shall not profit them.

[7] For the Egyptians shall help in vain, and to no purpose: therefore have I cried concerning this, Their strength is to sit still.

[8] Now go, write it before them in a table, and note it in a book, that it may be for the time to come for ever and ever:

[9] That this is a rebellious people, lying children, children that will not hear the law of the LORD:

[10] Which say to the seers, See not; and to the prophets, Prophesy not unto us right things, speak unto us smooth things, prophesy deceits:

[11] Get you out of the way, turn aside out of the path, cause the Holy One of Israel to cease from before us.

30:6 The burden of the beasts of the south: Into the land of trouble and anguish, from whence come the young and old lion, the viper, and fiery flying serpent, they will carry their riches upon the shoulders of young asses and their treasures upon the bunches of camels to a people that shall not profit them.

30:7 For the Egyptians shall help in vain and to no purpose; therefore have I cried concerning this: Their strength is to sit still.

30:8 Now go, write it before them in a table, and note it in a book, that it may be for the time to come forever and ever,

30:9 That this is a rebellious people, lying children, children that will not hear the law of the Lord,

30:10 Which say to the seers, See not; and to the prophets, Prophesy not unto us right things; speak unto us smooth things; prophesy deceits;

30:11 Get you out of the way; turn aside out of the path; cause the Holy One of Israel to cease from before us.

[12] Wherefore thus saith the Holy One of Israel, Because ye despise this word, and trust in oppression and perverseness, and stay thereon:

[13] Therefore this iniquity shall be to you as a breach ready to fall, swelling out in a high wall, whose breaking cometh suddenly at an instant.

[14] And he shall break it as the breaking of the potters' vessel that is broken in pieces; he shall not spare: so that there shall not be found in the bursting of it a sherd to take fire from the hearth, or to take water withal out of the pit.

[15] For thus saith the Lord GOD, the Holy One of Israel; In returning and rest shall ye be saved; in quietness and in confidence shall be your strength: and ye would not.

[16] But ye said, No; for we will flee upon horses; therefore shall ye flee: and, We will ride upon the swift; therefore shall they that pursue you be swift.

30:12 Wherefore, thus saith the Holy One of Israel, Because ye despise this word, and trust in oppression and perverseness, and stay thereon,

30:13 Therefore, this iniquity shall be to you as a breach ready to fall, swelling out in a high wall, whose breaking cometh suddenly, at an instant.

30:14 And he shall break it as the breaking of the potters' vessel that is broken in pieces; he shall not spare; so that there shall not be found in the bursting of it a sherd to take fire from the hearth or to take water withal out of the pit.

30:15 For thus saith the Lord God, the Holy One of Israel, In returning and rest shall ye be saved; in quietness and in confidence shall be your strength; and ye would not.

30:16 But ye said, No; for we will flee upon horses; therefore shall ye flee; and, We will ride upon the swift; therefore shall they that pursue you be swift.

[17] One thousand shall flee at the rebuke of one; at the rebuke of five shall ye flee: till ye be left as a beacon upon the top of a mountain, and as an ensign on an hill.

[18] And therefore will the LORD wait, that he may be gracious unto you, and therefore will he be exalted, that he may have mercy upon you: for the LORD is a God of judgment: blessed are all they that wait for him.

[19] For the people shall dwell in Zion at Jerusalem: thou shalt weep no more: he will be very gracious unto thee at the voice of thy cry; when he shall hear it, he will answer thee.

[20] And though the Lord give you the bread of adversity, and the water of affliction, yet shall not thy teachers be removed into a corner any more, but thine eyes shall see thy teachers:

[21] And thine ears shall hear a word behind thee, saying, This is the way, walk ye in it, when ye turn to the right hand, and when ye turn to the left.

30:17 One thousand shall flee at the rebuke of one; at the rebuke of five shall ye flee till ye be left as a beacon upon the top of a mountain and as an ensign on a hill.

30:18 And therefore will the Lord wait, that he may be gracious unto you, and therefore will he be exalted, that he may have mercy upon you; for the Lord is a God of judgment; blessed are all they that wait for him.

30:19 For the people shall dwell in Zion at Jerusalem; thou shalt weep no more; he will be very gracious unto thee at the voice of thy cry; when he shall hear it, he will answer thee.

30:20 And though the Lord give you the bread of adversity and the water of affliction, yet shall not thy teachers be removed into a corner any more; but thine eyes shall see thy teachers;

30:21 And thine ears shall hear a word behind thee, saying, This is the way; walk ye in it, when ye turn to the right hand and when ye turn to the left.

[22] Ye shall defile also the covering of thy graven images of silver, and the ornament of thy molten images of gold: thou shalt cast them away as a menstruous cloth; thou shalt say unto it, Get thee hence.

[23] Then shall he give the rain of thy seed, that thou shalt sow the ground withal; and bread of the increase of the earth, and it shall be fat and plenteous: in that day shall thy cattle feed in large pastures.

[24] The oxen likewise and the young asses that ear the ground shall eat clean provender, which hath been winnowed with the shovel and with the fan.

[25] And there shall be upon every high mountain, and upon every high hill, rivers and streams of waters in the day of the great slaughter, when the towers fall.

[26] Moreover the light of the moon shall be as the light of the sun, and the light of the sun shall be sevenfold, as the light of seven days, in the day that the LORD bindeth up the breach of his people, and healeth the stroke of their wound.

30:22 Ye shall defile also the covering of thy graven images of silver and the ornament of thy molten images of gold; thou shalt cast them away as a menstruous cloth; thou shalt say unto it, Get thee hence.

30:23 Then shall he give the rain of thy seed, that thou shalt sow the ground withal, and bread of the increase of the earth; and it shall be fat and plenteous; in that day shall thy cattle feed in large pastures.

30:24 The oxen, likewise, and the young asses that ear the ground shall eat clean provender, which hath been winnowed with the shovel and with the fan.

30:25 And there shall be, upon every high mountain and upon every high hill, rivers and streams of waters in the day of the great slaughter, when the towers fall.

30:26 Moreover, the light of the moon shall be as the light of the sun; and the light of the sun shall be sevenfold, as the light of seven days, in the day that the Lord bindeth up the breach of his people and healeth the stroke of their wound.

[27] Behold, the name of the LORD cometh from far, burning with his anger, and the burden thereof is heavy: his lips are full of indignation, and his tongue as a devouring fire:

[28] And his breath, as an overflowing stream, shall reach to the midst of the neck, to sift the nations with the sieve of vanity: and there shall be a bridle in the jaws of the people, causing them to err.

[29] Ye shall have a song, as in the night when a holy solemnity is kept; and gladness of heart, as when one goeth with a pipe to come into the mountain of the LORD, to the mighty One of Israel.

[30] And the LORD shall cause his glorious voice to be heard, and shall shew the lighting down of his arm, with the indignation of his anger, and with the flame of a devouring fire, with scattering, and tempest, and hailstones.

[31] For through the voice of the LORD shall the Assyrian be beaten down, which smote with a rod.

30:27 Behold, the name of the Lord cometh from far, burning with his anger, and the burden thereof is heavy; his lips are full of indignation, and his tongue as a devouring fire;

30:28 And his breath, as an overflowing stream, shall reach to the midst of the neck, to sift the nations with the sieve of vanity; and there shall be a bridle in the jaws of the people, causing them to err.

30:29 Ye shall have a song, as in the night when a holy solemnity is kept, and gladness of heart, as when one goeth with a pipe to come unto the mountain of the Lord, to the Mighty One of Israel.

30:30 And the Lord shall cause his glorious voice to be heard and shall show the lighting down of his arm, with the indignation of his anger, and with the flame of a devouring fire, with scattering, and tempest, and hailstones.

30:31 For through the voice of the Lord shall the Assyrian be beaten down, which smote with a rod.

[32] And in every place where the grounded staff shall pass, which the LORD shall lay upon him, it shall be with tabrets and harps: and in battles of shaking will he fight with it.

[33] For Tophet is ordained of old; yea, for the king it is prepared; he hath made it deep and large: the pile thereof is fire and much wood; the breath of the LORD, like a stream of brimstone, doth kindle it.

.31

[1] Woe to them that go down to Egypt for help; and stay on horses, and trust in chariots, because they are many; and in horsemen, because they are very strong; but they look not unto the Holy One of Israel, neither seek the LORD!

[2] Yet he also is wise, and will bring evil, and will not call back his words: but will arise against the house of the evildoers, and against the help of them that work iniquity.

30:32 And in every place where the grounded staff shall pass, which the Lord shall lay upon him, it shall be with tabrets and harps; and in battles of shaking will he fight with it.

30:33 For Tophet is ordained of old; yea, for the king it is prepared; he hath made it deep and large; the pile thereof is fire and much wood; the breath of the Lord, like a stream of brimstone, doth kindle it.

Chapter 31

31:1 Woe to them that go down to Egypt for help, and stay on horses, and trust in chariots, because they are many, and in horsemen, because they are very strong; but they look not unto the Holy One of Israel, neither seek the Lord.

31:2 Yet he also is wise, and will bring evil, and will not call back his words, but will arise against the house of the evildoers and against the help of them that work iniquity.

[3] Now the Egyptians are men, and not God; and their horses flesh, and not spirit. When the LORD shall stretch out his hand, both he that helpeth shall fall, and he that is holpen shall fall down, and they all shall fail together.

[4] For thus hath the LORD spoken unto me, Like as the lion and the young lion roaring on his prey, when a multitude of shepherds is called forth against him, he will not be afraid of their voice, nor abase himself for the noise of them: so shall the LORD of hosts come down to fight for mount Zion, and for the hill thereof.

[5] As birds flying, so will the LORD of hosts defend Jerusalem; defending also he will deliver it; and passing over he will preserve it.

[6] Turn ye unto him from whom the children of Israel have deeply revolted.

[7] For in that day every man shall cast away his idols of silver, and his idols of gold, which your own hands have made unto you for a sin.

31:3 Now the Egyptians are men and not God; and their horses flesh and not spirit. When the Lord shall stretch out his hand, both he that helpeth shall fall, and he that is helped shall fall down, and they all shall fail together.

31:4 For thus hath the Lord spoken unto me, Like as the lion and the young lion roaring on his prey, when a multitude of shepherds is called forth against him, he will not be afraid of their voice nor abase himself for the noise of them; so shall the Lord of hosts come down to fight for Mount Zion and for the hill thereof.

31:5 As birds flying, so will the Lord of hosts defend Jerusalem; defending, also, he will deliver it; and passing over, he will preserve it.

31:6 Turn ye unto him from whom the children of Israel have deeply revolted.

31:7 For in that day every man shall cast away his idols of silver and his idols of gold, which your own hands have made unto you for a sin.

[8] Then shall the Assyrian fall with the sword, not of a mighty man; and the sword, not of a mean man, shall devour him: but he shall flee from the sword, and his young men shall be discomfited.

[9] And he shall pass over to his strong hold for fear, and his princes shall be afraid of the ensign, saith the LORD, whose fire is in Zion, and his furnace in Jerusalem.

.32

[1] Behold, a king shall reign in righteousness, and princes shall rule in judgment.

[2] And a man shall be as an hiding place from the wind, and a covert from the tempest; as rivers of water in a dry place, as the shadow of a great rock in a weary land.

[3] And the eyes of them that see shall not be dim, and the ears of them that hear shall hearken.

31:8 Then shall the Assyrian fall with the sword, not of a mighty man; and the sword, not of a mean man, shall devour him; but he shall flee from the sword, and his young men shall be discomfited.

31:9 And he shall pass over to his stronghold for fear, and his princes shall be afraid of the ensign, saith the Lord, whose fire is in Zion, and his furnace in Jerusalem.

Chapter 32

32:1 Behold, a King shall reign in righteousness, and princes shall rule in judgment.

32:2 And a man shall be as a hiding place from the wind and a covert from the tempest, as rivers of water in a dry place, as the shadow of a great rock in a weary land.

32:3 And the eyes of them that see shall not be dim, and the ears of them that hear shall hearken.

[4] The heart also of the rash shall understand knowledge, and the tongue of the stammerers shall be ready to speak plainly.

[5] The vile person shall be no more called liberal, nor the churl said to be bountiful.

[6] For the vile person will speak villany, and his heart will work iniquity, to practise hypocrisy, and to utter error against the LORD, to make empty the soul of the hungry, and he will cause the drink of the thirsty to fail.

[7] The instruments also of the churl are evil: he deviseth wicked devices to destroy the poor with lying words, even when the needy speaketh right.

[8] But the liberal deviseth liberal things; and by liberal things shall he stand.

[9] Rise up, ye women that are at ease; hear my voice, ye careless daughters; give ear unto my speech.

32:4 The heart also of the rash shall understand knowledge, and the tongue of the stammerers shall be ready to speak plainly.

32:5 The vile person shall be no more called liberal, nor the churl said to be bountiful.

32:6 For the vile person will speak villany, and his heart will work iniquity, to practice hypocrisy and to utter error against the Lord, to make empty the soul of the hungry; and he will cause the drink of the thirsty to fail.

32:7 The instruments also of the churl are evil; he deviseth wicked devices to destroy the poor with lying words, even when the needy speaketh right.

32:8 But the liberal deviseth liberal things; and by liberal things shall he stand.

32:9 Rise up, ye women that are at ease; hear my voice, ye careless daughters; give ear unto my speech.

[10] Many days and years shall ye be troubled, ye careless women: for the vintage shall fail, the gathering shall not come.

[11] Tremble, ye women that are at ease; be troubled, ye careless ones: strip you, and make you bare, and gird sackcloth upon your loins.

[12] They shall lament for the teats, for the pleasant fields, for the fruitful vine.

[13] Upon the land of my people shall come up thorns and briers; yea, upon all the houses of joy in the joyous city:

[14] Because the palaces shall be forsaken; the multitude of the city shall be left; the forts and towers shall be for dens for ever, a joy of wild asses, a pasture of flocks;

[15] Until the spirit be poured upon us from on high, and the wilderness be a fruitful field, and the fruitful field be counted for a forest.

[16] Then judgment shall dwell in the wilderness, and righteousness remain in the fruitful field.

32:10 Many days and years shall ye be troubled, ye careless women; for the vintage shall fail; the gathering shall not come.

32:11 Tremble, ye women that are at ease; be troubled, ye careless ones; strip you, and make you bare, and gird sackcloth upon your loins.

32:12 They shall lament for the teats, for the pleasant fields, for the fruitful vine.

32:13 Upon the land of my people shall come up thorns and briers, yea, upon all the houses of joy in the joyous city,

32:14 Because the palaces shall be forsaken; the houses of the city shall be left desolate; the forts and towers shall be for dens forever, a joy of wild asses, a pasture of flocks,

32:15 Until the Spirit be poured upon us from on high, and the wilderness be a fruitful field, and the fruitful field be counted for a forest.

32:16 Then judgment shall dwell in the wilderness, and righteousness remain in the fruitful field.

[17] And the work of righteousness shall be peace; and the effect of righteousness quietness and assurance for ever.

[18] And my people shall dwell in a peaceable habitation, and in sure dwellings, and in quiet resting places;

[19] When it shall hail, coming down on the forest; and the city shall be low in a low place.

[20] Blessed are ye that sow beside all waters, that send forth thither the feet of the ox and the ass.

.33

[1] Woe to thee that spoilest, and thou wast not spoiled; and dealest treacherously, and they dealt not treacherously with thee! when thou shalt cease to spoil, thou shalt be spoiled; and when thou shalt make an end to deal treacherously, they shall deal treacherously with thee.

[2] O LORD, be gracious unto us; we have waited for thee: be thou their arm every morning, our salvation also in the time of trouble.

32:17 And the work of righteousness shall be peace; and the effect of righteousness, quietness and assurance forever.

32:18 And my people shall dwell in a peaceable habitation, and in sure dwellings, and in quiet resting places,

32:19 When it shall hail, coming down on the forest; and the city shall be low in a low place.

32:20 Blessed are ye that sow beside all waters, that send forth thither the feet of the ox and the ass.

Chapter 33

33:1 Woe to thee that spoilest, and thou wast not spoiled, and dealest treacherously, and they dealt not treacherously with thee! When thou shalt cease to spoil, thou shalt be spoiled; and when thou shalt make an end to deal treacherously, they shall deal treacherously with thee.

33:2 O Lord, be gracious unto us; we have waited for thee; be thou their arm every morning, their salvation also in the time of trouble.

[3] At the noise of the tumult the people fled; at the lifting up of thyself the nations were scattered.

[4] And your spoil shall be gathered like the gathering of the caterpiller: as the running to and fro of locusts shall he run upon them.

[5] The LORD is exalted; for he dwelleth on high: he hath filled Zion with judgment and righteousness.

[6] And wisdom and knowledge shall be the stability of thy times, and strength of salvation: the fear of the LORD is his treasure.

[7] Behold, their valiant ones shall cry without: the ambassadors of peace shall weep bitterly.

[8] The highways lie waste, the wayfaring man ceaseth: he hath broken the covenant, he hath despised the cities, he regardeth no man.

33:3 At the noise of the tumult the people fled; at the lifting up of thyself the nations were scattered.

33:4 And your spoil shall be gathered like the gathering of the caterpillar; as the running to and fro of locusts shall he run upon them.

33:5 The Lord is exalted, for he dwelleth on high; he hath filled Zion with judgment and righteousness.

33:6 And wisdom and knowledge shall be the stability of thy times, and strength of salvation; the fear of the Lord is his treasure.

33:7 Behold, their valiant ones shall cry without; the ambassadors of peace shall weep bitterly.

33:8 The highways lie waste; the wayfaring man ceaseth; he hath broken the covenant; he hath despised the cities; he regardeth no man.

[9] The earth mourneth and languisheth: Lebanon is ashamed and hewn down: Sharon is like a wilderness; and Bashan and Carmel shake off their fruits.

[10] Now will I rise, saith the LORD; now will I be exalted; now will I lift up myself.

[11] Ye shall conceive chaff, ye shall bring forth stubble: your breath, as fire, shall devour you.

[12] And the people shall be as the burnings of lime: as thorns cut up shall they be burned in the fire.

[13] Hear, ye that are far off, what I have done; and, ye that are near, acknowledge my might.

[14] The sinners in Zion are afraid; fearfulness hath surprised the hypocrites. Who among us shall dwell with the devouring fire? who among us shall dwell with everlasting burnings?

9 The earth mourneth and languisheth; Lebanon is ashamed and hewn down; Sharon is like a wilderness; and Bashan and Carmel shake off their fruits.

33:10 Now will I rise, saith the Lord; now will I be exalted; now will I lift up myself.

33:11 Ye shall conceive chaff; ye shall bring forth stubble; your breath, as fire, shall devour you.

33:12 And the people shall be as the burnings of lime; as thorns cut up shall they be burned in the fire.

33:13 Hear, ye that are far off, what I have done; and ye that are near, acknowledge my might.

33:14 The sinners in Zion are afraid; fearfulness hath surprised the hypocrites. Who among us shall dwell with the devouring fire? Who among us shall dwell with everlasting burnings?

[15] He that walketh righteously, and speaketh uprightly; he that despiseth the gain of oppressions, that shaketh his hands from holding of bribes, that stoppeth his ears from hearing of blood, and shutteth his eyes from seeing evil;

[16] He shall dwell on high: his place of defence shall be the munitions of rocks: bread shall be given him; his waters shall be sure.

[17] Thine eyes shall see the king in his beauty: they shall behold the land that is very far off.

[18] Thine heart shall meditate terror. Where is the scribe? where is the receiver? where is he that counted the towers?

[19] Thou shalt not see a fierce people, a people of a deeper speech than thou canst perceive; of a stammering tongue, that thou canst not understand.

33:15 He that walketh righteously and speaketh uprightly; he that despiseth the gain of oppressions, that shaketh his hands from holding of bribes, that stoppeth his ears from hearing of blood, and shutteth his eyes from seeing evil;

33:16 He shall dwell on high; his place of defense shall be the munitions of rocks; bread shall be given him; his waters shall be sure.

33:17 Thine eyes shall see the King in his beauty; they shall behold the land that is very far off.

33:18 Thine heart shall meditate in terror. Where is the scribe? Where is the receiver? Where is he that counted the towers?

33:19 Thou shalt not see a fierce people, a people of a deeper speech than thou canst perceive, of a stammering tongue that thou canst not understand.

[20] Look upon Zion, the city of our solemnities: thine eyes shall see Jerusalem a quiet habitation, a tabernacle that shall not be taken down; not one of the stakes thereof shall ever be removed, neither shall any of the cords thereof be broken.

[21] But there the glorious LORD will be unto us a place of broad rivers and streams; wherein shall go no galley with oars, neither shall gallant ship pass thereby.

[22] For the LORD is our judge, the LORD is our lawgiver, the LORD is our king; he will save us.

[23] Thy tacklings are loosed; they could not well strengthen their mast, they could not spread the sail: then is the prey of a great spoil divided; the lame take the prey.

[24] And the inhabitant shall not say, I am sick: the people that dwell therein shall be forgiven their iniquity.

33:20 Look upon Zion, the city of our solemnities; thine eyes shall see Jerusalem a quiet habitation, a tabernacle that shall not be taken down; not one of the stakes thereof shall ever be removed; neither shall any of the cords thereof be broken.

33:21 But there the glorious Lord will be unto us a place of broad rivers and streams, wherein shall go no galley with oars; neither shall gallant ship pass thereby.

33:22 For the Lord is our judge; the Lord is our lawgiver; the Lord is our King; he will save us.

33:23 Thy tacklings are loosed; they could not well strengthen their mast; they could not spread the sail; then is the prey of a great spoil divided; the lame take the prey.

33:24 And the inhabitant shall not say, I am sick. The people that dwell therein shall be forgiven their iniquity.

.34

[1] Come near, ye nations, to hear; and hearken, ye people: let the earth hear, and all that is therein; the world, and all things that come forth of it.

[2] For the indignation of the LORD is upon all nations, and his fury upon all their armies: he hath utterly destroyed them, he hath delivered them to the slaughter.

[3] Their slain also shall be cast out, and their stink shall come up out of their carcases, and the mountains shall be melted with their blood.

[4] And all the host of heaven shall be dissolved, and the heavens shall be rolled together as a scroll: and all their host shall fall down, as the leaf falleth off from the vine, and as a falling fig from the fig tree.

[5] For my sword shall be bathed in heaven: behold, it shall come down upon Idumea, and upon the people of my curse, to judgment.

Chapter 34

34:1 Come near, ye nations, to hear; and hearken, ye people; let the earth hear and all that is therein, the world and all things that come forth of it.

34:2 For the indignation of the Lord is upon all nations, and his fury upon all their armies; he hath utterly destroyed them; he hath delivered them to the slaughter.

34:3 Their slain also shall be cast out, and their stink shall come up out of their carcasses; and the mountains shall be melted with their blood.

34:4 And all the host of heaven shall be dissolved, and the heavens shall be rolled together as a scroll; and all their host shall fall down, as the leaf falleth off from the vine and as a falling fig from the fig tree.

34:5 For my sword shall be bathed in heaven; behold, it shall come down upon Idumea and upon the people of my curse, to judgment.

[6] The sword of the LORD is filled with blood, it is made fat with fatness, and with the blood of lambs and goats, with the fat of the kidneys of rams: for the LORD hath a sacrifice in Bozrah, and a great slaughter in the land of Idumea.

[7And the unicorns shall come down with them, and the bullocks with the bulls; and their land shall be soaked with blood, and their dust made fat with fatness.

[8] For it is the day of the LORD's vengeance, and the year of recompences for the controversy of Zion.

[9] And the streams thereof shall be turned into pitch, and the dust thereof into brimstone, and the land thereof shall become burning pitch.

[10] It shall not be quenched night nor day; the smoke thereof shall go up for ever: from generation to generation it shall lie waste; none shall pass through it for ever and ever.

34:6 The sword of the Lord is filled with blood; it is made fat with fatness, and with the blood of lambs and goats, with the fat of the kidneys of rams; for the Lord hath a sacrifice in Bozrah and a great slaughter in the land of Idumea.

34:7 And the reem shall come down with them, and the bullocks with the bulls; and their land shall be soaked with blood, and their dust made fat with fatness.

34:8 For it is the day of the Lord's vengeance and the year of recompenses for the controversy of Zion.

34:9 And the streams thereof shall be turned into pitch, and the dust thereof into brimstone; and the land thereof shall become burning pitch.

34:10 It shall not be quenched night nor day; the smoke thereof shall go up forever; from generation to generation it shall lie waste; none shall pass through it forever and ever.

[11] But the cormorant and the bittern shall possess it; the owl also and the raven shall dwell in it: and he shall stretch out upon it the line of confusion, and the stones of emptiness.

[12] They shall call the nobles thereof to the kingdom, but none shall be there, and all her princes shall be nothing.

[13] And thorns shall come up in her palaces, nettles and brambles in the fortresses thereof: and it shall be an habitation of dragons, and a court for owls.

[14] The wild beasts of the desert shall also meet with the wild beasts of the island, and the satyr shall cry to his fellow; the screech owl also shall rest there, and find for herself a place of rest.

[15] There shall the great owl make her nest, and lay, and hatch, and gather under her shadow: there shall the vultures also be gathered, every one with her mate.

34:11 But the cormorant and the bittern shall possess it; the owl also and the raven shall dwell in it; and he shall stretch out upon it the line of confusion and the stones of emptiness.

34:12 They shall call the nobles thereof to the kingdom, but none shall be there; and all her princes shall be nothing.

34:13 And thorns shall come up in her palaces, nettles and brambles in the fortresses thereof; and it shall be a habitation of dragons and a court for owls.

34:14 The wild beasts of the desert shall also meet with the wild beasts of the island, and the satyr shall cry to his fellow; the screech owl also shall rest there and find for herself a place of rest.

34:15 There shall the great owl make her nest, and lay, and hatch, and gather under her shadow; there shall the vultures also be gathered, every one with her mate.

[16] Seek ye out of the book of the LORD, and read: no one of these shall fail, none shall want her mate: for my mouth it hath commanded, and his spirit it hath gathered them.

[17] And he hath cast the lot for them, and his hand hath divided it unto them by line: they shall possess it for ever, from generation to generation shall they dwell therein.

.35

[1] The wilderness and the solitary place shall be glad for them; and the desert shall rejoice, and blossom as the rose.

[2] It shall blossom abundantly, and rejoice even with joy and singing: the glory of Lebanon shall be given unto it, the excellency of Carmel and Sharon, they shall see the glory of the LORD, and the excellency of our God.

[3] Strengthen ye the weak hands, and confirm the feeble knees.

34:16 Seek ye out of the book of the Lord, and read the names written therein; no one of these shall fail; none shall want their mate; for my mouth it hath commanded, and my Spirit it hath gathered them.

34:17 And I have cast the lot for them, and I have divided it unto them by line; they shall possess it forever; from generation to generation they shall dwell therein.

Chapter 35

35:1 The wilderness and the solitary place shall be glad for them; and the desert shall rejoice and blossom as the rose.

35:2 It shall blossom abundantly and rejoice, even with joy and singing; the glory of Lebanon shall be given unto it, the excellency of Carmel and Sharon; they shall see the glory of the Lord and the excellency of our God.

35:3 Strengthen ye the weak hands, and confirm the feeble knees.

[4] Say to them that are of a fearful heart, Be strong, fear not: behold, your God will come with vengeance, even God with a recompence; he will come and save you.

[5] Then the eyes of the blind shall be opened, and the ears of the deaf shall be unstopped.

[6] Then shall the lame man leap as an hart, and the tongue of the dumb sing: for in the wilderness shall waters break out, and streams in the desert.

[7] And the parched ground shall become a pool, and the thirsty land springs of water: in the habitation of dragons, where each lay, shall be grass with reeds and rushes.

[8] And an highway shall be there, and a way, and it shall be called The way of holiness; the unclean shall not pass over it; but it shall be for those: the wayfaring men, though fools, shall not err therein.

35:4 Say to them that are of a fearful heart, Be strong; fear not; behold, your God will come with vengeance, even God with a recompense; he will come and save you.

35:5 Then the eyes of the blind shall be opened, and the ears of the deaf shall be unstopped.

35:6 Then shall the lame man leap as a hart, and the tongue of the dumb sing; for in the wilderness shall waters break out, and streams in the desert.

35:7 And the parched ground shall become a pool, and the thirsty land springs of water; in the habitation of dragons, where each lay, shall be grass with reeds and rushes.

35:8 And a highway shall be there; for a way shall be cast up, and it shall be called the way of holiness. The unclean shall not pass over upon it; but it shall be cast up for those who are clean; and the wayfaring men, though they are accounted fools, shall not err therein.

[9] No lion shall be there, nor any ravenous beast shall go up thereon, it shall not be found there; but the redeemed shall walk there:

[10] And the ransomed of the LORD shall return, and come to Zion with songs and everlasting joy upon their heads: they shall obtain joy and gladness, and sorrow and sighing shall flee away.

.36

[1] Now it came to pass in the fourteenth year of king Hezekiah, that Sennacherib king of Assyria came up against all the defenced cities of Judah, and took them.

[2] And the king of Assyria sent Rabshakeh from Lachish to Jerusalem unto king Hezekiah with a great army. And he stood by the conduit of the upper pool in the highway of the fuller's field.

[3] Then came forth unto him Eliakim, Hilkiah's son, which was over the house, and Shebna the scribe, and Joah, Asaph's son, the recorder.

35:9 No lion shall be there, nor any ravenous beast shall go up thereon; it shall not be found there; but the redeemed shall walk there.

35:10 And the ransomed of the Lord shall return and come to Zion with songs and everlasting joy upon their heads; they shall obtain joy and gladness, and sorrow and sighing shall flee away.

Chapter 36

36:1 Now it came to pass in the fourteenth year of King Hezekiah, that Sennacherib, king of Assyria, came up against all the defensed cities of Judah and took them.

36:2 And the king of Assyria sent Rabshakeh from Lachish to Jerusalem unto King Hezekiah with a great army. And he stood by the conduit of the upper pool in the highway of the fuller's field.

36:3 Then came forth unto him Eliakim, Hilkiah's son, which was over the house, and Shebna, the scribe, and Joah, Asaph's son, the recorder.

[4] And Rabshakeh said unto them, Say ye now to Hezekiah, Thus saith the great king, the king of Assyria, What confidence is this wherein thou trustest?

[5] I say, sayest thou, (but they are but vain words) I have counsel and strength for war: now on whom dost thou trust, that thou rebellest against me?

[6] Lo, thou trustest in the staff of this broken reed, on Egypt; whereon if a man lean, it will go into his hand, and pierce it: so is Pharaoh king of Egypt to all that trust in him.

[7] But if thou say to me, We trust in the LORD our God: is it not he, whose high places and whose altars Hezekiah hath taken away, and said to Judah and to Jerusalem, Ye shall worship before this altar?

[8] Now therefore give pledges, I pray thee, to my master the king of Assyria, and I will give thee two thousand horses, if thou be able on thy part to set riders upon them.

36:4 And Rabshakeh said unto them, Say ye now to Hezekiah, Thus saith the great king, the king of Assyria, What confidence is this wherein thou trustest?

36:5 I say, thy words are but vain when thou sayest, I have counsel and strength for war. Now, on whom dost thou trust that thou rebellest against me?

36:6 Lo, thou trustest in the staff of this broken reed, on Egypt, whereon if a man lean, it will go into his hand and pierce it; so is Pharaoh, king of Egypt, to all that trust in him.

36:7 But if thou say to me, We trust in the Lord, our God, is it not he, whose high places and whose altars Hezekiah hath taken away and said to Judah and to Jerusalem, Ye shall worship before this altar?

36:8 Now, therefore, give pledges, I pray thee, to my master, the king of Assyria; and I will give thee two thousand horses if thou be able on thy part to set riders upon them.

[9] How then wilt thou turn away the face of one captain of the least of my master's servants, and put thy trust on Egypt for chariots and for horsemen?

[10] And am I now come up without the LORD against this land to destroy it? the LORD said unto me, Go up against this land, and destroy it.

[11] Then said Eliakim and Shebna and Joah unto Rabshakeh, Speak, I pray thee, unto thy servants in the Syrian language; for we understand it: and speak not to us in the Jews' language, in the ears of the people that are on the wall.

[12] But Rabshakeh said, Hath my master sent me to thy master and to thee to speak these words? hath he not sent me to the men that sit upon the wall, that they may eat their own dung, and drink their own piss with you?

[13] Then Rabshakeh stood, and cried with a loud voice in the Jews' language, and said, Hear ye the words of the great king, the king of Assyria.

36:9 How then wilt thou turn away the face of one captain of the least of my master's servants and put thy trust on Egypt for chariots and for horsemen?

36:10 And am I now come up without the Lord against this land to destroy it? The Lord said unto me, Go up against this land, and destroy it.

36:11 Then said Eliakim, and Shebna, and Joah unto Rabshakeh, Speak, I pray thee, unto thy servants in the Syrian language; for we understand it; and speak not to us in the Jews' language, in the ears of the people that are on the wall.

36:12 But Rabshakeh said, Hath my master sent me to thy master and to thee to speak these words? Hath he not sent me to the men that sit upon the wall, that they may eat their own dung and drink their own piss with you?

36:13 Then Rabshakeh stood, and cried with a loud voice in the Jews' language, and said, Hear ye the words of the great king, the king of Assyria.

[**14**] Thus saith the king, Let not Hezekiah deceive you: for he shall not be able to deliver you.

[**15**] Neither let Hezekiah make you trust in the LORD, saying, The LORD will surely deliver us: this city shall not be delivered into the hand of the king of Assyria.

[**16**] Hearken not to Hezekiah: for thus saith the king of Assyria, Make an agreement with me by a present, and come out to me: and eat ye every one of his vine, and every one of his fig tree, and drink ye every one the waters of his own cistern;

[**17**] Until I come and take you away to a land like your own land, a land of corn and wine, a land of bread and vineyards.

[**18**] Beware lest Hezekiah persuade you, saying, The LORD will deliver us. Hath any of the gods of the nations delivered his land out of the hand of the king of Assyria?

36:14 Thus saith the king, Let not Hezekiah deceive you; for he shall not be able to deliver you.

36:15 Neither let Hezekiah make you trust in the Lord, saying, The Lord will surely deliver us; this city shall not be delivered into the hand of the king of Assyria.

36:16 Hearken not to Hezekiah; for thus saith the king of Assyria, Make an agreement with me by a present, and come out to me; and eat ye everyone of his vine, and everyone of his fig tree, and drink ye everyone the waters of his own cistern,

36:17 Until I come and take you away to a land like your own land, a land of corn and wine, a land of bread and vineyards.

36:18 Beware lest Hezekiah persuade you, saying, The Lord will deliver us. Hath any of the gods of the nations delivered his land out of the hand of the king of Assyria?

[19] Where are the gods of Hamath and Arphad? where are the gods of Sepharvaim? and have they delivered Samaria out of my hand?

[20] Who are they among all the gods of these lands, that have delivered their land out of my hand, that the LORD should deliver Jerusalem out of my hand?

[21] But they held their peace, and answered him not a word: for the king's commandment was, saying, Answer him not.

[22] Then came Eliakim, the son of Hilkiah, that was over the household, and Shebna the scribe, and Joah, the son of Asaph, the recorder, to Hezekiah with their clothes rent, and told him the words of Rabshakeh.

.37

[1] And it came to pass, when king Hezekiah heard it, that he rent his clothes, and covered himself with sackcloth, and went into the house of the LORD.

36:19 Where are the gods of Hamath and Arpad? Where are the gods of Sepharvaim? And have they delivered Samaria out of my hand?

36:20 Who are they among all the gods of these lands that have delivered their land out of my hand, that the Lord should deliver Jerusalem out of my hand?

36:21 But they held their peace and answered him not a word; for the king's commandment was, saying, Answer him not.

36:22 Then came Eliakim, the son of Hilkiah, that was over the household, and Shebna, the scribe, and Joah, the son of Asaph, the recorder, to Hezekiah with their clothes rent and told him the words of Rabshakeh.

Chapter 37

37:1 And it came to pass, when King Hezekiah heard it, that he rent his clothes, and covered himself with sackcloth, and went into the house of the Lord.

[2] And he sent Eliakim, who was over the household, and Shebna the scribe, and the elders of the priests covered with sackcloth, unto Isaiah the prophet the son of Amoz.

[3] And they said unto him, Thus saith Hezekiah, This day is a day of trouble, and of rebuke, and of blasphemy: for the children are come to the birth, and there is not strength to bring forth.

[4] It may be the LORD thy God will hear the words of Rabshakeh, whom the king of Assyria his master hath sent to reproach the living God, and will reprove the words which the LORD thy God hath heard: wherefore lift up thy prayer for the remnant that is left.

[5] So the servants of king Hezekiah came to Isaiah.

[6] And Isaiah said unto them, Thus shall ye say unto your master, Thus saith the LORD, Be not afraid of the words that thou hast heard, wherewith the servants of the king of Assyria have blasphemed me.

37:2 And he sent Eliakim, who was over the household, and Shebna, the scribe, and the elders of the priests, covered with sackcloth, unto Isaiah, the prophet, the son of Amoz.

37:3 And they said unto him, Thus saith Hezekiah, This day is a day of trouble, and of rebuke, and of blasphemy; for the children are come to the birth, and there is not strength to bring forth.

37:4 It may be the Lord, thy God, will hear the words of Rabshakeh, whom the king of Assyria, his master, hath sent to reproach the living God, and will reprove the words which the Lord, thy God, hath heard; wherefore, lift up thy prayer for the remnant that is left.

37:5 So the servants of King Hezekiah came to Isaiah.

37:6 And Isaiah said unto them, Thus shall ye say unto your master, Thus saith the Lord, Be not afraid of the words that thou hast heard, wherewith the servants of the king of Assyria have blasphemed me.

[7] Behold, I will send a blast upon him, and he shall hear a rumour, and return to his own land; and I will cause him to fall by the sword in his own land.

[8] So Rabshakeh returned, and found the king of Assyria warring against Libnah: for he had heard that he was departed from Lachish.

[9] And he heard say concerning Tirhakah king of Ethiopia, He is come forth to make war with thee. And when he heard it, he sent messengers to Hezekiah, saying,

[10] Thus shall ye speak to Hezekiah king of Judah, saying, Let not thy God, in whom thou trustest, deceive thee, saying, Jerusalem shall not be given into the hand of the king of Assyria.

[11] Behold, thou hast heard what the kings of Assyria have done to all lands by destroying them utterly; and shalt thou be delivered?

37:7 Behold, I will send a blast upon him, and he shall hear a rumor and return to his own land; and I will cause him to fall by the sword in his own land.

37:8 So Rabshakeh returned and found the king of Assyria warring against Libnah, for he had heard that he was departed from Lachish.

37:9 And he heard say concerning Tirhakah, king of Ethiopia, He is come forth to make war with thee. And when he heard it, he sent messengers to Hezekiah, saying,

37:10 Thus shall ye speak to Hezekiah, king of Judah, saying, Let not thy God, in whom thou trustest, deceive thee, saying, Jerusalem shall not be given into the hand of the king of Assyria.

37:11 Behold, thou hast heard what the kings of Assyria have done to all lands by destroying them utterly. And shalt thou be delivered?

[12] Have the gods of the nations delivered them which my fathers have destroyed, as Gozan, and Haran, and Rezeph, and the children of Eden which were in Telassar?

[13] Where is the king of Hamath, and the king of Arphad, and the king of the city of Sepharvaim, Hena, and Ivah?

[14] And Hezekiah received the letter from the hand of the messengers, and read it: and Hezekiah went up unto the house of the LORD, and spread it before the LORD.

[15] And Hezekiah prayed unto the LORD, saying,

[16] O LORD of hosts, God of Israel, that dwellest between the cherubims, thou art the God, even thou alone, of all the kingdoms of the earth: thou hast made heaven and earth.

[17] Incline thine ear, O LORD, and hear; open thine eyes, O LORD, and see: and hear all the words of Sennacherib, which hath sent to reproach the living God.

37:12 Have the gods of the nations delivered them which my fathers have destroyed, as Gozan, and Haran, and Rezeph, and the children of Eden which were in Telassar?

37:13 Where is the king of Hamath, and the king of Arpad, and the king of the city of Sepharvaim, Hena, and Ivah?

37:14 And Hezekiah received the letter from the hand of the messengers and read it; and Hezekiah went up unto the house of the Lord and spread it before the Lord.

37:15 And Hezekiah prayed unto the Lord, saying,

37:16 O Lord of hosts, God of Israel, that dwellest between the cherubim, thou art the God, even thou alone, of all the kingdoms of the earth; thou hast made heaven and earth.

37:17 Incline thine ear, O Lord, and hear; open thine eyes, O Lord, and see; and hear all the words of Sennacherib, which he hath sent to reproach the living God.

[**18**] Of a truth, LORD, the kings of Assyria have laid waste all the nations, and their countries,

[**19**] And have cast their gods into the fire: for they were no gods, but the work of men's hands, wood and stone: therefore they have destroyed them.

[**20**] Now therefore, O LORD our God, save us from his hand, that all the kingdoms of the earth may know that thou art the LORD, even thou only.

[**21**] Then Isaiah the son of Amoz sent unto Hezekiah, saying, Thus saith the LORD God of Israel, Whereas thou hast prayed to me against Sennacherib king of Assyria:

[**22**] This is the word which the LORD hath spoken concerning him; The virgin, the daughter of Zion, hath despised thee, and laughed thee to scorn; the daughter of Jerusalem hath shaken her head at thee.

[**23**] Whom hast thou reproached and blasphemed? and against whom hast thou exalted thy voice, and lifted up thine eyes on high? even against the Holy One of Israel.

37:18 Of a truth, Lord, the kings of Assyria have laid waste all the nations and their countries,

37:19 And have cast their gods into the fire; for they were no gods, but the work of men's hands, wood and stone; therefore they have destroyed them.

37:20 Now, therefore, O Lord, our God, save us from his hand, that all the kingdoms of the earth may know that thou art the Lord, even thou only.

37:21 Then Isaiah, the son of Amoz, sent unto Hezekiah, saying, Thus saith the Lord God of Israel, Whereas thou hast prayed to me against Sennacherib, king of Assyria,

22 This is the word which the Lord hath spoken concerning him: The virgin, the daughter of Zion, hath despised thee and laughed thee to scorn; the daughter of Jerusalem hath shaken her head at thee.

37:23 Whom hast thou reproached and blasphemed? And against whom hast thou exalted thy voice and lifted up thine eyes on high? Even against the Holy One of Israel.

[24] By thy servants hast thou reproached the Lord, and hast said, By the multitude of my chariots am I come up to the height of the mountains, to the sides of Lebanon; and I will cut down the tall cedars thereof, and the choice fir trees thereof: and I will enter into the height of his border, and the forest of his Carmel.

[25] I have digged, and drunk water; and with the sole of my feet have I dried up all the rivers of the besieged places.

[26] Hast thou not heard long ago, how I have done it; and of ancient times, that I have formed it? now have I brought it to pass, that thou shouldest be to lay waste defenced cities into ruinous heaps.

[27] Therefore their inhabitants were of small power, they were dismayed and confounded: they were as the grass of the field, and as the green herb, as the grass on the housetops, and as corn blasted before it be grown up.

[28] But I know thy abode, and thy going out, and thy coming in, and thy rage against me.

37:24 By thy servants hast thou reproached the Lord and hast said, By the multitude of my chariots am I come up to the height of the mountains, to the sides of Lebanon; and I will cut down the tall cedars thereof and the choice fir trees thereof; and I will enter into the height of his border and the forest of his Carmel.

37:25 I have digged and drunk water; and with the sole of my feet have I dried up all the rivers of the besieged places.

37:26 Hast thou not heard, long ago, how I have done it and, of ancient times, that I have formed it? Now have I brought it to pass, that thou shouldest be to lay waste defensed cities into ruinous heaps.

37:27 Therefore, their inhabitants were of small power; they were dismayed and confounded; they were as the grass of the field and as the green herb, as the grass on the housetops and as corn blasted before it be grown up.

37:28 But I know thy abode, and thy going out, and thy coming in, and thy rage against me.

[29] Because thy rage against me, and thy tumult, is come up into mine ears, therefore will I put my hook in thy nose, and my bridle in thy lips, and I will turn thee back by the way by which thou camest.

[30] And this shall be a sign unto thee, Ye shall eat this year such as groweth of itself; and the second year that which springeth of the same: and in the third year sow ye, and reap, and plant vineyards, and eat the fruit thereof.

[31] And the remnant that is escaped of the house of Judah shall again take root downward, and bear fruit upward:

[32] For out of Jerusalem shall go forth a remnant, and they that escape out of mount Zion: the zeal of the LORD of hosts shall do this.

[33] Therefore thus saith the LORD concerning the king of Assyria, He shall not come into this city, nor shoot an arrow there nor come before it with shields, nor cast a bank against it.

37:29 Because thy rage against me and thy tumult is come up into mine ears, therefore will I put my hook in thy nose and my bridle in thy lips, and I will turn thee back by the way by which thou camest.

37:30 And this shall be a sign unto thee: Ye shall eat this year such as groweth of itself; and the second year that which springeth of the same; and in the third year sow ye, and reap, and plant vineyards, and eat the fruit thereof.

37:31 And the remnant that is escaped of the house of Judah shall again take root downward and bear fruit upward,

37:32 For out of Jerusalem shall go forth a remnant; and they that escape out of Jerusalem shall come up upon Mount Zion; the zeal of the Lord of hosts shall do this.

37:33 Therefore, thus saith the Lord concerning the king of Assyria, He shall not come into this city, nor shoot an arrow there, nor come before it with shields, nor cast a bank against it.

[34] By the way that he came, by the same shall he return, and shall not come into this city, saith the LORD.

[35] For I will defend this city to save it for mine own sake, and for my servant David's sake.

[36] Then the angel of the LORD went forth, and smote in the camp of the Assyrians a hundred and fourscore and five thousand: and when they arose early in the morning, behold, they were all dead corpses.

[37] So Sennacherib king of Assyria departed, and went and returned, and dwelt at Nineveh.

[38] And it came to pass, as he was worshipping in the house of Nisroch his god, that Adrammelech and Sharezer his sons smote him with the sword; and they escaped into the land of Armenia: and Esar-haddon his son reigned in his stead.

.38

37:34 By the way that he came, by the same shall he return and shall not come into this city, saith the Lord.

37:35 For I will defend this city to save it for mine own sake and for my servant David's sake.

37:36 Then the angel of the Lord went forth and smote in the camp of the Assyrians a hundred and fourscore and five thousand; and when they who were left arose early in the morning, behold, they were all dead corpses.

37:37 So Sennacherib, king of Assyria, departed, and went, and returned, and dwelt at Nineveh.

37:38 And it came to pass, as he was worshiping in the house of Nisroch, his god, that Adrammelech and Sharezer, his sons, smote him with the sword; and they escaped into the land of Armenia; and Esar-haddon, his son, reigned in his stead.

Chapter 38

[1] In those days was Hezekiah sick unto death. And Isaiah the prophet the son of Amoz came unto him, and said unto him, Thus saith the LORD, Set thine house in order: for thou shalt die, and not live.

[2] Then Hezekiah turned his face toward the wall, and prayed unto the LORD,

[3] And said, Remember now, O LORD, I beseech thee, how I have walked before thee in truth and with a perfect heart, and have done that which is good in thy sight. And Hezekiah wept sore.

[4] Then came the word of the LORD to Isaiah, saying,

[5] Go, and say to Hezekiah, Thus saith the LORD, the God of David thy father, I have heard thy prayer, I have seen thy tears: behold, I will add unto thy days fifteen years.

[6] And I will deliver thee and this city out of the hand of the king of Assyria: and I will defend this city.

[7] And this shall be a sign unto thee from the LORD, that the LORD will do this thing that he hath spoken;

38:1 In those days was Hezekiah sick unto death. And Isaiah, the prophet, the son of Amoz, came unto him and said unto him, Thus saith the Lord, Set thine house in order, for thou shalt die and not live.

2 Then Hezekiah turned his face toward the wall and prayed unto the Lord,

38:3 And said, Remember now, O Lord, I beseech thee, how I have walked before thee in truth and with a perfect heart and have done that which is good in thy sight. And Hezekiah wept sore.

38:4 Then came the word of the Lord to Isaiah, saying,

38:5 Go, and say to Hezekiah, Thus saith the Lord, the God of David, thy father, I have heard thy prayer; I have seen thy tears; behold, I will add unto thy days fifteen years.

38:6 And I will deliver thee and this city out of the hand of the king of Assyria; and I will defend this city.

38:7 And this shall be a sign unto thee from the Lord, that the Lord will do this thing that he hath spoken:

[8] Behold, I will bring again the shadow of the degrees, which is gone down in the sun dial of Ahaz, ten degrees backward. So the sun returned ten degrees, by which degrees it was gone down.

[9] The writing of Hezekiah king of Judah, when he had been sick, and was recovered of his sickness:

[10] I said in the cutting off of my days, I shall go to the gates of the grave: I am deprived of the residue of my years.

[11] I said, I shall not see the LORD, even the LORD, in the land of the living: I shall behold man no more with the inhabitants of the world.

[12] Mine age is departed, and is removed from me as a shepherd's tent: I have cut off like a weaver my life: he will cut me off with pining sickness: from day even to night wilt thou make an end of me.

[13] I reckoned till morning, that, as a lion, so will he break all my bones: from day even to night wilt thou make an end of me.

8 Behold, I will bring again the shadow of the degrees, which is gone down in the sundial of Ahaz, ten degrees backward. So the sun returned ten degrees, by which degrees it was gone down.

38:9 The writing of Hezekiah, king of Judah, when he had been sick and was recovered of his sickness:

38:10 I said in the cutting off of my days, I shall go to the gates of the grave; I am deprived of the residue of my years.

38:11 I said, I shall not see the Lord, even the Lord, in the land of the living; I shall behold man no more with the inhabitants of the world.

38:12 Mine age is departed and is removed from me as a shepherd's tent; I have cut off, like a weaver, my life; he will cut me off with pining sickness; from day even to night wilt thou make an end of me.

38:13 I reckoned till morning that, as a lion, so will he break all my bones; from day even to night wilt thou make an end of me.

[14] Like a crane or a swallow, so did I chatter: I did mourn as a dove: mine eyes fail with looking upward: O LORD, I am oppressed; undertake for me.

[15] What shall I say? he hath both spoken unto me, and himself hath done it: I shall go softly all my years in the bitterness of my soul.

[16] O Lord, by these things men live, and in all these things is the life of my spirit: so wilt thou recover me, and make me to live.

[17] Behold, for peace I had great bitterness: but thou hast in love to my soul delivered it from the pit of corruption: for thou hast cast all my sins behind thy back.

[18] For the grave cannot praise thee, death can not celebrate thee: they that go down into the pit cannot hope for thy truth.

[19] The living, the living, he shall praise thee, as I do this day: the father to the children shall make known thy truth.

38:14 Like a crane or swallow, so did I chatter; I did mourn as a dove; mine eyes fail with looking upward; O Lord, I am oppressed; undertake for me.

38:15 What shall I say? He hath both spoken unto me and himself hath healed me. I shall go softly all my years, that I may not walk in the bitterness of my soul.

38:16 O Lord, thou who art the life of my spirit, in whom I live, so wilt thou recover me and make me to live; and in all these things I will praise thee.

38:17 Behold, I had great bitterness instead of peace; but thou hast in love to my soul saved me from the pit of corruption, for thou hast cast all my sins behind thy back.

38:18 For the grave cannot praise thee; death cannot celebrate thee; they that go down into the pit cannot hope for thy truth.

38:19 The living, the living, he shall praise thee as I do this day; the father to the children shall make known thy truth.

[20] The LORD was ready to save me: therefore we will sing my songs to the stringed instruments all the days of our life in the house of the LORD.

[21] For Isaiah had said, Let them take a lump of figs, and lay it for a plaister upon the boil, and he shall recover.

[22] Hezekiah also had said, What is the sign that I shall go up to the house of the LORD?

.39

[1] At that time Merodach-baladan, the son of Baladan, king of Babylon, sent letters and a present to Hezekiah: for he had heard that he had been sick, and was recovered.

[2] And Hezekiah was glad of them, and shewed them the house of his precious things, the silver, and the gold, and the spices, and the precious ointment, and all the house of his armour, and all that was found in his treasures: there was nothing in his house, nor in all his dominion, that Hezekiah shewed them not.

38:20 The Lord was ready to save me; therefore, we will sing my songs to the stringed instruments all the days of our life in the house of the Lord.

38:21 For Isaiah had said, Let them take a lump of figs and lay it for a plaster upon the boil, and he shall recover.

38:22 Hezekiah also had said, What is the sign that I shall go up to the house of the Lord?

Chapter 39

39:1 At that time Merodach-baladan, the son of Baladan, king of Babylon, sent letters and a present to Hezekiah; for he had heard that he had been sick and was recovered.

39:2 And Hezekiah was glad of them and showed them the house of his precious things--the silver, and the gold, and the spices, and the precious ointment, and all the house of his armor, and all that was found in his treasures; there was nothing in his house nor in all his dominion that Hezekiah showed him not.

[3] Then came Isaiah the prophet unto king Hezekiah, and said unto him, What said these men? and from whence came they unto thee? And Hezekiah said, They are come from a far country unto me, even from Babylon.

[4] Then said he, What have they seen in thine house? And Hezekiah answered, All that is in mine house have they seen: there is nothing among my treasures that I have not shewed them.

[5] Then said Isaiah to Hezekiah, Hear the word of the LORD of hosts:

[6] Behold, the days come, that all that is in thine house, and that which thy fathers have laid up in store until this day, shall be carried to Babylon: nothing shall be left, saith the LORD.

[7] And of thy sons that shall issue from thee, which thou shalt beget, shall they take away; and they shall be eunuchs in the palace of the king of Babylon.

[8] Then said Hezekiah to Isaiah, Good is the word of the LORD which thou hast spoken. He said moreover, For there shall be peace and truth in my days.

39:3 Then came Isaiah, the prophet, unto King Hezekiah and said unto him, What said these men? And from whence came they unto thee? And Hezekiah said, They are come from a far country unto me, even from Babylon.

39:4 Then said he, What have they seen in thine house? And Hezekiah answered, All that is in mine house have they seen; there is nothing among my treasures that I have not showed them.

39:5 Then said Isaiah to Hezekiah, Hear the word of the Lord of hosts:

39:6 Behold, the days come that all that is in thine house, and that which thy fathers have laid up in store until this day, shall be carried to Babylon; nothing shall be left, saith the Lord.

39:7 And of thy sons that shall issue from thee, which thou shalt beget, shall they take away; and they shall be eunuchs in the palace of the king of Babylon.

39:8 Then said Hezekiah to Isaiah, Good is the word of the Lord which thou hast spoken. He said, moreover, For there shall be peace and truth in my days.

.40

[1] Comfort ye, comfort ye my people, saith your God.

[2] Speak ye comfortably to Jerusalem, and cry unto her, that her warfare is accomplished, that her iniquity is pardoned: for she hath received of the LORD's hand double for all her sins.

[3] The voice of him that crieth in the wilderness, Prepare ye the way of the LORD, make straight in the desert a highway for our God.

[4] Every valley shall be exalted, and every mountain and hill shall be made low: and the crooked shall be made straight, and the rough places plain:

[5] And the glory of the LORD shall be revealed, and all flesh shall see it together: for the mouth of the LORD hath spoken it.

[6] The voice said, Cry. And he said, What shall I cry? All flesh is grass, and all the goodliness thereof is as the flower of the field:

Chapter 40

40:1 Comfort ye, comfort ye, my people, saith your God.

40:2 Speak ye comfortably to Jerusalem and cry unto her that her warfare is accomplished, that her iniquity is pardoned; for she hath received of the Lord's hand double for all her sins.

40:3 The voice of him that crieth in the wilderness, Prepare ye the way of the Lord; make straight in the desert a highway for our God.

40:4 Every valley shall be exalted, and every mountain and hill shall be made low; and the crooked shall be made straight, and the rough places plain;

40:5 And the glory of the Lord shall be revealed, and all flesh shall see it together; for the mouth of the Lord hath spoken it.

40:6 The voice said, Cry. And he said, What shall I cry? All flesh is grass, and all the goodliness thereof is as the flower of the field;

(1 Ne 10:8 – Paraphrased)
Yea, even he should go forth and cry in the wilderness: ªPrepare ye the way of the Lord, and make his paths straight; for there standeth one among you whom ye know not; and he is mightier than I, whose shoe's latchet I am not worthy to unloose.

[7] The grass withereth, the flower fadeth: because the spirit of the LORD bloweth upon it: surely the people is grass.

[8] The grass withereth, the flower fadeth: but the word of our God shall stand for ever.

[9] O Zion, that bringest good tidings, get thee up into the high mountain; O Jerusalem, that bringest good tidings, lift up thy voice with strength; lift it up, be not afraid; say unto the cities of Judah, Behold your God!

[10] Behold, the Lord GOD will come with strong hand, and his arm shall rule for him: behold, his reward is with him, and his work before him.

[11] He shall feed his flock like a shepherd: he shall gather the lambs with his arm, and carry them in his bosom, and shall gently lead those that are with young.

40:7 The grass withereth; the flower fadeth because the Spirit of the Lord bloweth upon it; surely the people is grass.

40:8 The grass withereth; the flower fadeth; but the word of our God shall stand forever.

40:9 O Zion, that bringest good tidings, get thee up into the high mountain; O Jerusalem, that bringest good tidings, lift up thy voice with strength; lift it up; be not afraid; say unto the cities of Judah, Behold your God!

40:10 Behold, the Lord God will come with strong hand, and his arm shall rule for him; behold, his reward is with him, and his work before him.

40:11 He shall feed his flock like a shepherd; he shall gather the lambs with his arm, and carry them in his bosom, and shall gently lead those that are with young.

[12] Who hath measured the waters in the hollow of his hand, and meted out heaven with the span, and comprehended the dust of the earth in a measure, and weighed the mountains in scales, and the hills in a balance?

[13] Who hath directed the Spirit of the LORD, or being his counseller hath taught him?

[14] With whom took he counsel, and who instructed him, and taught him in the path of judgment, and taught him knowledge, and shewed to him the way of understanding?

[15] Behold, the nations are as a drop of a bucket, and are counted as the small dust of the balance: behold, he taketh up the isles as a very little thing.
[
16] And Lebanon is not sufficient to burn, nor the beasts thereof sufficient for a burnt offering.

[17] All nations before him are as nothing; and they are counted to him less than nothing, and vanity.

40:12 Who hath measured the waters in the hollow of his hand, and meted out heaven with the span, and comprehended the dust of the earth in a measure, and weighed the mountains in scales and the hills in a balance?

40:13 Who hath directed the Spirit of the Lord or, being his counselor, hath taught him?

40:14 With whom took he counsel, and who instructed him, and taught him in the path of judgment, and taught him knowledge, and showed to him the way of understanding?

40:15 Behold, the nations are as a drop of a bucket and are counted as the small dust of the balance; behold, he taketh up the isles as a very little thing.

40:16 And Lebanon is not sufficient to burn nor the beasts thereof sufficient for a burnt offering.

40:17 All nations before him are as nothing; and they are counted to him less than nothing and vanity.

[**18**] To whom then will ye liken God? or what likeness will ye compare unto him?

[**19**] The workman melteth a graven image, and the goldsmith spreadeth it over with gold, and casteth silver chains.

[**20**] He that is so impoverished that he hath no oblation chooseth a tree that will not rot; he seeketh unto him a cunning workman to prepare a graven image, that shall not be moved.

[**21**] Have ye not known? have ye not heard? hath it not been told you from the beginning? have ye not understood from the foundations of the earth?

[**22**] It is he that sitteth upon the circle of the earth, and the inhabitants thereof are as grasshoppers; that stretcheth out the heavens as a curtain, and spreadeth them out as a tent to dwell in:

[**23**] That bringeth the princes to nothing; he maketh the judges of the earth as vanity.

18 To whom then will ye liken God? Or what likeness will ye compare unto him?

40:19 The workman melteth a graven image, and the goldsmith spreadeth it over with gold and casteth silver chains.

40:20 He that is so impoverished that he hath no oblation chooseth a tree that will not rot; he seeketh unto him a cunning workman to prepare a graven image that shall not be moved.

40:21 Have ye not known? Have ye not heard? Hath it not been told you from the beginning? Have ye not understood from the foundations of the earth?

40:22 It is he that sitteth upon the circle of the earth--and the inhabitants thereof are as grasshoppers--that stretcheth out the heavens as a curtain and spreadeth them out as a tent to dwell in,

40:23 That bringeth the princes to nothing; he maketh the judges of the earth as vanity.

[24] Yea, they shall not be planted; yea, they shall not be sown: yea, their stock shall not take root in the earth: and he shall also blow upon them, and they shall wither, and the whirlwind shall take them away as stubble.

[25] To whom then will ye liken me, or shall I be equal? saith the Holy One.

[26] Lift up your eyes on high, and behold who hath created these things, that bringeth out their host by number: he calleth them all by names by the greatness of his might, for that he is strong in power; not one faileth.

[27] Why sayest thou, O Jacob, and speakest, O Israel, My way is hid from the LORD, and my judgment is passed over from my God?

[28] Hast thou not known? hast thou not heard, that the everlasting God, the Lord, the Creator of the ends of the earth, fainteth not, neither is weary? there is no searching of his understanding.

[29] He giveth power to the faint; and to them that have no might he increaseth strength.

40:24 Yea, they shall not be planted; yea, they shall not be sown; yea, their stock shall not take root in the earth. And he shall also blow upon them; and they shall wither, and the whirlwind shall take them away as stubble.

40:25 To whom then will ye liken me, or shall I be equal? saith the Holy One.

40:26 Lift up your eyes on high, and behold who hath created these things, that bringeth out their host by number; he calleth them all by names by the greatness of his might, for that he is strong in power; not one faileth.

40:27 Why sayest thou, O Jacob, and speakest, O Israel, My way is hid from the Lord, and my judgment is passed over from my God?

40:28 Hast thou not known? Hast thou not heard that the everlasting God, the Lord, the Creator of the ends of the earth, fainteth not, neither is weary? There is no searching of his understanding.

40:29 He giveth power to the faint; and to them that have no might he increaseth strength.

[30] Even the youths shall faint and be weary, and the young men shall utterly fall:

[31] But they that wait upon the LORD shall renew their strength; they shall mount up with wings as eagles; they shall run, and not be weary; and they shall walk, and not faint.

.41

[1] Keep silence before me, O islands; and let the people renew their strength: let them come near; then let them speak: let us come near together to judgment.

[2] Who raised up the righteous man from the east, called him to his foot, gave the nations before him, and made him rule over kings? he gave them as the dust to his sword, and as driven stubble to his bow.

[3] He pursued them, and passed safely; even by the way that he had not gone with his feet.

40:30 Even the youths shall faint and be weary, and the young men shall utterly fall;

40:31 But they that wait upon the Lord shall renew their strength; they shall mount up with wings as eagles; they shall run and not be weary; and they shall walk and not faint.

Chapter 41

41:1 Keep silence before me, O islands; and let the people renew their strength; let them come near; then let them speak; let us come near together to judgment.

41:2 Who raised up the righteous man from the east, called him to his foot, gave the nations before him, and made him rule over kings? He gave them as the dust to his sword and as driven stubble to his bow.

41:3 He pursued them and passed safely, even by the way that he had not gone with his feet.

[4] Who hath wrought and done it, calling the generations from the beginning? I the LORD, the first, and with the last; I am he.

[5] The isles saw it, and feared; the ends of the earth were afraid, drew near, and came.

[6] They helped every one his neighbour; and every one said to his brother, Be of good courage.

[7] So the carpenter encouraged the goldsmith, and he that smootheth with the hammer him that smote the anvil, saying, It is ready for the sodering: and he fastened it with nails, that it should not be moved.

[8] But thou, Israel, art my servant, Jacob whom I have chosen, the seed of Abraham my friend.

[9] Thou whom I have taken from the ends of the earth, and called thee from the chief men thereof, and said unto thee, Thou art my servant; I have chosen thee, and not cast thee away.

41:4 Who hath wrought and done it, calling the generations from the beginning? I, the Lord, the first and with the last; I am he.

41:5 The isles saw it and feared; the ends of the earth were afraid, drew near, and came.

41:6 They helped everyone his neighbor; and everyone said to his brother, Be of good courage.

41:7 So the carpenter encouraged the goldsmith, and he that smootheth with the hammer him that smote the anvil, saying, It is ready for the soldering; and he fastened it with nails, that it should not be moved.

41:8 But thou, Israel, art my servant, Jacob, whom I have chosen, the seed of Abraham, my friend,

41:9 Thou whom I have taken from the ends of the earth, and called thee from the chief men thereof, and said unto thee, Thou art my servant; I have chosen thee and not cast thee away.

[10] Fear thou not; for I am with thee: be not dismayed; for I am thy God: I will strengthen thee; yea, I will help thee; yea, I will uphold thee with the right hand of my righteousness.

[11] Behold, all they that were incensed against thee shall be ashamed and confounded: they shall be as nothing; and they that strive with thee shall perish.

[12] Thou shalt seek them, and shalt not find them, even them that contended with thee: they that war against thee shall be as nothing, and as a thing of nought.

[13] For I the LORD thy God will hold thy right hand, saying unto thee, Fear not; I will help thee.

[14] Fear not, thou worm Jacob, and ye men of Israel; I will help thee, saith the LORD, and thy redeemer, the Holy One of Israel.

[15] Behold, I will make thee a new sharp threshing instrument having teeth: thou shalt thresh the mountains, and beat them small, and shalt make the hills as chaff.

41:10 Fear thou not, for I am with thee; be not dismayed, for I am thy God; I will strengthen thee; yea, I will help thee; yea, I will uphold thee with the right hand of my righteousness.

41:11 Behold, all they that were incensed against thee shall be ashamed and confounded; they shall be as nothing; and they that strive with thee shall perish.

41:12 Thou shalt seek them and shalt not find them, even them that contended with thee; they that war against thee shall be as nothing and as a thing of naught.

41:13 For I, the Lord, thy God, will hold thy right hand, saying unto thee, Fear not; I will help thee.

41:14 Fear not, thou worm Jacob and ye men of Israel; I will help thee, saith the Lord and thy Redeemer, the Holy One of Israel.

41:15 Behold, I will make thee a new sharp threshing instrument having teeth; thou shalt thresh the mountains, and beat them small, and shalt make the hills as chaff.

[16] Thou shalt fan them, and the wind shall carry them away, and the whirlwind shall scatter them: and thou shalt rejoice in the LORD, and shalt glory in the Holy One of Israel.

[17] When the poor and needy seek water, and there is none, and their tongue faileth for thirst, I the LORD will hear them, I the God of Israel will not forsake them.

[18] I will open rivers in high places, and fountains in the midst of the valleys: I will make the wilderness a pool of water, and the dry land springs of water.

[19] I will plant in the wilderness the cedar, the shittah tree, and the myrtle, and the oil tree; I will set in the desert the fir tree, and the pine, and the box tree together:

[20] That they may see, and know, and consider, and understand together, that the hand of the LORD hath done this, and the Holy One of Israel hath created it.

[21] Produce your cause, saith the LORD; bring forth your strong reasons, saith the King of Jacob.

41:16 Thou shalt fan them; and the wind shall carry them away, and the whirlwind shall scatter them; and thou shalt rejoice in the Lord and shalt glory in the Holy One of Israel.

41:17 When the poor and needy seek water, and there is none, and their tongue faileth for thirst, I, the Lord, will hear them. I, the God of Israel, will not forsake them.

41:18 I will open rivers in high places and fountains in the midst of the valleys; I will make the wilderness a pool of water and the dry land springs of water.

41:19 I will plant in the wilderness the cedar, the shittah tree, and the myrtle, and the oil tree; I will set in the desert the fir tree, and the pine, and the box tree together,

41:20 That they may see, and know, and consider, and understand together, that the hand of the Lord hath done this, and the Holy One of Israel hath created it.

41:21 Produce your cause, saith the Lord; bring forth your strong reasons, saith the King of Jacob.

[22] Let them bring them forth, and shew us what shall happen: let them shew the former things, what they be, that we may consider them, and know the latter end of them; or declare us things for to come.

[23] Shew the things that are to come hereafter, that we may know that ye are gods: yea, do good, or do evil, that we may be dismayed, and behold it together.

[24] Behold, ye are of nothing, and your work of nought: an abomination is he that chooseth you.

[25] I have raised up one from the north, and he shall come: from the rising of the sun shall he call upon my name: and he shall come upon princes as upon morter, and as the potter treadeth clay.

[26] Who hath declared from the beginning, that we may know? and beforetime, that we may say, He is righteous? yea, there is none that sheweth, yea, there is none that declareth, yea, there is none that heareth your words.

41:22 Let them bring them forth and show us what shall happen; let them show the former things, what they be, that we may consider them and know the latter end of them; or declare us things for to come.

41:23 Show the things that are to come hereafter, that we may know that ye are gods; yea, do good or do evil, that we may be dismayed and behold it together.

41:24 Behold, ye are of nothing, and your work of naught; an abomination is he that chooseth you.

41:25 I have raised up one from the north, and he shall come; from the rising of the sun shall he call upon my name; and he shall come upon princes as upon mortar, and as the potter treadeth clay.

41:26 Who hath declared from the beginning, that we may know; and beforetime, that we may say, He is righteous? Yea, there is none that showeth; yea, there is none that declareth; yea, there is none that heareth your words.

[27] The first shall say to Zion, Behold, behold them: and I will give to Jerusalem one that bringeth good tidings.

[28] For I beheld, and there was no man; even among them, and there was no counseller, that, when I asked of them, could answer a word.

[29] Behold, they are all vanity; their works are nothing: their molten images are wind and confusion.

.42

[1] Behold my servant, whom I uphold; mine elect, in whom my soul delighteth; I have put my spirit upon him: he shall bring forth judgment to the Gentiles.

[2] He shall not cry, nor lift up, nor cause his voice to be heard in the street.

[3] A bruised reed shall he not break, and the smoking flax shall he not quench: he shall bring forth judgment unto truth.

[4] He shall not fail nor be discouraged, till he have set judgment in the earth: and the isles shall wait for his law.

41:27 The first shall say to Zion, Behold, behold them; and I will give to Jerusalem one that bringeth good tidings.

41:28 For I beheld, and there was no man, even among men; and there was no counselor that, when I asked of them, could answer a word.

41:29 Behold, they are all vanity; their works are nothing; their molten images are wind and confusion.

Chapter 42

42:1 Behold my servant, whom I uphold, mine elect, in whom my soul delighteth; I have put my Spirit upon him; he shall bring forth judgment to the Gentiles.

42:2 He shall not cry, nor lift up, nor cause his voice to be heard in the street.

42:3 A bruised reed shall he not break, and the smoking flax shall he not quench; he shall bring forth judgment unto truth.

42:4 He shall not fail nor be discouraged till he have set judgment in the earth; and the isles shall wait for his law.

[5] Thus saith God the LORD, he that created the heavens, and stretched them out; he that spread forth the earth, and that which cometh out of it; he that giveth breath unto the people upon it, and spirit to them that walk therein:

[6] I the LORD have called thee in righteousness, and will hold thine hand, and will keep thee, and give thee for a covenant of the people, for a light of the Gentiles;

[7] To open the blind eyes, to bring out the prisoners from the prison, and them that sit in darkness out of the prison house.

[8] I am the LORD: that is my name: and my glory will I not give to another, neither my praise to graven images.

[9] Behold, the former things are come to pass, and new things do I declare: before they spring forth I tell you of them.

[10] Sing unto the LORD a new song, and his praise from the end of the earth, ye that go down to the sea, and all that is therein; the isles, and the inhabitants thereof.

42:5 Thus saith God, the Lord, he that created the heavens and stretched them out, he that spread forth the earth and that which cometh out of it, he that giveth breath unto the people upon it and spirit to them that walk therein:

42:6 I, the Lord, have called thee in righteousness, and will hold thine hand, and will keep thee, and give thee for a covenant of the people, for a light of the Gentiles,

42:7 To open the blind eyes, to bring out the prisoners from the prison, and them that sit in darkness out of the prison house.

42:8 I am the Lord; that is my name; and my glory will I not give to another, neither my praise to graven images.

9 Behold, the former things are come to pass, and new things do I declare; before they spring forth, I tell you of them.

42:10 Sing unto the Lord a new song and his praise from the end of the earth, ye that go down to the sea and all that is therein--the isles and the inhabitants thereof.

[11] Let the wilderness and the cities thereof lift up their voice, the villages that Kedar doth inhabit: let the inhabitants of the rock sing, let them shout from the top of the mountains.

[12] Let them give glory unto the LORD, and declare his praise in the islands.

[13] The LORD shall go forth as a mighty man, he shall stir up jealousy like a man of war: he shall cry, yea, roar; he shall prevail against his enemies.

[14] I have long time holden my peace; I have been still, and refrained myself: now will I cry like a travailing woman; I will destroy and devour at once.

[15] I will make waste mountains and hills, and dry up all their herbs; and I will make the rivers islands, and I will dry up the pools.

[16] And I will bring the blind by a way that they knew not; I will lead them in paths that they have not known: I will make darkness light before them, and crooked things straight. These things will I do unto them, and not forsake them.

42:11 Let the wilderness and the cities thereof lift up their voice, the villages that Kedar doth inhabit; let the inhabitants of the rock sing; let them shout from the top of the mountains.

42:12 Let them give glory unto the Lord and declare his praise in the islands.

42:13 The Lord shall go forth as a mighty man; he shall stir up jealousy like a man of war; he shall cry, yea, roar; he shall prevail against his enemies.

42:14 I have long time holden my peace; I have been still and refrained myself; now will I cry like a travailing woman; I will destroy and devour at once.

42:15 I will make waste mountains and hills and dry up all their herbs; and I will make the rivers islands, and I will dry up the pools.

42:16 And I will bring the blind by a way that they knew not; I will lead them in paths that they have not known; I will make darkness light before them and crooked things straight. These things will I do unto them and not forsake them.

[17] They shall be turned back, they shall be greatly ashamed, that trust in graven images, that say to the molten images, Ye are our gods.

[18] Hear, ye deaf; and look, ye blind, that ye may see.

[19] Who is blind, but my servant? or deaf, as my messenger that I sent? who is blind as he that is perfect, and blind as the LORD's servant?

[20] Seeing many things, but thou observest not; opening the ears, but he heareth not.

[21] The LORD is well pleased for his righteousness' sake; he will magnify the law, and make it honourable.

[22] But this is a people robbed and spoiled; they are all of them snared in holes, and they are hid in prison houses: they are for a prey, and none delivereth; for a spoil, and none saith, Restore.

42:17 They shall be turned back; they shall be greatly ashamed that trust in graven images, that say to the molten images, Ye are our gods.

42:18 Hear, ye deaf, and look, ye blind, that ye may see.

42:19 For I will send my servant unto you who are blind, yea, a messenger to open the eyes of the blind and unstop the ears of the deaf;

42:20 And they shall be made perfect, notwithstanding their blindness, if they will hearken unto the messenger, the Lord's servant.

42:21 Thou art a people, seeing many things, but thou observest not; opening the ears to hear, but thou hearest not.

42:22 The Lord is not well pleased with such a people, but for his righteousness' sake he will magnify the law and make it honorable.

[23] Who among you will give ear to this? who will hearken and hear for the time to come?

42:23 Thou art a people robbed and spoiled; thine enemies, all of them, have snared thee in holes, and they have hid thee in prison houses; they have taken thee for a prey, and none delivereth; for a spoil, and none saith, Restore.

[24] Who gave Jacob for a spoil, and Israel to the robbers? did not the LORD, he against whom we have sinned? for they would not walk in his ways, neither were they obedient unto his law.

42:24 Who among them will give ear unto thee or hearken and hear thee for the time to come? And who gave Jacob for a spoil, and Israel to the robbers? Did not the Lord, he against whom they have sinned?

[25] Therefore he hath poured upon him the fury of his anger, and the strength of battle: and it hath set him on fire round about, yet he knew not; and it burned him, yet he laid it not to heart.

42:25 For they would not walk in his ways; neither were they obedient unto his law; therefore, he hath poured upon them the fury of his anger and the strength of battle; and they have set them on fire round about; yet they knew not, and it burned them; yet they laid it not to heart.

.43

Chapter 43

[1] But now thus saith the LORD that created thee, O Jacob, and he that formed thee, O Israel, Fear not: for I have redeemed thee, I have called thee by thy name; thou art mine.

43:1 But now thus saith the Lord that created thee, O Jacob, and he that formed thee, O Israel, Fear not; for I have redeemed thee, I have called thee by thy name; thou art mine.

[2] When thou passest through the waters, I will be with thee; and through the rivers, they shall not overflow thee: when thou walkest through the fire, thou shalt not be burned; neither shall the flame kindle upon thee.

[3] For I am the LORD thy God, the Holy One of Israel, thy Saviour: I gave Egypt for thy ransom, Ethiopia and Seba for thee.

[4] Since thou wast precious in my sight, thou hast been honourable, and I have loved thee: therefore will I give men for thee, and people for thy life.

[5] Fear not: for I am with thee: I will bring thy seed from the east, and gather thee from the west;

[6] I will say to the north, Give up; and to the south, Keep not back: bring my sons from far, and my daughters from the ends of the earth;

[7] Even every one that is called by my name: for I have created him for my glory, I have formed him; yea, I have made him.

43:2 When thou passest through the waters, I will be with thee; and through the rivers, they shall not overflow thee; when thou walkest through the fire, thou shalt not be burned; neither shall the flame kindle upon thee.

43:3 For I am the Lord, thy God, the Holy One of Israel, thy Savior; I gave Egypt for thy ransom, Ethiopia and Seba for thee.

43:4 Since thou wast precious in my sight, thou hast been honorable, and I have loved thee; therefore will I give men for thee, and people for thy life.

43:5 Fear not, for I am with thee; I will bring thy seed from the east and gather thee from the west;

43:6 I will say to the north, Give up; and to the south, Keep not back; bring my sons from far, and my daughters from the ends of the earth,

43:7 Even everyone that is called by my name; for I have created him for my glory; I have formed him; yea, I have made him.

[8] Bring forth the blind people that have eyes, and the deaf that have ears.

[9] Let all the nations be gathered together, and let the people be assembled: who among them can declare this, and shew us former things? let them bring forth their witnesses, that they may be justified: or let them hear, and say, It is truth.

[10] Ye are my witnesses, saith the LORD, and my servant whom I have chosen: that ye may know and believe me, and understand that I am he: before me there was no God formed, neither shall there be after me.

[11] I, even I, am the LORD; and beside me there is no saviour.

[12] I have declared, and have saved, and I have shewed, when there was no strange god among you: therefore ye are my witnesses, saith the LORD, that I am God.

[13] Yea, before the day was I am he; and there is none that can deliver out of my hand: I will work, and who shall let it?

43:8 Bring forth the blind people that have eyes and the deaf that have ears.

43:9 Let all the nations be gathered together, and let the people be assembled. Who among them can declare this and show us former things? Let them bring forth their witnesses, that they may be justified; or let them hear and say, It is truth.

43:10 Ye are my witnesses, saith the Lord, and my servant whom I have chosen, that ye may know, and believe me, and understand that I am he; before me there was no God formed; neither shall there be after me.

43:11 I, even I, am the Lord; and beside me there is no savior.

43:12 I have declared and have saved, and I have showed when there was no strange god among you; therefore, ye are my witnesses, saith the Lord, that I am God.

43:13 Yea, before the day was, I am he; and there is none that can deliver out of my hand; I will work. And who shall hinder it?

[14] Thus saith the LORD, your redeemer, the Holy One of Israel; For your sake I have sent to Babylon, and have brought down all their nobles, and the Chaldeans, whose cry is in the ships.

[15] I am the LORD, your Holy One, the creator of Israel, your King.

[16] Thus saith the LORD, which maketh a way in the sea, and a path in the mighty waters;

[17] Which bringeth forth the chariot and horse, the army and the power; they shall lie down together, they shall not rise: they are extinct, they are quenched as tow.

[18] Remember ye not the former things, neither consider the things of old.

[19] Behold, I will do a new thing; now it shall spring forth; shall ye not know it? I will even make a way in the wilderness, and rivers in the desert.

43:14 Thus saith the Lord, your Redeemer, the Holy One of Israel: For your sake I have sent to Babylon and have brought down all their nobles, and the Chaldeans, whose cry is in the ships.

43:15 I am the Lord, your Holy One, the Creator of Israel, your King.

43:16 Thus saith the Lord, which maketh a way in the sea and a path in the mighty waters,

43:17 Which bringeth forth the chariot and horse, the army and the power; they shall lie down together; they shall not rise; they are extinct; they are quenched as tow.

43:18 Remember ye not the former things; neither consider the things of old.

43:19 Behold, I will do a new thing; now it shall spring forth. Shall ye not know it? I will even make a way in the wilderness and rivers in the desert.

[20] The beast of the field shall honour me, the dragons and the owls: because I give waters in the wilderness, and rivers in the desert, to give drink to my people, my chosen.

[21] This people have I formed for myself; they shall shew forth my praise.

[22] But thou hast not called upon me, O Jacob; but thou hast been weary of me, O Israel.

[23] Thou hast not brought me the small cattle of thy burnt offerings; neither hast thou honoured me with thy sacrifices. I have not caused thee to serve with an offering, nor wearied thee with incense.

[24] Thou hast bought me no sweet cane with money, neither hast thou filled me with the fat of thy sacrifices: but thou hast made me to serve with thy sins, thou hast wearied me with thine iniquities.

[25] I, even I, am he that blotteth out thy transgressions for mine own sake, and will not remember thy sins.

43:20 The beast of the field shall honor me, the dragons and the owls, because I give waters in the wilderness and rivers in the desert to give drink to my people, my chosen.

43:21 This people have I formed for myself; they shall show forth my praise.

43:22 But thou hast not called upon me, O Jacob; but thou hast been weary of me, O Israel.

43:23 Thou hast not brought me the small cattle of thy burnt offerings; neither hast thou honored me with thy sacrifices. I have not caused thee to serve with an offering nor wearied thee with incense.

43:24 Thou hast bought me no sweet cane with money; neither hast thou filled me with the fat of thy sacrifices; but thou hast made me to serve with thy sins; thou hast wearied me with thine iniquities.

43:25 I, even I, am he that blotteth out thy transgressions for mine own sake and will not remember thy sins.

[26] Put me in remembrance: let us plead together: declare thou, that thou mayest be justified.

[27] Thy first father hath sinned, and thy teachers have transgressed against me.

[28] Therefore I have profaned the princes of the sanctuary, and have given Jacob to the curse, and Israel to reproaches.

.44

[1] Yet now hear, O Jacob my servant; and Israel, whom I have chosen:

[2] Thus saith the LORD that made thee, and formed thee from the womb, which will help thee; Fear not, O Jacob, my servant; and thou, Jesurun, whom I have chosen.

[3] For I will pour water upon him that is thirsty, and floods upon the dry ground: I will pour my spirit upon thy seed, and my blessing upon thine offspring:

[4] And they shall spring up as among the grass, as willows by the water courses.

43:26 Put me in remembrance; let us plead together; declare thou, that thou mayest be justified.

27 Thy first father hath sinned, and thy teachers have transgressed against me.

43:28 Therefore, I have profaned the princes of the sanctuary and have given Jacob to the curse, and Israel to reproaches.

Chapter 44

44:1 Yet now hear, O Jacob, my servant, and Israel, whom I have chosen,

44:2 Thus saith the Lord that made thee and formed thee from the womb, which will help thee: Fear not, O Jacob, my servant, and thou, Jeshurun, whom I have chosen.

44:3 For I will pour water upon him that is thirsty and floods upon the dry ground; I will pour my Spirit upon thy seed, and my blessing upon thine offspring;

44:4 And they shall spring up as among the grass, as willows by the water courses.

165

[5] One shall say, I am the LORD's; and another shall call himself by the name of Jacob; and another shall subscribe with his hand unto the LORD, and surname himself by the name of Israel.

[6] Thus saith the LORD the King of Israel, and his redeemer the LORD of hosts; I am the first, and I am the last; and beside me there is no God.

[7] And who, as I, shall call, and shall declare it, and set it in order for me, since I appointed the ancient people? and the things that are coming, and shall come, let them shew unto them.

[8] Fear ye not, neither be afraid: have not I told thee from that time, and have declared it? ye are even my witnesses. Is there a God beside me? yea, there is no God; I know not any.

[9] They that make a graven image are all of them vanity; and their delectable things shall not profit; and they are their own witnesses; they see not, nor know; that they may be ashamed.
[

44:5 One shall say, I am the Lord's; and another shall call himself by the name of Jacob; and another shall subscribe with his hand unto the Lord and surname himself by the name of Israel.

44:6 Thus saith the Lord, the King of Israel, and his Redeemer, the Lord of hosts: I am the first, and I am the last; and besides me there is no God.

44:7 And who, as I, shall call, and shall declare it, and set it in order for me, since I appointed the ancient people? And the things that are coming and shall come, let them show unto them.

44:8 Fear ye not; neither be afraid. Have not I told thee from that time and have declared it? Ye are even my witnesses. Is there a God besides me? Yea, there is no God; I know not any.

44:9 They that make a graven image are all of them vanity; and their delectable things shall not profit; and they are their own witnesses; they see not, nor know, that they may be ashamed.

10] Who hath formed a god, or molten a graven image that is profitable for nothing?

[11] Behold, all his fellows shall be ashamed: and the workmen, they are of men: let them all be gathered together, let them stand up; yet they shall fear, and they shall be ashamed together.

[12] The smith with the tongs both worketh in the coals, and fashioneth it with hammers, and worketh it with the strength of his arms: yea, he is hungry, and his strength faileth: he drinketh no water, and is faint.

[13] The carpenter stretcheth out his rule; he marketh it out with a line; he fitteth it with planes, and he marketh it out with the compass, and maketh it after the figure of a man, according to the beauty of a man; that it may remain in the house.

[14] He heweth him down cedars, and taketh the cypress and the oak, which he strengtheneth for himself among the trees of the forest: he planteth an ash, and the rain doth nourish it.

44:10 Who hath formed a god or molten a graven image that is profitable for nothing?

44:11 Behold, all his fellows shall be ashamed; and the workmen, they are of men; let them all be gathered together; let them stand up; yet they shall fear, and they shall be ashamed together.

44:12 The smith with the tongs both worketh in the coals, and fashioneth it with hammers, and worketh it with the strength of his arms; yea, he is hungry, and his strength faileth; he drinketh no water and is faint.

44:13 The carpenter stretcheth out his rule; he marketh it out with a line; he fitteth it with planes, and he marketh it out with the compass and maketh it after the figure of a man, according to the beauty of a man, that it may remain in the house.

44:14 He heweth him down cedars and taketh the cypress and the oak, which he strengtheneth for himself among the trees of the forest; he planteth an ash, and the rain doth nourish it.

[15] Then shall it be for a man to burn: for he will take thereof, and warm himself; yea, he kindleth it, and baketh bread; yea, he maketh a god, and worshippeth it; he maketh it a graven image, and falleth down thereto.

[16] He burneth part thereof in the fire; with part thereof he eateth flesh; he roasteth roast, and is satisfied: yea, he warmeth himself, and saith, Aha, I am warm, I have seen the fire:

[17] And the residue thereof he maketh a god, even his graven image: he falleth down unto it, and worshippeth it, and prayeth unto it, and saith, Deliver me; for thou art my god.

[18] They have not known nor understood: for he hath shut their eyes, that they cannot see; and their hearts, that they cannot understand.

44:15 Then shall it be for a man to burn; for he will take thereof and warm himself; yea, he kindleth it and baketh bread; yea, he maketh a god and worshipeth it; he maketh it a graven image and falleth down thereto.

44:16 He burneth part thereof in the fire; with part thereof he eateth flesh; he roasteth roast and is satisfied; yea, he warmeth himself and saith, Aha, I am warm; I have seen the fire;

44:17 And the residue thereof he maketh a god, even his graven image; he falleth down unto it, and worshipeth it, and prayeth unto it, and saith, Deliver me, for thou art my god.

44:18 They have not known nor understood; for he hath shut their eyes, that they cannot see, and their hearts, that they cannot understand.

[19] And none considereth in his heart, neither is there knowledge nor understanding to say, I have burned part of it in the fire; yea, also I have baked bread upon the coals thereof; I have roasted flesh, and eaten it: and shall I make the residue thereof an abomination? shall I fall down to the stock of a tree?

[20] He feedeth on ashes: a deceived heart hath turned him aside, that he cannot deliver his soul, nor say, Is there not a lie in my right hand?

[21] Remember these, O Jacob and Israel; for thou art my servant: I have formed thee; thou art my servant: O Israel, thou shalt not be forgotten of me.

[22] I have blotted out, as a thick cloud, thy transgressions, and, as a cloud, thy sins: return unto me; for I have redeemed thee.

[23] Sing, O ye heavens; for the LORD hath done it: shout, ye lower parts of the earth: break forth into singing, ye mountains, O forest, and every tree therein: for the LORD hath redeemed Jacob, and glorified himself in Israel.

44:19 And none considereth in his heart; neither is there knowledge nor understanding to say, I have burned part of it in the fire; yea, also I have baked bread upon the coals thereof; I have roasted flesh and eaten it. And shall I make the residue thereof an abomination? Shall I fall down to the stock of a tree?

44:20 He feedeth on ashes; a deceived heart hath turned him aside, that he cannot deliver his soul nor say, Is there not a lie in my right hand?

44:21 Remember these, O Jacob and Israel, for thou art my servant; I have formed thee; thou art my servant; O Israel, thou shalt not be forgotten of me.

44:22 I have blotted out, as a thick cloud, thy transgressions, and, as a cloud, thy sins; return unto me, for I have redeemed thee.

44:23 Sing, O ye heavens, for the Lord hath done it; shout, ye lower parts of the earth; break forth into singing, ye mountains, O forest, and every tree therein; for the Lord hath redeemed Jacob and glorified himself in Israel.

[24] Thus saith the LORD, thy redeemer, and he that formed thee from the womb, I am the LORD that maketh all things; that stretcheth forth the heavens alone; that spreadeth abroad the earth by myself;

[25] That frustrateth the tokens of the liars, and maketh diviners mad; that turneth wise men backward, and maketh their knowledge foolish;

[26] That confirmeth the word of his servant, and performeth the counsel of his messengers; that saith to Jerusalem, Thou shalt be inhabited; and to the cities of Judah, Ye shall be built, and I will raise up the decayed places thereof:

[27] That saith to the deep, Be dry, and I will dry up thy rivers:

[28] That saith of Cyrus, He is my shepherd, and shall perform all my pleasure: even saying to Jerusalem, Thou shalt be built; and to the temple, Thy foundation shall be laid.

.45

44:24 Thus saith the Lord, thy Redeemer, and he that formed thee from the womb: I am the Lord that maketh all things; that stretcheth forth the heavens alone; that spreadeth abroad the earth by myself;

44:25 That frustrateth the tokens of the liars and maketh diviners mad; that turneth wise men backward and maketh their knowledge foolish;

44:26 That confirmeth the word of his servant and performeth the counsel of his messengers; that saith to Jerusalem, Thou shalt be inhabited; and to the cities of Judah, Ye shall be built, and I will raise up the decayed places thereof;

44:27 That saith to the deep, Be dry, and I will dry up thy rivers;

44:28 That saith of Cyrus, He is my shepherd and shall perform all my pleasure, even saying to Jerusalem, Thou shalt be built; and to the temple, Thy foundation shall be laid.

Chapter 45

[1] Thus saith the LORD to his anointed, to Cyrus, whose right hand I have holden, to subdue nations before him; and I will loose the loins of kings, to open before him the two leaved gates; and the gates shall not be shut;

[2] I will go before thee, and make the crooked places straight: I will break in pieces the gates of brass, and cut in sunder the bars of iron:

[3] And I will give thee the treasures of darkness, and hidden riches of secret places, that thou mayest know that I, the LORD, which call thee by thy name, am the God of Israel.

[4] For Jacob my servant's sake, and Israel mine elect, I have even called thee by thy name: I have surnamed thee, though thou hast not known me.

[5] I am the LORD, and there is none else, there is no God beside me: I girded thee, though thou hast not known me:

[6] That they may know from the rising of the sun, and from the west, that there is none beside me. I am the LORD, and there is none else.

45:1 Thus saith the Lord to his anointed, to Cyrus--whose right hand I have holden, to subdue nations before him; and I will loose the loins of kings, to open before him the two-leaved gates; and the gates shall not be shut--

45:2 I will go before thee and make the crooked places straight; I will break in pieces the gates of brass and cut in sunder the bars of iron;

45:3 And I will give thee the treasures of darkness and hidden riches of secret places, that thou mayest know that I, the Lord, which call thee by thy name, am the God of Israel.

45:4 For Jacob, my servant's sake, and Israel, mine elect, I have even called thee by thy name; I have surnamed thee though thou hast not known me.

45:5 I am the Lord, and there is none else; there is no God besides me; I girded thee, though thou hast not known me,

45:6 That they may know from the rising of the sun and from the west that there is none besides me. I am the Lord, and there is none else.

[7] I form the light, and create darkness: I make peace, and create evil: I the LORD do all these things.

[8] Drop down, ye heavens, from above, and let the skies pour down righteousness: let the earth open, and let them bring forth salvation, and let righteousness spring up together; I the LORD have created it.

[9] Woe unto him that striveth with his Maker! Let the potsherd strive with the potsherds of the earth. Shall the clay say to him that fashioneth it, What makest thou? or thy work, He hath no hands?

[10] Woe unto him that saith unto his father, What begettest thou? or to the woman, What hast thou brought forth?

[11] Thus saith the LORD, the Holy One of Israel, and his Maker, Ask me of things to come concerning my sons, and concerning the work of my hands command ye me.

[12] I have made the earth, and created man upon it: I, even my hands, have stretched out the heavens, and all their host have I commanded.

45:7 I form the light and create darkness; I make peace and create evil; I, the Lord, do all these things.

45:8 Drop down, ye heavens, from above, and let the skies pour down righteousness; let the earth open, and let them bring forth salvation, and let righteousness spring up together; I, the Lord, have created it.

45:9 Woe unto him that striveth with his Maker! Let the potsherd strive with the potsherds of the earth. Shall the clay say to him that fashioneth it, What makest thou? Or thy work, He hath no hands?

45:10 Woe unto him that saith unto his father, What begettest thou? Or to the woman, What hast thou brought forth?

45:11 Thus saith the Lord, the Holy One of Israel, and his Maker, Ask me of things to come concerning my sons; and concerning the work of my hands, command ye me.

45:12 I have made the earth and created man upon it; I, even my hands, have stretched out the heavens, and all their hosts have I commanded.

[13] I have raised him up in righteousness, and I will direct all his ways: he shall build my city, and he shall let go my captives, not for price nor reward, saith the LORD of hosts.

[14] Thus saith the LORD, The labour of Egypt and merchandise of Ethiopia and of the Sabeans, men of stature, shall come over unto thee, and they shall be thine: they shall come after thee; in chains they shall come over, and they shall fall down unto thee, they shall make supplication unto thee, saying, Surely God is in thee; and there is none else, there is no God.

[15] Verily thou art a God that hidest thyself, O God of Israel, the Saviour.

[16] They shall be ashamed, and also confounded, all of them: they shall go to confusion together that are makers of idols.

[17] But Israel shall be saved in the LORD with an everlasting salvation: ye shall not be ashamed nor confounded world without end.

45:13 I have raised him up in righteousness, and I will direct all his ways; he shall build my city, and he shall let go my captives, not for price nor reward, saith the Lord of hosts.

45:14 Thus saith the Lord, The labor of Egypt and merchandise of Ethiopia and of the Sabeans, men of stature, shall come over unto thee, and they shall be thine; they shall come after thee; in chains they shall come over, and they shall fall down unto thee; they shall make supplication unto thee, saying, Surely God is in thee; and there is none else; there is no god.

45:15 Verily, thou art a God that hidest thyself, O God of Israel, the Savior.

45:16 They shall be ashamed and also confounded, all of them; they shall go to confusion together that are makers of idols.

45:17 But Israel shall be saved in the Lord with an everlasting salvation; ye shall not be ashamed nor confounded, world without end.

[18] For thus saith the LORD that created the heavens; God himself that formed the earth and made it; he hath established it, he created it not in vain, he formed it to be inhabited: I am the LORD; and there is none else.

[19] I have not spoken in secret, in a dark place of the earth: I said not unto the seed of Jacob, Seek ye me in vain: I the LORD speak righteousness, I declare things that are right.

[20] Assemble yourselves and come; draw near together, ye that are escaped of the nations: they have no knowledge that set up the wood of their graven image, and pray unto a god that cannot save.

[21] Tell ye, and bring them near; yea, let them take counsel together: who hath declared this from ancient time? who hath told it from that time? have not I the LORD? and there is no God else beside me; a just God and a Saviour; there is none beside me.

[22] Look unto me, and be ye saved, all the ends of the earth: for I am God, and there is none else.

45:18 For thus saith the Lord that created the heavens--God himself that formed the earth and made it; he hath established it; he created it not in vain; he formed it to be inhabited--I am the Lord, and there is none else.

45:19 I have not spoken in secret, in a dark place of the earth; I said not unto the seed of Jacob, Seek ye me in vain; I, the Lord, speak righteousness; I declare things that are right.

45:20 Assemble yourselves and come; draw near together, ye that are escaped of the nations; they have no knowledge that set up the wood of their graven image and pray unto a god that cannot save.

45:21 Tell ye, and bring them near; yea, let them take counsel together. Who hath declared this from ancient time? Who hath told it from that time? Have not I, the Lord? And there is no god else beside me, a just God and a Savior; there is none beside me.

45:22 Look unto me, and be ye saved, all the ends of the earth; for I am God, and there is none else.

[23] I have sworn by myself, the word is gone out of my mouth in righteousness, and shall not return, That unto me every knee shall bow, every tongue shall swear.

[24] Surely, shall one say, in the LORD have I righteousness and strength: even to him shall men come; and all that are incensed against him shall be ashamed.

[25] In the LORD shall all the seed of Israel be justified, and shall glory.

.46

[1] Bel boweth down, Nebo stoopeth, their idols were upon the beasts, and upon the cattle: your carriages were heavy loaden; they are a burden to the weary beast.

[2] They stoop, they bow down together; they could not deliver the burden, but themselves are gone into captivity.

[3] Hearken unto me, O house of Jacob, and all the remnant of the house of Israel, which are borne by me from the belly, which are carried from the womb:

45:23 I have sworn by myself; the word is gone out of my mouth in righteousness and shall not return: That unto me every knee shall bow, every tongue shall swear.

45:24 Surely shall one say, In the Lord have I righteousness and strength; even to him shall men come; and all that are incensed against him shall be ashamed.

45:25 In the Lord shall all the seed of Israel be justified and shall glory.

Chapter 46

46:1 Bel boweth down; Nebo stoopeth; their idols were upon the beasts and upon the cattle; your carriages were heavy laden; they are a burden to the weary beast.

46:2 They stoop; they bow down together; they could not deliver the burden, but themselves are gone into captivity.

46:3 Hearken unto me, O house of Jacob, and all the remnant of the house of Israel, which are borne by me from the belly, which are carried from the womb;

[4] And even to your old age I am he; and even to hoar hairs will I carry you: I have made, and I will bear; even I will carry, and will deliver you.

[5] To whom will ye liken me, and make me equal, and compare me, that we may be like?

[6] They lavish gold out of the bag, and weigh silver in the balance, and hire a goldsmith; and he maketh it a god: they fall down, yea, they worship.

[7] They bear him upon the shoulder, they carry him, and set him in his place, and he standeth; from his place shall he not remove: yea, one shall cry unto him, yet can he not answer, nor save him out of his trouble.

[8] Remember this, and shew yourselves men: bring it again to mind, O ye transgressors.

[9] Remember the former things of old: for I am God, and there is none else; I am God, and there is none like me,

46:4 And even to your old age I am he; and even to hoar hairs will I carry you; I have made, and I will bear; even I will carry and will deliver you.

46:5 To whom will ye liken me, and make me equal, and compare me, that we may be like?

46:6 They lavish gold out of the bag, and weigh silver in the balance, and hire a goldsmith; and he maketh it a god; they fall down; yea, they worship.

46:7 They bear him upon the shoulder; they carry him and set him in his place, and he standeth; from his place shall he not remove; yea, one shall cry unto him; yet can he not answer nor save him out of his trouble.

46:8 Remember this, and show yourselves men; bring it again to mind, O ye transgressors.

46:9 Remember the former things of old; for I am God, and there is none else; I am God, and there is none like me,

[10] Declaring the end from the beginning, and from ancient times the things that are not yet done, saying, My counsel shall stand, and I will do all my pleasure:

[11] Calling a ravenous bird from the east, the man that executeth my counsel from a far country: yea, I have spoken it, I will also bring it to pass; I have purposed it, I will also do it.

[12] Hearken unto me, ye stouthearted, that are far from righteousness:

[13] I bring near my righteousness; it shall not be far off, and my salvation shall not tarry: and I will place salvation in Zion for Israel my glory.

.47

[1] Come down, and sit in the dust, O virgin daughter of Babylon, sit on the ground: there is no throne, O daughter of the Chaldeans: for thou shalt no more be called tender and delicate.

[2] Take the millstones, and grind meal: uncover thy locks, make bare the leg, uncover the thigh, pass over the rivers.

46:10 Declaring the end from the beginning, and from ancient times the things that are not yet done, saying, My counsel shall stand, and I will do all my pleasure,

46:11 Calling a ravenous bird from the east, the man that executeth my counsel from a far country; yea, I have spoken it; I will also bring it to pass; I have purposed it; I will also do it.

46:12 Hearken unto me, ye stouthearted, that are far from righteousness;

46:13 I bring near my righteousness; it shall not be far off, and my salvation shall not tarry; and I will place salvation in Zion for Israel, my glory.

Chapter 47

47:1 Come down, and sit in the dust, O virgin daughter of Babylon; sit on the ground; there is no throne, O daughter of the Chaldeans; for thou shalt no more be called tender and delicate.

47:2 Take the millstones, and grind meal; uncover thy locks; make bare the leg; uncover the thigh; pass over the rivers.

[3] Thy nakedness shall be uncovered, yea, thy shame shall be seen: I will take vengeance, and I will not meet thee as a man.

[4] As for our redeemer, the LORD of hosts is his name, the Holy One of Israel.

[5] Sit thou silent, and get thee into darkness, O daughter of the Chaldeans: for thou shalt no more be called, The lady of kingdoms.

[6] I was wroth with my people, I have polluted mine inheritance, and given them into thine hand: thou didst shew them no mercy; upon the ancient hast thou very heavily laid thy yoke.

[7] And thou saidst, I shall be a lady for ever: so that thou didst not lay these things to thy heart, neither didst remember the latter end of it.

[8] Therefore hear now this, thou that art given to pleasures, that dwellest carelessly, that sayest in thine heart, I am, and none else beside me; I shall not sit as a widow, neither shall I know the loss of children:

47:3 Thy nakedness shall be uncovered; yea, thy shame shall be seen; I will take vengeance, and I will not meet thee as a man.

47:4 As for our Redeemer, the Lord of hosts is his name, the Holy One of Israel.

47:5 Sit thou silent, and get thee into darkness, O daughter of the Chaldeans; for thou shalt no more be called the lady of kingdoms.

47:6 I was wroth with my people; I have polluted mine inheritance and given them into thine hand; thou didst show them no mercy; upon the ancient hast thou very heavily laid thy yoke.

47:7 And thou saidst, I shall be a lady forever, so that thou didst not lay these things to thy heart, neither didst remember the latter end of it.

47:8 Therefore hear now this, thou that art given to pleasures, that dwellest carelessly, that sayest in thine heart, I am and none else besides me; I shall not sit as a widow; neither shall I know the loss of children;

[9] But these two things shall come to thee in a moment in one day, the loss of children, and widowhood: they shall come upon thee in their perfection for the multitude of thy sorceries, and for the great abundance of thine enchantments.

[10] For thou hast trusted in thy wickedness: thou hast said, None seeth me. Thy wisdom and thy knowledge, it hath perverted thee; and thou hast said in thine heart, I am, and none else beside me.

[11] Therefore shall evil come upon thee; thou shalt not know from whence it riseth: and mischief shall fall upon thee; thou shalt not be able to put it off: and desolation shall come upon thee suddenly, which thou shalt not know.

[12] Stand now with thine enchantments, and with the multitude of thy sorceries, wherein thou hast laboured from thy youth; if so be thou shalt be able to profit, if so be thou mayest prevail.

47:9 But these two things shall come to thee in a moment in one day: the loss of children and widowhood; they shall come upon thee in their perfection for the multitude of thy sorceries and for the great abundance of thine enchantments.

47:10 For thou hast trusted in thy wickedness; thou hast said, None seeth me. Thy wisdom and thy knowledge, it hath perverted thee; and thou hast said in thine heart, I am and none else besides me.

47:11 Therefore shall evil come upon thee; thou shalt not know from whence it riseth; and mischief shall fall upon thee; thou shalt not be able to put it off; and desolation shall come upon thee suddenly, which thou shalt not know.

47:12 Stand now with thine enchantments and with the multitude of thy sorceries wherein thou hast labored from thy youth--if so be thou shalt be able to profit, if so be thou mayest prevail.

[13] Thou art wearied in the multitude of thy counsels. Let now the astrologers, the stargazers, the monthly prognosticators, stand up, and save thee from these things that shall come upon thee.

[14] Behold, they shall be as stubble; the fire shall burn them; they shall not deliver themselves from the power of the flame: there shall not be a coal to warm at, nor fire to sit before it.

[15] Thus shall they be unto thee with whom thou hast laboured, even thy merchants, from thy youth: they shall wander every one to his quarter; none shall save thee.

.48

[1] Hear ye this, O house of Jacob, which are called by the name of Israel, and are come forth out of the waters of Judah, which swear by the name of the LORD, and make mention of the God of Israel, but not in truth, nor in righteousness.

13 Thou art wearied in the multitude of thy counsels. Let now the astrologers, the stargazers, the monthly prognosticators stand up and save thee from these things that shall come upon thee.

47:14 Behold, they shall be as stubble; the fire shall burn them; they shall not deliver themselves from the power of the flame; there shall not be a coal to warm at nor fire to sit before it.

47:15 Thus shall they be unto thee with whom thou hast labored, even thy merchants, from thy youth; they shall wander, everyone to his quarter; none shall save thee.

Chapter 48

48:1 Hear ye this, O house of Jacob, which are called by the name of Israel and are come forth out of the waters of Judah, which swear by the name of the Lord and make mention of the God of Israel--but not in truth nor in righteousness.

1 Ne 20:1-22

1 ᵃHearken and hear this, O house of Jacob, who are called by the name of Israel, and are come forth out of the waters of Judah, or out of the waters of ᵇbaptism, who ᶜswear by the name of the Lord, and make mention of the God of Israel, yet they swear ᵈnot in truth nor in righteousness.

[2] For they call themselves of the holy city, and stay themselves upon the God of Israel; The LORD of hosts is his name.	48:2 For they call themselves of the holy city and stay themselves upon the God of Israel. The Lord of hosts is his name.	2 Nevertheless, they call themselves of the *a*holy city, but they do *b*not stay themselves upon the God of Israel, who is the Lord of Hosts; yea, the Lord of Hosts is his name.
[3] I have declared the former things from the beginning; and they went forth out of my mouth, and I shewed them; I did them suddenly, and they came to pass.	48:3 I have declared the former things from the beginning; and they went forth out of my mouth, and I showed them; I did them suddenly, and they came to pass,	3 Behold, I have declared the *a*former things from the beginning; and they went forth out of my mouth, and I showed them. I did show them suddenly.
[4] Because I knew that thou art obstinate, and thy neck is an iron sinew, and thy brow brass;	48:4 Because I knew that thou art obstinate, and thy neck is an iron sinew, and thy brow brass,	4 And I did it because I knew that thou art obstinate, and thy *a*neck is an iron sinew, and thy brow brass;
[5] I have even from the beginning declared it to thee; before it came to pass I shewed it thee: lest thou shouldest say, Mine idol hath done them, and my graven image, and my molten image, hath commanded them.	48:5 I have even from the beginning declared it to thee; before it came to pass, I showed it thee, lest thou shouldest say, Mine idol hath done them; and my graven image, and my molten image, hath commanded them.	5 And I have even from the beginning declared to thee; before it came to pass I *a*showed them thee; and I showed them for fear lest thou shouldst say—Mine idol hath done them, and my graven image, and my molten image hath commanded them.
[6] Thou hast heard, see all this; and will not ye declare it? I have shewed thee new things from this time, even hidden things, and thou didst not know them.	48:6 Thou hast heard; see all this. And will not ye declare it? I have showed thee new things from this time, even hidden things, and thou didst not know them.	6 Thou hast seen and heard all this; and will ye *a*not declare them? And that I have showed thee new things from this time, even hidden things, and thou didst not know them.

[7] They are created now, and not from the beginning; even before the day when thou heardest them not; lest thou shouldest say, Behold, I knew them.	48:7 They are created now, and not from the beginning, even before the day when thou heardest them not, lest thou shouldest say, Behold, I knew them.	7 They are created now, and not from the beginning, even before the day when thou heardest them not they were declared unto thee, lest thou shouldst say—Behold I knew them.
[8] Yea, thou heardest not; yea, thou knewest not; yea, from that time that thine ear was not opened: for I knew that thou wouldest deal very treacherously, and wast called a transgressor from the womb.	48:8 Yea, thou heardest not; yea, thou knewest not; yea, from that time that thine ear was not opened, for I knew that thou wouldest deal very treacherously and wast called a transgressor from the womb.	8 Yea, and thou heardest not; yea, thou knewest not; yea, from that time thine ear was not opened; for I knew that thou wouldst deal very treacherously, and wast called a *a*transgressor from the womb.
[9] For my name's sake will I defer mine anger, and for my praise will I refrain for thee, that I cut thee not off.	48:9 For my name's sake will I defer mine anger, and for my praise will I refrain for thee, that I cut thee not off.	9 Nevertheless, for my *a*name's sake will I defer mine anger, and for my praise will I refrain from thee, that I cut thee not off.
[10] Behold, I have refined thee, but not with silver; I have chosen thee in the furnace of affliction.	48:10 Behold, I have refined thee, but not with silver; I have chosen thee in the furnace of affliction.	10 For, behold, I have refined thee, I have chosen thee in the furnace of *a*affliction.
[11] For mine own sake, even for mine own sake, will I do it: for how should my name be polluted? and I will not give my glory unto another.	48:11 For mine own sake, even for mine own sake, will I do it. For how should my name be polluted? And I will not give my glory unto another.	11 For mine own sake, yea, for mine own sake will I do this, for I will not suffer my *a*name to be polluted, and I will *b*not give my glory unto another.
[12] Hearken unto me, O Jacob and Israel, my called; I am he; I am the first, I also am the last.	48:12 Hearken unto me, O Jacob and Israel, my called; I am he; I am the first; I also am the last.	12 Hearken unto me, O Jacob, and Israel my called, for I am he; I am the *a*first, and I am also the last.

[13] Mine hand also hath laid the foundation of the earth, and my right hand hath spanned the heavens: when I call unto them, they stand up together.	48:13 Mine hand also hath laid the foundation of the earth, and my right hand hath spanned the heavens; when I call unto them, they stand up together.	13 Mine hand hath also *a*laid the foundation of the earth, and my right hand hath spanned the heavens. I *b*call unto them and they stand up together.
[14] All ye, assemble yourselves, and hear; which among them hath declared these things? The LORD hath loved him: he will do his pleasure on Babylon, and his arm shall be on the Chaldeans.	48:14 All ye, assemble yourselves, and hear. Which among them hath declared these things? The Lord hath loved him; he will do his pleasure on Babylon, and his arm shall be on the Chaldeans.	14 All ye, assemble yourselves, and hear; who among them hath declared these things unto them? The Lord hath loved him; yea, and he will *a*fulfil his word which he hath declared by them; and he will do his pleasure on *b*Babylon, and his arm shall come upon the Chaldeans.
[15] I, even I, have spoken; yea, I have called him: I have brought him, and he shall make his way prosperous.	48:15 I, even I, have spoken; yea, I have called him; I have brought him, and he shall make his way prosperous.	15 Also, saith the Lord; I the Lord, yea, I have spoken; yea, I have called *a*him to declare, I have brought him, and he shall make his way prosperous.
[16] Come ye near unto me, hear ye this; I have not spoken in secret from the beginning; from the time that it was, there am I: and now the Lord GOD, and his Spirit, hath sent me.	48:16 Come ye near unto me; hear ye this: I have not spoken in secret from the beginning; from the time that it was, there am I; and now the Lord God and his Spirit hath sent me.	16 Come ye near unto me; I have not spoken in *a*secret; from the beginning, from the time that it was declared have I spoken; and the Lord God, and his *b*Spirit, hath sent me.
[17] Thus saith the LORD, thy Redeemer, the Holy One of Israel; I am the LORD thy God which teacheth thee to profit, which leadeth thee by the way that thou shouldest go.	48:17 Thus saith the Lord, thy Redeemer, the Holy One of Israel: I am the Lord, thy God, which teacheth thee to profit, which leadeth thee by the way that thou shouldest go.	17 And thus saith the Lord, thy *a*Redeemer, the Holy One of Israel; I have sent him, the Lord thy God who teacheth thee to profit, who *b*leadeth thee by the way thou shouldst go, hath done it.

[18] O that thou hadst hearkened to my commandments! then had thy peace been as a river, and thy righteousness as the waves of the sea:

[19] Thy seed also had been as the sand, and the offspring of thy bowels like the gravel thereof; his name should not have been cut off nor destroyed from before me.

[20] Go ye forth of Babylon, flee ye from the Chaldeans, with a voice of singing declare ye, tell this, utter it even to the end of the earth; say ye, The LORD hath redeemed his servant Jacob.

[21] And they thirsted not when he led them through the deserts: he caused the waters to flow out of the rock for them: he clave the rock also, and the waters gushed out.

[22] There is no peace, saith the LORD, unto the wicked.

48:18 Oh, that thou hadst hearkened to my commandments! Then had thy peace been as a river and thy righteousness as the waves of the sea;

19 Thy seed also had been as the sand, and the offspring of thy bowels like the gravel thereof; his name should not have been cut off nor destroyed from before me.

48:20 Go ye forth of Babylon; flee ye from the Chaldeans; with a voice of singing declare ye; tell this; utter it even to the end of the earth; say ye, The Lord hath redeemed his servant Jacob.

48:21 And they thirsted not when he led them through the deserts; he caused the waters to flow out of the rock for them; he clave the rock also, and the waters gushed out.

48:22 There is no peace, saith the Lord, unto the wicked.

18 O that thou hadst hearkened to my *a*commandments—then had thy *b*peace been as a river, and thy righteousness as the waves of the sea.

19 Thy *a*seed also had been as the sand; the offspring of thy bowels like the gravel thereof; his name should not have been cut off nor destroyed from before me.

20 *a*Go ye forth of Babylon, flee ye from the *b*Chaldeans, with a voice of singing declare ye, tell this, utter it to the end of the earth; say ye: The Lord hath redeemed his *c*servant Jacob.

21 And they *a*thirsted not; he led them through the deserts; he caused the waters to flow out of the *b*rock for them; he clave the rock also and the waters gushed out.

22 And notwithstanding he hath done all this, and greater also, there is no *a*peace, saith the Lord, unto the wicked.

.49

[1] Listen, O isles, unto me; and hearken, ye people, from far; The LORD hath called me from the womb; from the bowels of my mother hath he made mention of my name.

[2] And he hath made my mouth like a sharp sword; in the shadow of his hand hath he hid me, and made me a polished shaft; in his quiver hath he hid me;

[3] And said unto me, Thou art my servant, O Israel, in whom I will be glorified.

[4] Then I said, I have laboured in vain, I have spent my strength for nought, and in vain: yet surely my judgment is with the LORD, and my work with my God.

Chapter 49

49:1 Listen, O isles, unto me; and hearken, ye people, from far: The Lord hath called me from the womb; from the bowels of my mother hath he made mention of my name.

49:2 And he hath made my mouth like a sharp sword; in the shadow of his hand hath he hid me and made me a polished shaft; in his quiver hath he hid me,

49:3 And said unto me, Thou art my servant, O Israel, in whom I will be glorified.

49:4 Then I said, I have labored in vain; I have spent my strength for naught and in vain; yet surely my judgment is with the Lord and my work with my God.

1 Nephi 21:1-26

1 *a*And again: Hearken, O ye house of Israel, all ye that are broken off and are driven out because of the wickedness of the pastors of my people; yea, all ye that are broken off, that are scattered abroad, who are of my people, O house of Israel. Listen, O *b*isles, unto me, and hearken ye people from *c*far; the Lord hath called me from the womb; from the bowels of my mother hath he made mention of my name.

2 And he hath made my mouth like a sharp sword; in the shadow of his hand hath he hid me, and made me a polished shaft; in his quiver hath he hid me;

3 And said unto me: Thou art my *a*servant, O Israel, in whom I will be glorified.

4 Then I said, I have labored in *a*vain, I have spent my strength for naught and in vain; surely my judgment is with the Lord, and my work with my God.

[5] And now, saith the LORD that formed me from the womb to be his servant, to bring Jacob again to him, Though Israel be not gathered, yet shall I be glorious in the eyes of the LORD, and my God shall be my strength.

[6] And he said, It is a light thing that thou shouldest be my servant to raise up the tribes of Jacob, and to restore the preserved of Israel: I will also give thee for a light to the Gentiles, that thou mayest be my salvation unto the end of the earth.

[7] Thus saith the LORD, the Redeemer of Israel, and his Holy One, to him whom man despiseth, to him whom the nation abhorreth, to a servant of rulers, Kings shall see and arise, princes also shall worship, because of the LORD that is faithful, and the Holy One of Israel, and he shall choose thee.

49:5 And now, saith the Lord that formed me from the womb to be his servant, to bring Jacob again to him, Though Israel be not gathered, yet shall I be glorious in the eyes of the Lord, and my God shall be my strength.

49:6 And he said, It is a light thing that thou shouldest be my servant to raise up the tribes of Jacob and to restore the preserved of Israel; I will also give thee for a light to the Gentiles, that thou mayest be my salvation unto the end of the earth.

49:7 Thus saith the Lord, the Redeemer of Israel, and his Holy One, to him whom man despiseth, to him whom the nation abhorreth, to a servant of rulers, Kings shall see and arise; princes also shall worship because of the Lord that is faithful and the Holy One of Israel; and he shall choose thee.

5 And now, saith the Lord—
that _aformed_ me from the womb that I should be his servant, to bring Jacob again to him—though Israel be not gathered, yet shall I be glorious in the eyes of the Lord, and my God shall be my _bstrength_.

6 And he said: It is a light thing that thou shouldst be my servant to raise up the _atribes_ of Jacob, and to restore the preserved of Israel. I will also give thee for a _blight_ to the _cGentiles_, that thou mayest be my salvation unto the ends of the earth.

7 Thus saith the Lord, the Redeemer of Israel, his Holy One, to him whom man despiseth, to him whom the nations abhorreth, to servant of rulers: Kings shall see and arise, princes also shall worship, because of the Lord that is faithful.

[8] Thus saith the LORD, In an acceptable time have I heard thee, and in a day of salvation have I helped thee: and I will preserve thee, and give thee for a covenant of the people, to establish the earth, to cause to inherit the desolate heritages;

[9] That thou mayest say to the prisoners, Go forth; to them that are in darkness, Shew yourselves. They shall feed in the ways, and their pastures shall be in all high places.

[10] They shall not hunger nor thirst; neither shall the heat nor sun smite them: for he that hath mercy on them shall lead them, even by the springs of water shall he guide them.

[11] And I will make all my mountains a way, and my highways shall be exalted.

[12] Behold, these shall come from far: and lo, these from the north and from the west; and these from the land of Sinim.

49:8 Thus saith the Lord, In an acceptable time have I heard thee, and in a day of salvation have I helped thee; and I will preserve thee and give thee for a covenant of the people, to establish the earth, to cause to inherit the desolate heritages,

49:9 That thou mayest say to the prisoners, Go forth; to them that are in darkness, Show yourselves. They shall feed in the ways, and their pastures shall be in all high places.

49:10 They shall not hunger nor thirst; neither shall the heat nor sun smite them; for he that hath mercy on them shall lead them; even by the springs of water shall he guide them.

49:11 And I will make all my mountains a way, and my highways shall be exalted.

49:12 Behold, these shall come from far; and lo, these from the north and from the west; and these from the land of Sinim.

8 Thus saith the Lord: In an acceptable time have I heard thee, O isles of the sea, and in a day of salvation have I helped thee; and I will preserve thee, and give thee ᵃmy servant for a covenant of the people, to establish the earth, to cause to inherit the desolate heritages;

9 That thou mayest say to the ᵃprisoners: Go forth; to them that sit in ᵇdarkness: Show yourselves. They shall feed in the ways, and their ᶜpastures shall be in all high places.

10 They shall not hunger nor thirst, neither shall the heat nor the sun smite them; for he that hath mercy on them shall lead them, even by the springs of water shall he guide them.

11 And I will make all my mountains a way, and my ᵃhighways shall be exalted.

12 And then, O house of Israel, behold, ᵃthese shall come from far; and lo, these from the north and from the west; and these from the land of Sinim.

[13] Sing, O heavens; and be joyful, O earth; and break forth into singing, O mountains: for the LORD hath comforted his people, and will have mercy upon his afflicted.

[14] But Zion said, The LORD hath forsaken me, and my Lord hath forgotten me.

[15] Can a woman forget her sucking child, that she should not have compassion on the son of her womb? yea, they may forget, yet will I not forget thee.

[16] Behold, I have graven thee upon the palms of my hands; thy walls are continually before me.

[17] Thy children shall make haste; thy destroyers and they that made thee waste shall go forth of thee.

49:13 Sing, O heavens; and be joyful, O earth; and break forth into singing, O mountains; for the Lord hath comforted his people and will have mercy upon his afflicted.

49:14 But Zion said, The Lord hath forsaken me, and my Lord hath forgotten me.

49:15 Can a woman forget her sucking child, that she should not have compassion on the son of her womb? Yea, they may forget; yet will I not forget thee.

49:16 Behold, I have graven thee upon the palms of my hands; thy walls are continually before me.

49:17 Thy children shall make haste; thy destroyers and they that made thee waste shall go forth of thee.

---

13 *ª*Sing, O heavens; and be joyful, O earth; for the feet of those who are in the east shall be established; and *ᵇ*break forth into singing, O mountains; for they shall be smitten no more; for the Lord hath comforted his people, and will have mercy upon his *ᶜ*afflicted.

14 But, behold, Zion hath said: The Lord hath forsaken me, and my Lord hath forgotten me—but he will show that he hath not.

15 For can a *ª*woman forget her sucking child, that she should not have *ᵇ*compassion on the son of her womb? Yea, they may *ᶜ*forget, yet will I not forget thee, O house of Israel.

16 Behold, I have graven thee upon the *ª*palms of my hands; thy walls are continually before me.

17 Thy children shall make haste against thy destroyers; and they that made thee *ª*waste shall go forth of thee.

[18] Lift up thine eyes round about, and behold: all these gather themselves together, and come to thee. As I live, saith the LORD, thou shalt surely clothe thee with them all, as with an ornament, and bind them on thee, as a bride doeth.

[19] For thy waste and thy desolate places, and the land of thy destruction, shall even now be too narrow by reason of the inhabitants, and they that swallowed thee up shall be far away.

[20] The children which thou shalt have, after thou hast lost the other, shall say again in thine ears, The place is too strait for me: give place to me that I may dwell.

[21] Then shalt thou say in thine heart, Who hath begotten me these, seeing I have lost my children, and am desolate, a captive, and removing to and fro? and who hath brought up these? Behold, I was left alone; these, where had they been?

49:18 Lift up thine eyes round about, and behold; all these gather themselves together and come to thee. As I live, saith the Lord, thou shalt surely clothe thee with them all, as with an ornament, and bind them on thee, as a bride doeth.

49:19 For thy waste, and thy desolate places, and the land of thy destruction shall even now be too narrow by reason of the inhabitants; and they that swallowed thee up shall be far away.

49:20 The children which thou shalt have, after thou hast lost the other, shall say again in thine ears, The place is too strait for me; give place to me that I may dwell.

49:21 Then shalt thou say in thine heart, Who hath begotten me these, seeing I have lost my children and am desolate, a captive, and removing to and fro? And who hath brought up these? Behold, I was left alone. These, where had they been?

18 Lift up thine eyes round about and behold; all these *a*gather themselves together, and they shall come to thee. And as I live, saith the Lord, thou shalt surely clothe thee with them all, as with an ornament, and bind them on even as a bride.

19 For thy waste and thy desolate places, and the land of thy destruction, shall even now be too narrow by reason of the inhabitants; and they that swallowed thee up shall be far away.

20 The children whom thou shalt have, after thou hast lost the first, shall *a*again in thine ears say: The place is too strait for me; give place to me that I may dwell.

21 Then shalt thou say in thine heart: Who hath begotten me these, seeing I have lost my children, and am *a*desolate, a captive, and removing to and fro? And who hath brought up these? Behold, I was left alone; these, where have they been?

[22] Thus saith the Lord GOD, Behold, I will lift up mine hand to the Gentiles, and set up my standard to the people: and they shall bring thy sons in their arms, and thy daughters shall be carried upon their shoulders.

[23] And kings shall be thy nursing fathers, and their queens thy nursing mothers: they shall bow down to thee with their face toward the earth, and lick up the dust of thy feet; and thou shalt know that I am the LORD: for they shall not be ashamed that wait for me.

[24] Shall the prey be taken from the mighty, or the lawful captive delivered?

[25] But thus saith the LORD, Even the captives of the mighty shall be taken away, and the prey of the terrible shall be delivered: for I will contend with him that contendeth with thee, and I will save thy children.

49:22 Thus saith the Lord God, Behold, I will lift up mine hand to the Gentiles and set up my standard to the people; and they shall bring thy sons in their arms, and thy daughters shall be carried upon their shoulders.

49:23 And kings shall be thy nursing fathers and their queens thy nursing mothers; they shall bow down to thee with their faces toward the earth and lick up the dust of thy feet; and thou shalt know that I am the Lord, for they shall not be ashamed that wait for me.

49:24 Shall the prey be taken from the mighty or the lawful captive delivered?

25 But thus saith the Lord, Even the captives of the mighty shall be taken away, and the prey of the terrible shall be delivered; for the mighty God shall deliver his covenant people. For thus saith the Lord, I will contend with them that contend with thee, and I will save thy children.

22 Thus saith the Lord God: Behold, I will lift up mine hand to the *ª*Gentiles, and set up my *ᵇ*standard to the people; and they shall bring thy sons in their *ᶜ*arms, and thy daughters shall be carried upon their shoulders.

23 And *ª*kings shall be thy *ᵇ*nursing fathers, and their queens thy nursing mothers; they shall bow down to thee with their face towards the earth, and lick up the dust of thy feet; and thou shalt know that I am the Lord; for they shall not be ashamed that *ᶜ*wait for me.

24 For shall the prey be taken from the mighty, or the *ª*lawful captives delivered?

25 But thus saith the Lord, even the captives of the mighty shall be taken away, and the prey of the terrible shall be delivered; for I will contend with him that contendeth with thee, and I will save thy children.

[26] And I will feed them that oppress thee with their own flesh; and they shall be drunken with their own blood, as with sweet wine: and all flesh shall know that I the LORD am thy Saviour and thy Redeemer, the mighty One of Jacob.

.50

[1] Thus saith the LORD, Where is the bill of your mother's divorcement, whom I have put away? or which of my creditors is it to whom I have sold you? Behold, for your iniquities have ye sold yourselves, and for your transgressions is your mother put away.

[2] Wherfore, when I came, was there no man? when I called, was there none to answer? Is my hand shortened at all, that it cannot redeem? or have I no power to deliver? behold, at my rebuke I dry up the sea, I make the rivers a wilderness: their fish stinketh, because there is no water, and dieth for thirst.

[3] I clothe the heavens with blackness, and I make sackcloth their covering.

49:26 And I will feed them that oppress thee with their own flesh; and they shall be drunken with their own blood, as with sweet wine; and all flesh shall know that I, the Lord, am thy Savior and thy Redeemer, the Mighty One of Jacob.

Chapter 50

50:1 Yea, for thus saith the Lord, Have I put thee away, or have I cast thee off forever? For thus saith the Lord, Where is the bill of your mother's divorcement? To whom have I put thee away, or to which of my creditors have I sold you? Yea, to whom have I sold you?

50:2 Behold, for your iniquities have ye sold yourselves, and for your transgressions is your mother put away; wherefore, when I came there was no man; when I called there was none to answer. O house of Israel, is my hand shortened at all, that it cannot redeem? Or have I no power to deliver?

50:3 Behold, at my rebuke I dry up the sea; I make their rivers a wilderness and their fish to stink because the waters are dried up, and they die because of thirst. I

26 And I will *a*feed them that oppress thee with their own flesh; they shall be drunken with their own blood as with sweet wine; and all flesh shall *b*know that I, the Lord, am thy *c*Savior and thy Redeemer, the *d*Mighty One of Jacob.

2 Nephi 7:1-11

1 *a*Yea, for thus saith the Lord: Have I put thee away, or have I cast thee off forever? For thus saith the Lord: Where is the *b*bill of your mother's *c*divorcement? To whom have I put thee away, or to which of my *d*creditors have I *e*sold you? Yea, to whom have I sold you? Behold, for your iniquities have ye sold yourselves, and for your transgressions is your mother put away.

2 Wherefore, when I came, there was no man; when I *a*called, yea, there was none to answer. O house of Israel, is my hand shortened at all that it cannot redeem, or have I no power to deliver? Behold, at my rebuke I *b*dry up the *c*sea, I make their *d*rivers a wilderness and their *e*fish to stink because the waters are dried up, and they die because of thirst.

[4] The Lord GOD hath given me the tongue of the learned, that I should know how to speak a word in season to him that is weary: he wakeneth morning by morning, he wakeneth mine ear to hear as the learned.

[5] The Lord GOD hath opened mine ear, and I was not rebellious, neither turned away back.

[6] I gave my back to the smiters, and my cheeks to them that plucked off the hair: I hid not my face from shame and spitting.

[7] For the Lord GOD will help me; therefore shall I not be confounded: therefore have I set my face like a flint, and I know that I shall not be ashamed.

clothe the heavens with blackness, and I make sackcloth their covering.

50:4 The Lord God hath given me the tongue of the learned, that I should know how to speak a word in season unto thee, O house of Israel, when ye are weary. He waketh morning by morning; he waketh mine ear to hear as the learned.

50:5 The Lord God hath appointed mine ears, and I was not rebellious, neither turned away back. I gave my back to the smiters, and my cheeks to them that plucked off the hair. I hid not my face from shame and spitting, for the Lord God will help me; therefore shall I not be confounded; therefore have I set my face like a flint, and I know that I shall not be ashamed; and the Lord is near, and he justifieth me.

3 I clothe the heavens with ^ablackness, and I make ^bsackcloth their covering.

4 The Lord God hath given me the ^atongue of the learned, that I should know how to speak a word in season unto thee, O house of Israel. When ye are weary he waketh morning by morning. He waketh mine ear to hear as the learned.

5 The Lord God hath opened mine ^aear, and I was not rebellious, neither turned away back.

6 I gave my back to the ^asmiter, and my cheeks to them that plucked off the hair. I hid not my face from ^bshame and spitting.

7 For the Lord God will help me, therefore shall I not be confounded. Therefore have I set my face like a flint, and I know that I shall not be ^aashamed.

[8] He is near that justifieth me; who will contend with me? let us stand together: who is mine adversary? let him come near to me.

[9] Behold, the Lord GOD will help me; who is he that shall condemn me? lo, they all shall wax old as a garment; the moth shall eat them up.

[10] Who is among you that feareth the LORD, that obeyeth the voice of his servant, that walketh in darkness, and hath no light? let him trust in the name of the LORD, and stay upon his God.

[11] Behold, all ye that kindle a fire, that compass yourselves about with sparks: walk in the light of your fire, and in the sparks that ye have kindled. This shall ye have of mine hand; ye shall lie down in sorrow.

50:6 Who will contend with me? Let us stand together. Who is mine adversary? Let him come near me, and I will smite him with the strength of my mouth; for the Lord God will help me; and all they which shall condemn me, behold, all they shall wax old as a garment, and the moth shall eat them up.

50:7 Who is among you that feareth the Lord, that obeyeth the voice of his servant, that walketh in darkness, and hath no light? Let him trust in the name of the Lord, and stay upon his God.

50:8 Behold, all ye that kindleth fire, that compass yourselves about with sparks, walk in the light of your fire and in the sparks which ye have kindled; this shall ye have of mine hand; ye shall lie down in sorrow.

8 And the Lord is near, and he *ᵃjustifieth* me. Who will contend with me? Let us stand together. Who is mine adversary? Let him come near me, and I will *ᵇsmite* him with the strength of my mouth.

9 For the Lord God will help me. And all they who shall *ᵃcondemn* me, behold, all they shall *ᵇwax old* as a garment, and the moth shall eat them up.

10 Who is among you that feareth the Lord, that obeyeth the *ᵃvoice* of his servant, that *ᵇwalketh* in darkness and hath no light?

11 Behold all ye that kindle fire, that compass yourselves about with sparks, walk in the light of *ᵃyour* fire and in the sparks which ye have kindled. *ᵇThis* shall ye have of mine hand—ye shall lie down in sorrow.

51	Chapter 51	2 Nephi 8:1-23
[1] Hearken to me, ye that follow after righteousness, ye that seek the LORD: look unto the rock whence ye are hewn, and to the hole of the pit whence ye are digged.	51:1 Hearken unto me, ye that follow after righteousness; ye that seek the Lord, look unto the rock from whence ye were hewn and to the hole of the pit from whence ye are digged.	1 *a*Hearken unto me, ye that follow after righteousness. Look unto the *b*rock from whence ye are hewn, and to the hole of the pit from whence ye are digged.
[2] Look unto Abraham your father, and unto Sarah that bare you: for I called him alone, and blessed him, and increased him.	51:2 Look unto Abraham, your father, and unto Sarah that bare you; for I called him alone, and blessed him, and increased him.	2 Look unto Abraham, your *a*father, and unto *b*Sarah, she that bare you; for I called him alone, and blessed him.
[3] For the LORD shall comfort Zion: he will comfort all her waste places; and he will make her wilderness like Eden, and her desert like the garden of the LORD; joy and gladness shall be found therein, thanksgiving, and the voice of melody.	51:3 For the Lord shall comfort Zion; he will comfort all her waste places; and he will make her wilderness like Eden and her desert like the garden of the Lord; joy and gladness shall be found therein, thanksgiving, and the voice of melody.	3 For the Lord shall *a*comfort *b*Zion, he will comfort all her waste places; and he will make her *c*wilderness like *d*Eden, and her desert like the garden of the Lord. Joy and gladness shall be found therein, thanksgiving and the voice of melody.
[4] Hearken unto me, my people; and give ear unto me, O my nation: for a law shall proceed from me, and I will make my judgment to rest for a light of the people.	51:4 Hearken unto me, my people; and give ear unto me, O my nation; for a law shall proceed from me, and I will make my judgment to rest for a light of the people.	4 Hearken unto me, my people; and give ear unto me, O my nation; for a *a*law shall proceed from me, and I will make my judgment to rest for a *b*light for the people.
[5] My righteousness is near; my salvation is gone forth, and mine arms shall judge the people; the isles shall wait upon me, and on mine arm shall they trust.	51:5 My righteousness is near; my salvation is gone forth, and mine arms shall judge the people; the isles shall wait upon me, and on mine arm shall they trust.	5 My righteousness is near; my *a*salvation is gone forth, and mine arm shall *b*judge the people. The *c*isles shall wait upon me, and on mine arm shall they trust.

[6] Lift up your eyes to the heavens, and look upon the earth beneath: for the heavens shall vanish away like smoke, and the earth shall wax old like a garment, and they that dwell therein shall die in like manner: but my salvation shall be for ever, and my righteousness shall not be abolished.	51:6 Lift up your eyes to the heavens, and look upon the earth beneath; for the heavens shall vanish away like smoke, and the earth shall wax old like a garment; and they that dwell therein shall die in like manner; but my salvation shall be forever, and my righteousness shall not be abolished.	6 Lift up your eyes to the *a*heavens, and look upon the earth beneath; for the heavens shall *b*vanish away like smoke, and the earth shall *c*wax old like a garment; and they that dwell therein shall die in like manner. But my salvation shall be forever, and my righteousness shall not be abolished.
[7] Hearken unto me, ye that know righteousness, the people in whose heart is my law; fear ye not the reproach of men, neither be ye afraid of their revilings.	51:7 Hearken unto me, ye that know righteousness, the people in whose heart I have written my law; fear ye not the reproach of men; neither be ye afraid of their revilings.	7 Hearken unto me, ye that know righteousness, the people in whose heart I have written my law, *a*fear ye not the *b*reproach of men, neither be ye afraid of their *c*revilings.
[8] For the moth shall eat them up like a garment, and the worm shall eat them like wool: but my righteousness shall be for ever, and my salvation from generation to generation.	51:8 For the moth shall eat them up like a garment, and the worm shall eat them like wool; but my righteousness shall be forever, and my salvation from generation to generation.	8 For the *a*moth shall eat them up like a garment, and the worm shall eat them like wool. But my righteousness shall be forever, and my salvation from generation to generation.
[9] Awake, awake, put on strength, O arm of the LORD; awake, as in the ancient days, in the generations of old. Art thou not it that hath cut Rahab, and wounded the dragon?	51:9 Awake, awake; put on strength, O arm of the Lord; awake, as in the ancient days, in the generations of old. Art thou not it that hath cut Rahab and wounded the dragon?	9 *a*Awake, awake! Put on *b*strength, O arm of the Lord; awake as in the ancient days. Art thou not he that hath cut *c*Rahab, and wounded the *d*dragon?
[10] Art thou not it which hath dried the sea, the waters of the great deep; that hath made the depths of the sea a way for the ransomed to pass over?	51:10 Art thou not it which hath dried the sea, the waters of the great deep, that hath made the depths of the sea a way for the ransomed to pass over?	10 Art thou not he who hath dried the sea, the waters of the great deep; that hath made the depths of the sea a *a*way for the ransomed to pass over?

[11] Therefore the redeemed of the LORD shall return, and come with singing unto Zion; and everlasting joy shall be upon their head: they shall obtain gladness and joy; and sorrow and mourning shall flee away.

[12] I, even I, am he that comforteth you: who art thou, that thou shouldest be afraid of a man that shall die, and of the son of man which shall be made as grass;

[13] And forgettest the LORD thy maker, that hath stretched forth the heavens, and laid the foundations of the earth; and hast feared continually every day because of the fury of the oppressor, as if he were ready to destroy? and where is the fury of the oppressor?

[14] The captive exile hasteneth that he may be loosed, and that he should not die in the pit, nor that his bread should fail.

[15] But I am the LORD thy God, that divided the sea, whose waves roared: The LORD of hosts is his name.

51:11 Therefore, the redeemed of the Lord shall return and come with singing unto Zion; and everlasting joy and holiness shall be upon their heads; they shall obtain gladness and joy; and sorrow and mourning shall flee away.

51:12 I am he, yea, I am he that comforteth you. Behold, who art thou, that thou shouldest be afraid of a man that shall die, and of the son of man which shall be made as grass,

51:13 And forgettest the Lord, thy Maker--that hath stretched forth the heavens and laid the foundations of the earth-- and hast feared continually every day because of the fury of the oppressor, as if he were ready to destroy? And where is the fury of the oppressor?

51:14 The captive exile hasteneth, that he may be loosed, and that he should not die in the pit, nor that his bread should fail.

51:15 But I am the Lord, thy God, that divided the sea, whose waves roared; the Lord of hosts is his name.

11 Therefore, the *a*redeemed of the Lord shall *b*return, and come with *c*singing unto Zion; and everlasting joy and holiness shall be upon their heads; and they shall obtain gladness and joy; sorrow and *d*mourning shall flee away.

12 *a*I am he; yea, I am he that comforteth you. Behold, who art thou, that thou shouldst be *b*afraid of man, who shall die, and of the son of man, who shall be made like unto *c*grass?

13 And *a*forgettest the Lord thy maker, that hath *b*stretched forth the heavens, and laid the foundations of the earth, and hast feared continually every day, because of the fury of the *c*oppressor, as if he were ready to destroy? And where is the fury of the oppressor?

14 The *a*captive exile hasteneth, that he may be loosed, and that he should not die in the pit, nor that his bread should fail.

15 But I am the Lord thy God, whose *a*waves roared; the Lord of Hosts is my name.

[16] And I have put my words in thy mouth, and I have covered thee in the shadow of mine hand, that I may plant the heavens, and lay the foundations of the earth, and say unto Zion, Thou art my people.

[17] Awake, awake, stand up, O Jerusalem, which hast drunk at the hand of the LORD the cup of his fury; thou hast drunken the dregs of the cup of trembling, and wrung them out.

[18] There is none to guide her among all the sons whom she hath brought forth; neither is there any that taketh her by the hand of all the sons that she hath brought up.

[19] These two things are come unto thee; who shall be sorry for thee? desolation, and destruction, and the famine, and the sword: by whom shall I comfort thee?

[20] Thy sons have fainted, they lie at the head of all the streets, as a wild bull in a net: they are full of the fury of the LORD, the rebuke of thy God.

51:16 And I have put my words in thy mouth; and I have covered thee in the shadow of mine hand, that I may plant the heavens, and lay the foundations of the earth, and say unto Zion, Behold, thou art my people.

51:17 Awake, awake; stand up, O Jerusalem, which hast drunk at the hand of the Lord the cup of his fury; thou hast drunken the dregs of the cup of trembling and wrung them out.

51:18 And there is none to guide her among all the sons whom she hath brought forth; neither is there any that taketh her by the hand of all the sons that she hath brought up.

51:19 These two sons are come unto thee; they shall be sorry for thee, thy desolation, and destruction, and the famine, and the sword. And by whom shall I comfort thee?

51:20 Thy sons have fainted save these two; they lie at the head of all the streets as a wild bull in a net; they are full of the fury of the Lord, the rebuke of thy God.

---

16 And I have *a*put my words in thy mouth, and have covered thee in the shadow of mine hand, that I may plant the heavens and lay the foundations of the earth, and say unto Zion: Behold, thou art my *b*people.

17 Awake, awake, stand up, O Jerusalem, which hast drunk at the hand of the Lord the *a*cup of his *b*fury—thou hast drunken the dregs of the cup of trembling wrung out—

18 And none to guide her among all the sons she hath brought forth; neither that taketh her by the hand, of all the sons she hath brought up.

19 These two *a*sons are come unto thee, who shall be sorry for thee—thy desolation and destruction, and the famine and the sword—and by whom shall I comfort thee?

20 Thy sons have fainted, save these two; they lie at the head of all the streets; as a wild bull in a net, they are full of the fury of the Lord, the rebuke of thy God.

[21] Therefore hear now this, thou afflicted, and drunken, but not with wine:

[22] Thus saith thy Lord the LORD, and thy God that pleadeth the cause of his people, Behold, I have taken out of thine hand the cup of trembling, even the dregs of the cup of my fury; thou shalt no more drink it again:

[23] But I will put it into the hand of them that afflict thee; which have said to thy soul, Bow down, that we may go over: and thou hast laid thy body as the ground, and as the street, to them that went over.

.52

[1] Awake, awake; put on thy strength, O Zion; put on thy beautiful garments, O Jerusalem, the holy city: for henceforth there shall no more come into thee the uncircumcised and the unclean.

[2] Shake thyself from the dust; arise, and sit down, O Jerusalem: loose thyself from the bands of thy neck, O captive daughter of Zion.

51:21 Therefore, hear now this, thou afflicted and drunken, but not with wine;

51:22 Thus saith thy Lord, the Lord, and thy God that pleadeth the cause of his people, Behold, I have taken out of thine hand the cup of trembling, even the dregs of the cup of my fury; thou shalt no more drink it again;

51:23 But I will put it into the hand of them that afflict thee, which have said to thy soul, Bow down, that we may go over; and thou hast laid thy body as the ground and as the street to them that went over.

Chapter 52

52:1 Awake, awake; put on thy strength, O Zion; put on thy beautiful garments, O Jerusalem, the holy city; for henceforth there shall no more come into thee the uncircumcised and the unclean.

52:2 Shake thyself from the dust; arise, and sit down, O Jerusalem; loose thyself from the bands of thy neck, O captive daughter of Zion.

---

21 Therefore hear now this, thou afflicted, and *a*drunken, and not with wine:

22 Thus saith thy Lord, the Lord and thy God *a*pleadeth the cause of his people; behold, I have taken out of thine hand the cup of trembling, the dregs of the cup of my fury; thou shalt no more drink it again.

23 But *a*I will put it into the hand of them that afflict thee; who have said to thy soul: Bow down, that we may go over— and thou hast laid thy body as the ground and as the street to them that went over.

3 Nephi 20: 36-40

36 Awake, awake again, and put on thy strength, O Zion; put on thy beautiful garments, O Jerusalem, the holy city, for henceforth there shall no more come into thee the uncircumcised and the unclean.

37 Shake thyself from the dust; arise, sit down, O Jerusalem; loose thyself from the bands of thy neck, O captive daughter of Zion.

[3] For thus saith the LORD, Ye have sold yourselves for nought; and ye shall be redeemed without money.

[4] For thus saith the Lord GOD, My people went down aforetime into Egypt to sojourn there; and the Assyrian oppressed them without cause.

[5] Now therefore, what have I here, saith the LORD, that my people is taken away for nought? they that rule over them make them to howl, saith the LORD; and my name continually every day is blasphemed.

[6] Therefore my people shall know my name: therefore they shall know in that day that I am he that doth speak: behold, it is I.

[7] How beautiful upon the mountains are the feet of him that bringeth good tidings, that publisheth peace; that bringeth good tidings of good, that publisheth salvation; that saith unto Zion, Thy God reigneth!

52:3 For thus saith the Lord, Ye have sold yourselves for naught; and ye shall be redeemed without money.

52:4 For thus saith the Lord God, My people went down aforetime into Egypt to sojourn there; and the Assyrian oppressed them without cause.

52:5 Now, therefore, what have I here, saith the Lord, that my people is taken away for naught? They that rule over them make them to howl, saith the Lord; and my name continually every day is blasphemed.

52:6 Therefore, my people shall know my name; yea, in that day they shall know that I am he that doth speak; behold, it is I.

52:7 And then shall they say, How beautiful upon the mountains are the feet of him that bringeth good tidings unto them, that publisheth peace; that bringeth good tidings unto them of good, that publisheth salvation; that saith unto Zion, Thy God reigneth!

38 For thus saith the Lord: Ye have sold yourselves for naught, and ye shall be redeemed without money.

39 Verily, verily, I say unto you, that my people shall know my name; yea, in that day they shall know that I am he that doth speak.

40 And then shall they say: ^aHow beautiful upon the mountains are the feet of him that bringeth good tidings unto them, that ^bpublisheth peace; that bringeth good tidings unto them of good, that publisheth salvation; that saith unto Zion: Thy God reigneth!

[8] Thy watchmen shall lift up the voice; with the voice together shall they sing: for they shall see eye to eye, when the LORD shall bring again Zion.

[9] Break forth into joy, sing together, ye waste places of Jerusalem: for the LORD hath comforted his people, he hath redeemed Jerusalem.

[10] The LORD hath made bare his holy arm in the eyes of all the nations; and all the ends of the earth shall see the salvation of our God.

[11] Depart ye, depart ye, go ye out from thence, touch no unclean thing; go ye out of the midst of her; be ye clean, that bear the vessels of the LORD.

[12] For ye shall not go out with haste, nor go by flight: for the LORD will go before you; and the God of Israel will be your rereward.

52:8 Thy watchmen shall lift up the voice; with the voice together shall they sing; for they shall see eye to eye, when the Lord shall bring again Zion.

52:9 Break forth into joy; sing together, ye waste places of Jerusalem; for the Lord hath comforted his people; he hath redeemed Jerusalem.

52:10 The Lord hath made bare his holy arm in the eyes of all the nations; and all the ends of the earth shall see the salvation of our God.

52:11 Depart ye, depart ye; go ye out from thence; touch no unclean thing; go ye out of the midst of her; be ye clean that bear the vessels of the Lord.

52:12 For ye shall not go out with haste, nor go by flight; for the Lord will go before you; and the God of Israel will be your rearward.

3 Nephi 20:32
32 Then shall their *a*watchmen lift up their voice, and with the voice together shall they sing; for they shall see eye to eye.

3 Nephi 20:34-35
34 Then shall they break forth into joy— *a*Sing together, ye waste places of Jerusalem; for the Father hath comforted his people, he hath redeemed Jerusalem.

35 The Father hath made bare his holy arm in the eyes of all the nations; and all the ends of the earth shall see the salvation of the Father; and the Father and I are one.

3 Nephi 20:41-45
41 And then shall a cry go forth: *a*Depart ye, depart ye, go ye out from thence, touch not that which is *b*unclean; go ye out of the midst of her; be ye *c*clean that bear the vessels of the Lord.

42 For ye shall *a*not go out with *b*haste nor go by flight; for the Lord will go before you, and the God of Israel shall be your rearward.

[13] Behold, my servant shall deal prudently, he shall be exalted and extolled, and be very high.

[14] As many were astonied at thee; his visage was so marred more than any man, and his form more than the sons of men:

[15] So shall he sprinkle many nations; the kings shall shut their mouths at him: for that which had not been told them shall they see; and that which they had not heard shall they consider.

53

[1] Who hath believed our report? and to whom is the arm of the LORD revealed?

[2] For he shall grow up before him as a tender plant, and as a root out of a dry ground: he hath no form nor comeliness; and when we shall see him, there is no beauty that we should desire him.

52:13 Behold, my servant shall deal prudently; he shall be exalted, and extolled, and be very high.

52:14 As many were astonished at thee, his visage was so marred more than any man, and his form more than the sons of men;

52:15 So shall he gather many nations; the kings shall shut their mouths at him; for that which had not been told them shall they see; and that which they had not heard shall they consider.

Chapter 5

53:1 Who hath believed our report? And to whom is the arm of the Lord revealed?

53:2 For he shall grow up before him as a tender plant and as a root out of a dry ground; he hath no form nor comeliness; and when we shall see him, there is no beauty that we should desire him.

43 Behold, my servant shall deal prudently; he shall be exalted and extolled and be very high.

44 As many were astonished at thee—his visage was so marred, more than any man, and his form more than the sons of men—

45 So shall he ᵃsprinkle many nations; the kings shall shut their mouths at him, for that which had not been told them shall they see; and that which they had not heard shall they ᵇconsider.

Mosiah 14: 1-12

1 Yea, even doth not Isaiah say: Who hath ᵃbelieved our report, and to whom is the arm of the Lord revealed?

2 For he shall grow up before him as a tender plant, and as a root out of dry ground; he hath no form nor comeliness; and when we shall see him there is no beauty that we should desire him.

[3] He is despised and rejected of men; a man of sorrows, and acquainted with grief: and we hid as it were our faces from him; he was despised, and we esteemed him not.

[4] Surely he hath borne our griefs, and carried our sorrows: yet we did esteem him stricken, smitten of God, and afflicted.

[5] But he was wounded for our transgressions, he was bruised for our iniquities: the chastisement of our peace was upon him; and with his stripes we are healed.

[6] All we like sheep have gone astray; we have turned every one to his own way; and the LORD hath laid on him the iniquity of us all.

[7] He was oppressed, and he was afflicted, yet he opened not his mouth: he is brought as a lamb to the slaughter, and as a sheep before her shearers is dumb, so he openeth not his mouth.

53:3 He is despised and rejected of men, a man of sorrows and acquainted with grief; and we hid, as it were, our faces from him; he was despised, and we esteemed him not.

53:4 Surely he hath borne our griefs and carried our sorrows; yet we did esteem him stricken, smitten of God, and afflicted.

53:5 But he was wounded for our transgressions; he was bruised for our iniquities; the chastisement of our peace was upon him; and with his stripes we are healed.

53:6 All we like sheep have gone astray; we have turned everyone to his own way; and the Lord hath laid on him the iniquity of us all.

53:7 He was oppressed, and he was afflicted; yet he opened not his mouth; he is brought as a lamb to the slaughter; and as a sheep before her shearers is dumb, so he openeth not his mouth.

3 He is ^adespised and rejected of men; a man of sorrows, and acquainted with grief; and we hid as it were our faces from him; he was despised, and we esteemed him not.

4 Surely he has ^aborne our ^bgriefs, and carried our sorrows; yet we did esteem him stricken, smitten of God, and afflicted.

5 But he was ^awounded for our ^btransgressions, he was bruised for our iniquities; the chastisement of our peace was upon him; and with his stripes we are ^chealed.

6 All we, like ^asheep, have gone astray; we have turned every one to his own way; and the Lord hath laid on him the iniquities of us all.

7 He was oppressed, and he was afflicted, yet he ^aopened not his mouth; he is brought as a ^blamb to the slaughter, and as a sheep before her shearers is dumb so he opened not his mouth.

[8] He was taken from prison and from judgment: and who shall declare his generation? for he was cut off out of the land of the living: for the transgression of my people was he stricken.

[9] And he made his grave with the wicked, and with the rich in his death; because he had done no violence, neither was any deceit in his mouth.

[10] Yet it pleased the LORD to bruise him; he hath put him to grief: when thou shalt make his soul an offering for sin, he shall see his seed, he shall prolong his days, and the pleasure of the LORD shall prosper in his hand.

[11] He shall see of the travail of his soul, and shall be satisfied: by his knowledge shall my righteous servant justify many; for he shall bear their iniquities.

[12] Therefore will I divide him a portion with the great, and he shall divide the spoil with the strong; because he hath poured out his soul unto death: and he was numbered with the transgressors; and he bare the sin of many, and made intercession for the transgressors.

53:8 He was taken from prison and from judgment. And who shall declare his generation? For he was cut off out of the land of the living; for the transgression of my people was he stricken.

53:9 And he made his grave with the wicked and with the rich in his death because he had done no violence; neither was any deceit in his mouth.

53:10 Yet it pleased the Lord to bruise him; he hath put him to grief; when thou shalt make his soul an offering for sin, he shall see his seed; he shall prolong his days, and the pleasure of the Lord shall prosper in his hand.

53:11 He shall see of the travail of his soul and shall be satisfied; by his knowledge shall my righteous servant justify many, for he shall bear their iniquities.

53:12 Therefore will I divide him a portion with the great, and he shall divide the spoil with the strong because he hath poured out his soul unto death; and he was numbered with the transgressors; and he bare the sin of many and made intercession for the transgressors.

8 He was taken from prison and from judgment; and who shall declare his generation? For he was cut off out of the land of the living; for the transgressions of my people was he stricken.

9 And he made his grave with the wicked, and with the *a*rich in his death; because he had done no *b*evil, neither was any deceit in his mouth.

10 Yet it pleased the Lord to *a*bruise him; he hath put him to grief; when thou shalt make his soul an offering for sin he shall see his *b*seed, he shall prolong his days, and the pleasure of the Lord shall prosper in his hand.

11 He shall see the travail of his soul, and shall be satisfied; by his knowledge shall my righteous servant justify many; for he shall *a*bear their iniquities.

12 Therefore will I divide him a portion with the *a*great, and *b*he shall divide the spoil with the strong; because he hath poured out his soul unto death; and he was numbered with the transgressors; and he bore the sins of many, and made *c*intercession for the transgressors.

54	Chapter 54	3 Nephi 22: 1-17
[1] Sing, O barren, thou that didst not bear; break forth into singing, and cry aloud, thou that didst not travail with child: for more are the children of the desolate than the children of the married wife, saith the LORD.	54:1 Sing, O barren, thou that didst not bear; break forth into singing, and cry aloud, thou that didst not travail with child; for more are the children of the desolate than the children of the married wife, saith the Lord.	1 And then shall that which is written come to pass: Sing, O *a*barren, thou that didst not bear; break forth into *b*singing, and cry aloud, thou that didst not travail with child; for more are the children of the *c*desolate than the children of the married wife, saith the Lord.
[2] Enlarge the place of thy tent, and let them stretch forth the curtains of thine habitations: spare not, lengthen thy cords, and strengthen thy stakes;	54:2 Enlarge the place of thy tent, and let them stretch forth the curtains of thine habitations; spare not, lengthen thy cords, and strengthen thy stakes;	2 Enlarge the place of thy tent, and let them stretch forth the curtains of thy habitations; spare not, lengthen thy cords and strengthen thy *a*stakes;
[3] For thou shalt break forth on the right hand and on the left; and thy seed shall inherit the Gentiles, and make the desolate cities to be inhabited.	54:3 For thou shalt break forth on the right hand and on the left; and thy seed shall inherit the Gentiles and make the desolate cities to be inhabited.	3 For thou shalt break forth on the right hand and on the left, and thy seed shall *a*inherit the *b*Gentiles and make the desolate cities to be inhabited.
[4] Fear not; for thou shalt not be ashamed: neither be thou confounded; for thou shalt not be put to shame: for thou shalt forget the shame of thy youth, and shalt not remember the reproach of thy widowhood any more.	54:4 Fear not, for thou shalt not be ashamed; neither be thou confounded; for thou shalt not be put to shame; for thou shalt forget the shame of thy youth and shalt not remember the reproach of thy widowhood any more.	4 Fear not, for thou shalt not be ashamed; neither be thou confounded, for thou shalt not be put to *a*shame; for thou shalt forget the *b*shame of thy youth, and shalt not remember the *c*reproach of thy youth, and shalt not remember the reproach of thy widowhood any more.

[5] For thy Maker is thine husband; the LORD of hosts is his name; and thy Redeemer the Holy One of Israel; The God of the whole earth shall he be called.

[6] For the LORD hath called thee as a woman forsaken and grieved in spirit, and a wife of youth, when thou wast refused, saith thy God.

[7] For a small moment have I forsaken thee; but with great mercies will I gather thee.

[8] In a little wrath I hid my face from thee for a moment; but with everlasting kindness will I have mercy on thee, saith the LORD thy Redeemer.

[9] For this is as the waters of Noah unto me: for as I have sworn that the waters of Noah should no more go over the earth; so have I sworn that I would not be wroth with thee, nor rebuke thee.

[10] For the mountains shall depart, and the hills be removed; but my kindness shall not depart from thee, neither shall the covenant of my peace be removed, saith the LORD that hath mercy on thee.

54:5 For thy Maker is thine husband; the Lord of hosts is his name, and thy Redeemer, the Holy One of Israel; the God of the whole earth shall he be called.

54:6 For the Lord hath called thee as a woman forsaken and grieved in spirit, and a wife of youth, when thou wast refused, saith thy God.

54:7 For a small moment have I forsaken thee; but with great mercies will I gather thee.

54:8 In a little wrath I hid my face from thee for a moment; but with everlasting kindness will I have mercy on thee, saith the Lord, thy Redeemer.

54:9 For this is as the waters of Noah unto me; for as I have sworn that the waters of Noah should no more go over the earth, so have I sworn that I would not be wroth with thee nor rebuke thee.

54:10 For the mountains shall depart, and the hills be removed; but my kindness shall not depart from thee; neither shall the covenant of my people be removed, saith the Lord that hath mercy on thee.

5 For thy maker, thy *ahusband*, the Lord of Hosts is his name; and thy Redeemer, the Holy One of Israel—the God of the whole earth shall he be called.

6 For the Lord hath called thee *aas* a woman forsaken and grieved in spirit, and a wife of youth, when thou wast refused, saith thy God.

7 For a small moment have I *aforsaken* thee, but with great mercies will I gather thee.

8 In a little wrath I hid my face from thee for a moment, but with everlasting *akindness* will I have *bmercy* on thee, saith the Lord thy Redeemer.

9 For *athis*, the *bwaters of Noah* unto me, for as I have sworn that the waters of Noah should no more go over the earth, so have I sworn that I would not be wroth with thee.

10 For the *amountains* shall depart and the hills be removed, but my *bkindness* shall not *cdepart* from thee, neither shall the covenant of my peace be removed, saith the Lord that hath mercy on thee.

[11] O thou afflicted, tossed with tempest, and not comforted, behold, I will lay thy stones with fair colours, and lay thy foundations with sapphires.

[12] And I will make thy windows of agates, and thy gates of carbuncles, and all thy borders of pleasant stones.

[13] And all thy children shall be taught of the LORD; and great shall be the peace of thy children.

[14] In righteousness shalt thou be established: thou shalt be far from oppression; for thou shalt not fear: and from terror; for it shall not come near thee.

[15] Behold, they shall surely gather together, but not by me: whosoever shall gather together against thee shall fall for thy sake.

[16] Behold, I have created the smith that bloweth the coals in the fire, and that bringeth forth an instrument for his work; and I have created the waster to destroy.

54:11 O thou afflicted, tossed with tempest and not comforted, behold, I will lay thy stones with fair colors and lay thy foundations with sapphires.

54:12 And I will make thy windows of agates, and thy gates of carbuncles, and all thy borders of pleasant stones.

54:13 And all thy children shall be taught of the Lord; and great shall be the peace of thy children.

54:14 In righteousness shalt thou be established; thou shalt be far from oppression, for thou shalt not fear, and from terror, for it shall not come near thee.

54:15 Behold, they shall surely gather together against thee, but not by me; whosoever shall gather together against thee shall fall for thy sake.

54:16 Behold, I have created the smith that bloweth the coals in the fire and that bringeth forth an instrument for his work; and I have created the waster to destroy.

11 O thou afflicted, tossed with tempest, and not comforted! Behold, I will lay thy *a*stones with fair colors, and lay thy foundations with sapphires.

12 And I will make thy windows of agates, and thy gates of carbuncles, and all thy borders of pleasant stones.

13 And *a*all thy children shall be taught of the Lord; and great shall be the *b*peace of thy children.

14 In *a*righteousness shalt thou be established; thou shalt be far from oppression for thou shalt not fear, and from terror for it shall not come near thee.

15 Behold, they shall surely gather together *a*against thee, not by me; whosoever shall gather together against thee shall fall for thy sake.

16 Behold, I have created the smith that bloweth the coals in the fire, and that bringeth forth an instrument for his work; and I have created the waster to destroy.

[17] No weapon that is formed against thee shall prosper; and every tongue that shall rise against thee in judgment thou shalt condemn. This is the heritage of the servants of the LORD, and their righteousness is of me, saith the LORD.

55

[1] Ho, every one that thirsteth, come ye to the waters, and he that hath no money; come ye, buy, and eat; yea, come, buy wine and milk without money and without price.

[2] Wherefore do ye spend money for that which is not bread? and your labour for that which satisfieth not? hearken diligently unto me, and eat ye that which is good, and let your soul delight itself in fatness.

[3] Incline your ear, and come unto me: hear, and your soul shall live; and I will make an everlasting covenant with you, even the sure mercies of David.

54:17 No weapon that is formed against thee shall prosper; and every tongue that shall rise against thee in judgment thou shalt condemn. This is the heritage of the servants of the Lord; and their righteousness is of me, saith the Lord.

Chapter 55

55:1 Ho, everyone that thirsteth, come ye to the waters; and he that hath no money, come ye, buy, and eat; yea, come; buy wine and milk without money and without price.

55:2 Wherefore do ye spend money for that which is not bread, and your labor for that which satisfieth not? Hearken diligently unto me, and eat ye that which is good; and let your soul delight itself in fatness.

55:3 Incline your ear, and come unto me; hear, and your soul shall live; and I will make an everlasting covenant with you, even the sure mercies of David.

17 No weapon that is formed against thee shall prosper; and every tongue that shall revile against thee in judgment thou shalt condemn. This is the heritage of the *ᵃ*servants of the Lord, and their righteousness is of me, saith the Lord.

2 Nephi 9:50 - 51

50 Come, my brethren, every one that *ᵃ*thirsteth, come ye to the *ᵇ*waters; and he that hath no *ᶜ*money, come buy and eat; yea, come buy wine and milk without money and without price.

51 Wherefore, do not spend money for that which is of no worth, nor your *ᵃ*labor for that which cannot *ᵇ*satisfy. Hearken diligently unto me, and remember the words which I have spoken; and come unto the Holy One of Israel, and *ᶜ*feast upon that which perisheth not, neither can be corrupted, and let your soul delight in fatness.

[4] Behold, I have given him for a witness to the people, a leader and commander to the people.

[5] Behold, thou shalt call a nation that thou knowest not, and nations that knew not thee shall run unto thee because of the LORD thy God, and for the Holy One of Israel; for he hath glorified thee.

[6] Seek ye the LORD while he may be found, call ye upon him while he is near:

[7] Let the wicked forsake his way, and the unrighteous man his thoughts: and let him return unto the LORD, and he will have mercy upon him; and to our God, for he will abundantly pardon.

[8] For my thoughts are not your thoughts, neither are your ways my ways, saith the LORD.

[9] For as the heavens are higher than the earth, so are my ways higher than your ways, and my thoughts than your thoughts.

55:4 Behold, I have given him for a witness to the people, a leader and commander to the people.

55:5 Behold, thou shalt call a nation that thou knowest not, and nations that knew not thee shall run unto thee because of the Lord, thy God, and for the Holy One of Israel; for he hath glorified thee.

55:6 Seek ye the Lord while he may be found; call ye upon him while he is near;

55:7 Let the wicked forsake his way, and the unrighteous man his thoughts; and let him return unto the Lord, and he will have mercy upon him, and to our God, for he will abundantly pardon.

55:8 For my thoughts are not your thoughts; neither are your ways my ways, saith the Lord.

55:9 For as the heavens are higher than the earth, so are my ways higher than your ways, and my thoughts than your thoughts.

[10] For as the rain cometh down, and the snow from heaven, and returneth not thither, but watereth the earth, and maketh it bring forth and bud, that it may give seed to the sower, and bread to the eater:

[11] So shall my word be that goeth forth out of my mouth: it shall not return unto me void, but it shall accomplish that which I please, and it shall prosper in the thing whereto I sent it.

[12] For ye shall go out with joy, and be led forth with peace: the mountains and the hills shall break forth before you into singing, and all the trees of the field shall clap their hands.

[13] Instead of the thorn shall come up the fir tree, and instead of the brier shall come up the myrtle tree: and it shall be to the LORD for a name, for an everlasting sign that shall not be cut off.

.56

[1] Thus saith the LORD, Keep ye judgment, and do justice: for my salvation is near to come, and my righteousness to be revealed.

55:10 For as the rain cometh down, and the snow from heaven, and returneth not thither, but watereth the earth, and maketh it bring forth and bud, that it may give seed to the sower and bread to the eater,

55:11 So shall my word be that goeth forth out of my mouth; it shall not return unto me void; but it shall accomplish that which I please, and it shall prosper in the thing whereto I sent it.

55:12 For ye shall go out with joy and be led forth with peace; the mountains and the hills shall break forth before you into singing, and all the trees of the field shall clap their hands.

55:13 Instead of the thorn shall come up the fir tree, and instead of the brier shall come up the myrtle tree; and it shall be to the Lord for a name, for an everlasting sign that shall not be cut off.

Chapter 56

56:1 Thus saith the Lord, Keep ye judgment, and do justice; for my salvation is near to come and my righteousness to be revealed.

[2] Blessed is the man that doeth this, and the son of man that layeth hold on it; that keepeth the sabbath from polluting it, and keepeth his hand from doing any evil.

[3] Neither let the son of the stranger, that hath joined himself to the LORD, speak, saying, The LORD hath utterly separated me from his people: neither let the eunuch say, Behold, I am a dry tree.

[4] For thus saith the LORD unto the eunuchs that keep my sabbaths, and choose the things that please me, and take hold of my covenant;

[5] Even unto them will I give in mine house and within my walls a place and a name better than of sons and of daughters: I will give them an everlasting name, that shall not be cut off.

[6] Also the sons of the stranger, that join themselves to the LORD, to serve him, and to love the name of the LORD, to be his servants, every one that keepeth the sabbath from polluting it, and taketh hold of my covenant;

56:2 Blessed is the man that doeth this and the son of man that layeth hold on it, that keepeth the sabbath, from polluting it, and keepeth his hand from doing any evil.

56:3 Neither let the son of the stranger, that hath joined himself to the Lord, speak, saying, The Lord hath utterly separated me from his people; neither let the eunuch say, Behold, I am a dry tree.

56:4 For thus saith the Lord unto the eunuchs that keep my sabbaths, and choose the things that please me, and take hold of my covenant,

56:5 Even unto them will I give in mine house and within my walls a place and a name better than of sons and of daughters; I will give them an everlasting name that shall not be cut off.

56:6 Also the sons of the stranger, that join themselves to the Lord--to serve him, and to love the name of the Lord, to be his servants, everyone that keepeth the sabbath, from polluting it, and taketh hold of my covenant--

[7] Even them will I bring to my holy mountain, and make them joyful in my house of prayer: their burnt offerings and their sacrifices shall be accepted upon mine altar; for mine house shall be called an house of prayer for all people.

[8] The Lord GOD which gathereth the outcasts of Israel saith, Yet will I gather others to him, beside those that are gathered unto him.

[9] All ye beasts of the field, come to devour, yea, all ye beasts in the forest.

[10] His watchmen are blind: they are all ignorant, they are all dumb dogs, they cannot bark; sleeping, lying down, loving to slumber.

[11] Yea, they are greedy dogs which can never have enough, and they are shepherds that cannot understand: they all look to their own way, every one for his gain, from his quarter.

[12] Come ye, say they, I will fetch wine, and we will fill ourselves with strong drink; and to morrow shall be as this day, and much more abundant.

56:7 Even them will I bring to my holy mountain, and make them joyful in my house of prayer; their burnt offerings and their sacrifices shall be accepted upon mine altar, for mine house shall be called a house of prayer for all people.

56:8 The Lord God which gathereth the outcasts of Israel saith, Yet will I gather others to him besides those that are gathered unto him.

56:9 All ye beasts of the field, come to devour, yea, all ye beasts in the forest.

56:10 His watchmen are blind; they are all ignorant; they are all dumb dogs; they cannot bark--sleeping, lying down, loving to slumber.

56:11 Yea, they are greedy dogs, which can never have enough; and they are shepherds that cannot understand; they all look to their own way, everyone for his gain, from his quarter.

56:12 Come ye, say they; I will fetch wine, and we will fill ourselves with strong drink; and tomorrow shall be as this day, and much more abundant.

.57

[1] The righteous perisheth, and no man layeth it to heart: and merciful men are taken away, none considering that the righteous is taken away from the evil to come.

[2] He shall enter into peace: they shall rest in their beds, each one walking in his uprightness.

[3] But draw near hither, ye sons of the sorceress, the seed of the adulterer and the whore.

[4] Against whom do ye sport yourselves? against whom make ye a wide mouth, and draw out the tongue? are ye not children of transgression, a seed of falsehood,

[5] Enflaming yourselves with idols under every green tree, slaying the children in the valleys under the clifts of the rocks?

Chapter 57

57:1 The righteous perisheth, and no man layeth it to heart; and merciful men are taken away, none considering that the righteous is taken away from the evil to come.

57:2 He shall enter into peace; they shall rest in their beds, each one walking in his uprightness.

57:3 But draw near hither, ye sons of the sorceress, the seed of the adulterer and the whore.

57:4 Against whom do ye sport yourselves? Against whom make ye a wide mouth, and draw out the tongue? Are ye not children of transgression, a seed of falsehood,

57:5 Inflaming yourselves with idols under every green tree, slaying the children in the valleys under the clefts of the rocks?

[6] Among the smooth stones of the stream is thy portion; they, they are thy lot: even to them hast thou poured a drink offering, thou hast offered a meat offering. Should I receive comfort in these?

[7] Upon a lofty and high mountain hast thou set thy bed: even thither wentest thou up to offer sacrifice.

[8] Behind the doors also and the posts hast thou set up thy remembrance: for thou hast discovered thyself to another than me, and art gone up; thou hast enlarged thy bed, and made thee a covenant with them; thou lovedst their bed where thou sawest it.

[9] And thou wentest to the king with ointment, and didst increase thy perfumes, and didst send thy messengers far off, and didst debase thyself even unto hell.

[10] Thou art wearied in the greatness of thy way; yet saidst thou not, There is no hope: thou hast found the life of thine hand; therefore thou wast not grieved.

57:6 Among the smooth stones of the stream is thy portion; they, they are thy lot; even to them hast thou poured a drink offering; thou hast offered a meat offering. Should I receive comfort in these?

57:7 Upon a lofty and high mountain hast thou set thy bed; even thither wentest thou up to offer sacrifice.

57:8 Behind the doors also and the posts hast thou set up thy remembrance; for thou hast discovered thyself to another than me and art gone up; thou hast enlarged thy bed and made thee a covenant with them; thou lovedst their bed where thou sawest it.

57:9 And thou wentest to the king with ointment, and didst increase thy perfumes, and didst send thy messengers far off, and didst debase thyself even unto hell.

57:10 Thou art wearied in the greatness of thy way, yet saidst thou not, There is no hope. Thou hast found the life of thine hand; therefore, thou wast not grieved.

[11] And of whom hast thou been afraid or feared, that thou hast lied, and hast not remembered me, nor laid it to thy heart? have not I held my peace even of old, and thou fearest me not?

[12] I will declare thy righteousness, and thy works; for they shall not profit thee.

[13] When thou criest, let thy companies deliver thee; but the wind shall carry them all away; vanity shall take them: but he that putteth his trust in me shall possess the land, and shall inherit my holy mountain;

[14] And shall say, Cast ye up, cast ye up, prepare the way, take up the stumblingblock out of the way of my people.

[15] For thus saith the high and lofty One that inhabiteth eternity, whose name is Holy; I dwell in the high and holy place, with him also that is of a contrite and humble spirit, to revive the spirit of the humble, and to revive the heart of the contrite ones.

57:11 And of whom hast thou been afraid or feared, that thou hast lied, and hast not remembered me, nor laid it to thy heart? Have not I held my peace even of old, and thou fearest me not?

57:12 I will declare thy righteousness and thy works, for they shall not profit thee.

57:13 When thou criest, let thy companies deliver thee; but the wind shall carry them all away; vanity shall take them; but he that putteth his trust in me shall possess the land, and shall inherit my holy mountain,

57:14 And shall say, Cast ye up, cast ye up; prepare the way; take up the stumbling-block out of the way of my people.

57:15 For thus saith the high and lofty One that inhabiteth eternity, whose name is Holy, I dwell in the high and holy place with him also that is of a contrite and humble spirit, to revive the spirit of the humble and to revive the heart of the contrite ones.

[16] For I will not contend for ever, neither will I be always wroth: for the spirit should fail before me, and the souls which I have made.

[17] For the iniquity of his covetousness was I wroth, and smote him: I hid me, and was wroth, and he went on frowardly in the way of his heart.

[18] I have seen his ways, and will heal him: I will lead him also, and restore comforts unto him and to his mourners.

[19] I create the fruit of the lips; Peace, peace to him that is far off, and to him that is near, saith the LORD; and I will heal him.

[20] But the wicked are like the troubled sea, when it cannot rest, whose waters cast up mire and dirt.

[21] There is no peace, saith my God, to the wicked.

.58
[1] Cry aloud, spare not, lift up thy voice like a trumpet, and shew my people their transgression, and the house of Jacob their sins.

57:16 For I will not contend forever; neither will I be always wroth; for the spirit should fail before me, and the souls which I have made.

57:17 For the iniquity of his covetousness was I wroth and smote him; I hid me and was wroth, and he went on frowardly in the way of his heart.

57:18 I have seen his ways and will heal him; I will lead him also and restore comforts unto him and to his mourners.

57:19 I create the fruit of the lips; Peace, peace to him that is far off, and to him that is near, saith the Lord, and I will heal him.

57:20 But the wicked are like the troubled sea when it cannot rest, whose waters cast up mire and dirt.

57:21 There is no peace, saith my God, to the wicked.

Chapter 58
58:1 Cry aloud; spare not; lift up thy voice like a trumpet, and show my people their transgression and the house of Jacob their sins.

[2] Yet they seek me daily, and delight to know my ways, as a nation that did righteousness, and forsook not the ordinance of their God: they ask of me the ordinances of justice; they take delight in approaching to God.

[3] Wherefore have we fasted, say they, and thou seest not? wherefore have we afflicted our soul, and thou takest no knowledge? Behold, in the day of your fast ye find pleasure, and exact all your labours.

[4] Behold, ye fast for strife and debate, and to smite with the fist of wickedness: ye shall not fast as ye do this day, to make your voice to be heard on high.

[5] Is it such a fast that I have chosen? a day for a man to afflict his soul? is it to bow down his head as a bulrush, and to spread sackcloth and ashes under him? wilt thou call this a fast, and an acceptable day to the LORD?

58:2 Yet they seek me daily and delight to know my ways, as a nation that did righteousness and forsook not the ordinance of their God; they ask of me the ordinances of justice; they take delight in approaching to God.

58:3 Wherefore have we fasted, say they, and thou seest not? Wherefore have we afflicted our soul, and thou takest no knowledge? Behold, in the day of your fast ye find pleasure and exact all your labors.

58:4 Behold, ye fast for strife, and debate, and to smite with the fist of wickedness; ye shall not fast as ye do this day, to make your voice to be heard on high.

58:5 Is it such a fast that I have chosen, a day for a man to afflict his soul? Is it to bow down his head as a bulrush and to spread sackcloth and ashes under him? Wilt thou call this a fast and an acceptable day to the Lord?

[6] Is not this the fast that I have chosen? to loose the bands of wickedness, to undo the heavy burdens, and to let the oppressed go free, and that ye break every yoke?

[7] Is it not to deal thy bread to the hungry, and that thou bring the poor that are cast out to thy house? when thou seest the naked, that thou cover him; and that thou hide not thyself from thine own flesh?

[8] Then shall thy light break forth as the morning, and thine health shall spring forth speedily: and thy righteousness shall go before thee; the glory of the LORD shall be thy rereward.

[9] Then shalt thou call, and the LORD shall answer; thou shalt cry, and he shall say, Here I am. If thou take away from the midst of thee the yoke, the putting forth of the finger, and speaking vanity;

[10] And if thou draw out thy soul to the hungry, and satisfy the afflicted soul; then shall thy light rise in obscurity, and thy darkness be as the noonday:

58:6 Is not this the fast that I have chosen--to loose the bands of wickedness, to undo the heavy burdens, and to let the oppressed go free, and that ye break every yoke?

58:7 Is it not to deal thy bread to the hungry, and that thou bring the poor that are cast out to thy house; when thou seest the naked, that thou cover him; and that thou hide not thyself from thine own flesh?

58:8 Then shall thy light break forth as the morning, and thine health shall spring forth speedily; and thy righteousness shall go before thee; the glory of the Lord shall be thy rearward.

58:9 Then shalt thou call, and the Lord shall answer; thou shalt cry, and he shall say, Here I am. If thou take away from the midst of thee the yoke, the putting forth of the finger, and speaking vanity,

58:10 And if thou draw out thy soul to the hungry and satisfy the afflicted soul, then shall thy light rise in obscurity and thy darkness be as the noonday;

[11] And the LORD shall guide thee continually, and satisfy thy soul in drought, and make fat thy bones: and thou shalt be like a watered garden, and like a spring of water, whose waters fail not.

[12] And they that shall be of thee shall build the old waste places: thou shalt raise up the foundations of many generations; and thou shalt be called, The repairer of the breach, The restorer of paths to dwell in.

[13] If thou turn away thy foot from the sabbath, from doing thy pleasure on my holy day; and call the sabbath a delight, the holy of the LORD, honourable; and shalt honour him, not doing thine own ways, nor finding thine own pleasure, nor speaking thine own words:

[14] Then shalt thou delight thyself in the LORD; and I will cause thee to ride upon the high places of the earth, and feed thee with the heritage of Jacob thy father: for the mouth of the LORD hath spoken it.

58:11 And the Lord shall guide thee continually, and satisfy thy soul in drought, and make fat thy bones; and thou shalt be like a watered garden and like a spring of water, whose waters fail not.

58:12 And they that shall be of thee shall build the old waste places; thou shalt raise up the foundations of many generations; and thou shalt be called, the repairer of the breach, the restorer of paths to dwell in.

58:13 If thou turn away thy foot from the sabbath, from doing thy pleasure on my holy day, and call the sabbath a delight, the holy of the Lord, honorable, and shalt honor him--not doing thine own ways, nor finding thine own pleasure, nor speaking thine own words--

58:14 Then shalt thou delight thyself in the Lord; and I will cause thee to ride upon the high places of the earth and feed thee with the heritage of Jacob, thy father; for the mouth of the Lord hath spoken it.

Chapter 59

[1] Behold, the LORD's hand is not shortened, that it cannot save; neither his ear heavy, that it cannot hear:

59:1 Behold, the Lord's hand is not shortened, that it cannot save; neither his ear heavy, that it cannot hear;

[2] But your iniquities have separated between you and your God, and your sins have hid his face from you, that he will not hear.

59:2 But your iniquities have separated between you and your God; and your sins have hid his face from you, that he will not hear.

[3] For your hands are defiled with blood, and your fingers with iniquity; your lips have spoken lies, your tongue hath muttered perverseness.

59:3 For your hands are defiled with blood, and your fingers with iniquity; your lips have spoken lies; your tongue hath muttered perverseness.

[4] None calleth for justice, nor any pleadeth for truth: they trust in vanity, and speak lies; they conceive mischief, and bring forth iniquity.

59:4 None calleth for justice, nor any pleadeth for truth; they trust in vanity and speak lies; they conceive mischief and bring forth iniquity.

[5] They hatch cockatrice' eggs, and weave the spider's web: he that eateth of their eggs dieth, and that which is crushed breaketh out into a viper.

59:5 They hatch cockatrice eggs and weave the spider's web; he that eateth of their eggs dieth, and that which is crushed breaketh out into a viper.

[6] Their webs shall not become garments, neither shall they cover themselves with their works: their works are works of iniquity, and the act of violence is in their hands.

59:6 Their webs shall not become garments; neither shall they cover themselves with their works; their works are works of iniquity, and the act of violence is in their hands.

[7] Their feet run to evil, and they make hast to shed innocent blood: their thoughts are thoughts of iniquity; wasting and destruction are in their paths.

[8] The way of peace they know not; and there is no judgment in their goings: they have made them crooked paths: whosoever goeth therein shall not know peace.

[9] Therefore is judgment far from us, neither doth justice overtake us: we wait for light, but behold obscurity; for brightness, but we walk in darkness.

[10] We grope for the wall like the blind, and we grope as if we had no eyes: we stumble at noonday as in the night; we are in desolate places as dead men.

[11] We roar all like bears, and mourn sore like doves: we look for judgment, but there is none; for salvation, but it is far off from us.

[12] For our transgressions are multiplied before thee, and our sins testify against us: for our transgressions are with us; and as for our iniquities, we know them;

59:7 Their feet run to evil, and they make haste to shed innocent blood; their thoughts are thoughts of iniquity; wasting and destruction are in their paths.

59:8 The way of peace they know not, and there is no judgment in their goings; they have made them crooked paths; whosoever goeth therein shall not know peace.

59:9 Therefore is judgment far from us; neither doth justice overtake us; we wait for light, but behold obscurity; for brightness, but we walk in darkness.

59:10 We grope for the wall like the blind, and we grope as if we had no eyes; we stumble at noonday as in the night; we are in desolate places as dead men.

59:11 We roar all like bears and mourn sore like doves; we look for judgment, but there is none; for salvation, but it is far off from us.

59:12 For our transgressions are multiplied before thee, and our sins testify against us; for our transgressions are with us; and as for our iniquities, we know them--

[13] In transgressing and lying against the LORD, and departing away from our God, speaking oppression and revolt, conceiving and uttering from the heart words of falsehood.

[14] And judgment is turned away backward, and justice standeth afar off: for truth is fallen in the street, and equity cannot enter.

[15] Yea, truth faileth; and he that departeth from evil maketh himself a prey: and the LORD saw it, and it displeased him that there was no judgment.

[16] And he saw that there was no man, and wondered that there was no intercessor: therefore his arm brought salvation unto him; and his righteousness, it sustained him.

[17] For he put on righteousness as a breastplate, and an helmet of salvation upon his head; and he put on the garments of vengeance for clothing, and was clad with zeal as a cloke.

59:13 In transgressing and lying against the Lord, and departing away from our God, speaking oppression and revolt, conceiving and uttering from the heart words of falsehood.

59:14 And judgment is turned away backward, and justice standeth afar off; for truth is fallen in the street, and equity cannot enter.

59:15 Yea, truth faileth; and he that departeth from evil maketh himself a prey; and the Lord saw it, and it displeased him that there was no judgment.

59:16 And he saw that there was no man and wondered that there was no intercessor; therefore, his arm brought salvation unto him; and his righteousness, it sustained him.

59:17 For he put on righteousness as a breastplate, and a helmet of salvation upon his head; and he put on the garments of vengeance for clothing and was clad with zeal as a cloak.

[18] According to their deeds, accordingly he will repay, fury to his adversaries, recompence to his enemies; to the islands he will repay recompence.

[19] So shall they fear the name of the LORD from the west, and his glory from the rising of the sun. When the enemy shall come in like a flood, the Spirit of the LORD shall lift up a standard against him.

[20] And the Redeemer shall come to Zion, and unto them that turn from transgression in Jacob, saith the LORD.

[21] As for me, this is my covenant with them, saith the LORD; My spirit that is upon thee, and my words which I have put in thy mouth, shall not depart out of thy mouth, nor out of the mouth of thy seed, nor out of the mouth of thy seed's seed, saith the LORD, from henceforth and for ever.

.60

[1] Arise, shine; for thy light is come, and the glory of the LORD is risen upon thee.

59:18 According to their deeds, accordingly he will repay: fury to his adversaries, recompense to his enemies; to the islands he will repay recompense.

59:19 So shall they fear the name of the Lord from the west and his glory from the rising of the sun. When the enemy shall come in like a flood, the Spirit of the Lord shall lift up a standard against him.

59:20 And the Redeemer shall come to Zion and unto them that turn from transgression in Jacob, saith the Lord.

59:21 As for me, this is my covenant with them, saith the Lord; my Spirit that is upon thee and my words which I have put in thy mouth shall not depart out of thy mouth, nor out of the mouth of thy seed, nor out of the mouth of thy seed's seed, saith the Lord, from henceforth and forever.

Chapter 60

60:1 Arise; shine; for thy light is come, and the glory of the Lord is risen upon thee.

[2] For, behold, the darkness shall cover the earth, and gross darkness the people: but the LORD shall arise upon thee, and his glory shall be seen upon thee.

[3] And the Gentiles shall come to thy light, and kings to the brightness of thy rising.

[4] Lift up thine eyes round about, and see: all they gather themselves together, they come to thee: thy sons shall come from far, and thy daughters shall be nursed at thy side.

[5] Then thou shalt see, and flow together, and thine heart shall fear, and be enlarged; because the abundance of the sea shall be converted unto thee, the forces of the Gentiles shall come unto thee.

[6] The multitude of camels shall cover thee, the dromedaries of Midian and Ephah; all they from Sheba shall come: they shall bring gold and incense; and they shall shew forth the praises of the LORD.

60:2 For behold, the darkness shall cover the earth, and gross darkness the people; but the Lord shall arise upon thee, and his glory shall be seen upon thee.

60:3 And the Gentiles shall come to thy light, and kings to the brightness of thy rising.

60:4 Lift up thine eyes round about, and see; all they gather themselves together; they come to thee; thy sons shall come from far, and thy daughters shall be nursed at thy side.

60:5 Then thou shalt see and flow together, and thine heart shall fear and be enlarged because the abundance of the sea shall be converted unto thee; the forces of the Gentiles shall come unto thee.

60:6 The multitude of camels shall cover thee, the dromedaries of Midian and Ephah; all they from Sheba shall come; they shall bring gold and incense, and they shall show forth the praises of the Lord.

[7] All the flocks of Kedar shall be gathered together unto thee, the rams of Nebaioth shall minister unto thee: they shall come up with acceptance on mine altar, and I will glorify the house of my glory.	60:7 All the flocks of Kedar shall be gathered together unto thee; the rams of Nebaioth shall minister unto thee; they shall come up with acceptance on mine altar, and I will glorify the house of my glory.
[8] Who are these that fly as a cloud, and as the doves to their windows?	60:8 Who are these that fly as a cloud and as the doves to their windows?
[9] Surely the isles shall wait for me, and the ships of Tarshish first, to bring thy sons from far, their silver and their gold with them, unto the name of the LORD thy God, and to the Holy One of Israel, because he hath glorified thee.	60:9 Surely the isles shall wait for me, and the ships of Tarshish first, to bring thy sons from far, their silver and their gold with them, unto the name of the Lord, thy God, and to the Holy One of Israel because he hath glorified thee.
[10] And the sons of strangers shall build up thy walls, and their kings shall minister unto thee: for in my wrath I smote thee, but in my favour have I had mercy on thee.	60:10 And the sons of strangers shall build up thy walls, and their kings shall minister unto thee; for in my wrath I smote thee, but in my favor have I had mercy on thee.
[11] Therefore thy gates shall be open continually; they shall not be shut day nor night; that men may bring unto thee the forces of the Gentiles, and that their kings may be brought.	60:11 Therefore, thy gates shall be open continually; they shall not be shut day nor night, that men may bring unto thee the forces of the Gentiles and that their kings may be brought.

[12] For the nation and kingdom that will not serve thee shall perish; yea, those nations shall be utterly wasted.

[13] The glory of Lebanon shall come unto thee, the fir tree, the pine tree, and the box together, to beautify the place of my sanctuary; and I will make the place of my feet glorious.

[14] The sons also of them that afflicted thee shall come bending unto thee; and all they that despised thee shall bow themselves down at the soles of thy feet; and they shall call thee, The city of the LORD, The Zion of the Holy One of Israel.

[15] Whereas thou hast been forsaken and hated, so that no man went through thee, I will make thee an eternal excellency, a joy of many generations.

[16] Thou shalt also suck the milk of the Gentiles, and shalt suck the breast of kings: and thou shalt know that I the LORD am thy Saviour and thy Redeemer, the mighty One of Jacob.

60:12 For the nation and kingdom that will not serve thee shall perish; yea, those nations shall be utterly wasted.

60:13 The glory of Lebanon shall come unto thee--the fir tree, the pine tree, and the box together, to beautify the place of my sanctuary; and I will make the place of my feet glorious.

60:14 The sons also of them that afflicted thee shall come bending unto thee; and all they that despised thee shall bow themselves down at the soles of thy feet; and they shall call thee, the city of the Lord, the Zion of the Holy One of Israel.

60:15 Whereas thou hast been forsaken and hated, so that no man went through thee, I will make thee an eternal excellency, a joy of many generations.

60:16 Thou shalt also suck the milk of the Gentiles and shalt suck the breast of kings; and thou shalt know that I, the Lord, am thy Savior and thy Redeemer, the Mighty One of Jacob.

[17] For brass I will bring gold, and for iron I will bring silver, and for wood brass, and for stones iron: I will also make thy officers peace, and thine exactors righteousness.

[18] Violence shall no more be heard in thy land, wasting nor destruction within thy borders; but thou shalt call thy walls Salvation, and thy gates Praise.

[19] The sun shall be no more thy light by day; neither for brightness shall the moon give light unto thee: but the LORD shall be unto thee an everlasting light, and thy God thy glory.

[20] Thy sun shall no more go down; neither shall thy moon withdraw itself: for the LORD shall be thine everlasting light, and the days of thy mourning shall be ended.

[21] Thy people also shall be all righteous: they shall inherit the land for ever, the branch of my planting, the work of my hands, that I may be glorified.

60:17 For brass I will bring gold, and for iron I will bring silver, and for wood brass, and for stones iron; I will also make thy officers peace and thine exactors righteousness.

60:18 Violence shall no more be heard in thy land, wasting nor destruction within thy borders; but thou shalt call thy walls Salvation and thy gates Praise.

60:19 The sun shall be no more thy light by day; neither for brightness shall the moon give light unto thee; but the Lord shall be unto thee an everlasting light, and thy God thy glory.

60:20 Thy sun shall no more go down; neither shall thy moon withdraw itself; for the Lord shall be thine everlasting light, and the days of thy mourning shall be ended.

60:21 Thy people also shall be all righteous; they shall inherit the land forever, the branch of my planting, the work of my hands, that I may be glorified.

[22] A little one shall become a thousand, and a small one a strong nation: I the LORD will hasten it in his time.

.61

[1] The Spirit of the Lord GOD is upon me; because the LORD hath anointed me to preach good tidings unto the meek; he hath sent me to bind up the brokenhearted, to proclaim liberty to the captives, and the opening of the prison to them that are bound;

[2] To proclaim the acceptable year of the LORD, and the day of vengeance of our God; to comfort all that mourn;

[3] To appoint unto them that mourn in Zion, to give unto them beauty for ashes, the oil of joy for mourning, the garment of praise for the spirit of heaviness; that they might be called trees of righteousness, the planting of the LORD, that he might be glorified.

60:22 A little one shall become a thousand, and a small one a strong nation; I, the Lord, will hasten it in my time.

Chapter 61

61:1 The Spirit of the Lord God is upon me because the Lord hath anointed me to preach good tidings unto the meek; he hath sent me to bind up the brokenhearted, to proclaim liberty to the captives, and the opening of the prison to them that are bound;

61:2 To proclaim the acceptable year of the Lord and the day of vengeance of our God; to comfort all that mourn;

61:3 To appoint unto them that mourn in Zion; to give unto them beauty for ashes, the oil of joy for mourning, the garment of praise for the spirit of heaviness, that they might be called trees of righteousness, the planting of the Lord, that he might be glorified.

[4] And they shall build the old wastes, they shall raise up the former desolations, and they shall repair the waste cities, the desolations of many generations.

[5] And strangers shall stand and feed your flocks, and the sons of the alien shall be your plowmen and your vinedressers.

[6] But ye shall be named the Priests of the LORD: men shall call you the Ministers of our God: ye shall eat the riches of the Gentiles, and in their glory shall ye boast yourselves.

[7] For your shame ye shall have double; and for confusion they shall rejoice in their portion: therefore in their land they shall possess the double: everlasting joy shall be unto them.

[8] For I the LORD love judgment, I hate robbery for burnt offering; and I will direct their work in truth, and I will make an everlasting covenant with them.

61:4 And they shall build the old wastes; they shall raise up the former desolations; and they shall repair the waste cities, the desolations of many generations.

61:5 And strangers shall stand and feed your flocks, and the sons of the alien shall be your plowmen and your vinedressers.

61:6 But ye shall be named the priests of the Lord; men shall call you the ministers of our God; ye shall eat the riches of the Gentiles, and in their glory shall ye boast yourselves.

61:7 For your shame ye shall have double; and for confusion they shall rejoice in their portion; therefore, in their land they shall possess the double; everlasting joy shall be unto them.

61:8 For I, the Lord, love judgment; I hate robbery for burnt offering; and I will direct their work in truth; and I will make an everlasting covenant with them.

[9] And their seed shall be known among the Gentiles, and their offspring among the people: all that see them shall acknowledge them, that they are the seed which the LORD hath blessed.

[10] I will greatly rejoice in the LORD, my soul shall be joyful in my God; for he hath clothed me with the garments of salvation, he hath covered me with the robe of righteousness, as a bridegroom decketh himself with ornaments, and as a bride adorneth herself with her jewels.

[11] For as the earth bringeth forth her bud, and as the garden causeth the things that are sown in it to spring forth; so the Lord GOD will cause righteousness and praise to spring forth before all the nations.

.62

[1] For Zion's sake will I not hold my peace, and for Jerusalem's sake I will not rest, until the righteousness thereof go forth as brightness, and the salvation thereof as a lamp that burneth.

61:9 And their seed shall be known among the Gentiles, and their offspring among the people; all that see them shall acknowledge them, that they are the seed which the Lord hath blessed.

61:10 I will greatly rejoice in the Lord; my soul shall be joyful in my God; for he hath clothed me with the garments of salvation; he hath covered me with the robe of righteousness, as a bridegroom decketh himself with ornaments and as a bride adorneth herself with her jewels.

61:11 For as the earth bringeth forth her bud, and as the garden causeth the things that are sown in it to spring forth, so the Lord God will cause righteousness and praise to spring forth before all the nations.

Chapter 62

62:1 For Zion's sake will I not hold my peace, and for Jerusalem's sake I will not rest until the righteousness thereof go forth as brightness, and the salvation thereof as a lamp that burneth.

[2] And the Gentiles shall see thy righteousness, and all kings thy glory: and thou shalt be called by a new name, which the mouth of the LORD shall name.	62:2 And the Gentiles shall see thy righteousness, and all kings thy glory; and thou shalt be called by a new name, which the mouth of the Lord shall name.
[3] Thou shalt also be a crown of glory in the hand of the LORD, and a royal diadem in the hand of thy God.	62:3 Thou shalt also be a crown of glory in the hand of the Lord and a royal diadem in the hand of thy God.
[4] Thou shalt no more be termed Forsaken; neither shall thy land any more be termed Desolate: but thou shalt be called Hephzi-bah, and thy land Beulah: for the LORD delighteth in thee, and thy land shall be married.	62:4 Thou shalt no more be termed Forsaken; neither shall thy land any more be termed Desolate; but thou shalt be called Delightful, and thy land Union; for the Lord delighteth in thee, and thy land shall be married.
[5] For as a young man marrieth a virgin, so shall thy sons marry thee: and as the bridegroom rejoiceth over the bride, so shall thy God rejoice over thee.	62:5 For as a young man marrieth a virgin, so shall thy God marry thee; and as the bridegroom rejoiceth over the bride, so shall thy God rejoice over thee.
[6] I have set watchmen upon thy walls, O Jerusalem, which shall never hold their peace day nor night: ye that make mention of the LORD, keep not silence,	62:6 I have set watchmen upon thy walls, O Jerusalem, which shall never hold their peace day nor night; ye that make mention of the Lord, keep not silence,
[7] And give him no rest, till he establish, and till he make Jerusalem a praise in the earth.	62:7 And give him no rest till he establish and till he make Jerusalem a praise in the earth.

[8] The LORD hath sworn by his right hand, and by the arm of his strength, Surely I will no more give thy corn to be meat for thine enemies; and the sons of the stranger shall not drink thy wine, for the which thou hast laboured:

[9] But they that have gathered it shall eat it, and praise the LORD; and they that have brought it together shall drink it in the courts of my holiness.

[10] Go through, go through the gates; prepare ye the way of the people; cast up, cast up the highway; gather out the stones; lift up a standard for the people.

[11] Behold, the LORD hath proclaimed unto the end of the world, Say ye to the daughter of Zion, Behold, thy salvation cometh; behold, his reward is with him, and his work before him.

[12] And they shall call them, The holy people, The redeemed of the LORD: and thou shalt be called, Sought out, A city not forsaken.

62:8 The Lord hath sworn by his right hand and by the arm of his strength, Surely I will no more give thy corn to be meat for thine enemies; and the sons of the stranger shall not drink thy wine, for the which thou hast labored;

62:9 But they that have gathered it shall eat it and praise the Lord; and they that have brought it together shall drink it in the courts of my holiness.

62:10 Go through, go through the gates; prepare ye the way of the people; cast up, cast up the highway; gather out the stones; lift up a standard for the people.

62:11 Behold, the Lord hath proclaimed unto the end of the world, Say ye to the daughter of Zion, Behold, thy salvation cometh; behold, his reward is with him, and his work before him.

62:12 And they shall call them the holy people, the redeemed of the Lord; and thou shalt be called Sought out, a city not forsaken.

63

[1] Who is this that cometh from Edom, with dyed garments from Bozrah? this that is glorious in his apparel, travelling in the greatness of his strength? I that speak in righteousness, mighty to save.

[2] Wherefore art thou red in thine apparel, and thy garments like him that treadeth in the winefat?

[3] I have trodden the winepress alone; and of the people there was none with me: for I will tread them in mine anger, and trample them in my fury; and their blood shall be sprinkled upon my garments, and I will stain all my raiment.

[4] For the day of vengeance is in mine heart, and the year of my redeemed is come.

[5] And I looked, and there was none to help; and I wondered that there was none to uphold: therefore mine own arm brought salvation unto me; and my fury, it upheld me.

Chapter 63

63:1 Who is this that cometh from Edom, with dyed garments from Bozrah--this that is glorious in his apparel, traveling in the greatness of his strength? I, that speak in righteousness, mighty to save.

63:2 Wherefore art thou red in thine apparel and thy garments like him that treadeth in the winefat?

63:3 I have trodden the winepress alone; and of the people there was none with me; for I will tread them in mine anger and trample them in my fury; and their blood shall be sprinkled upon my garments, and I will stain all my raiment.

63:4 For the day of vengeance is in mine heart, and the year of my redeemed is come.

63:5 And I looked, and there was none to help; and I wondered that there was none to uphold; therefore, mine own arm brought salvation unto me; and my fury, it upheld me.

[6] And I will tread down the people in mine anger, and make them drunk in my fury, and I will bring down their strength to the earth.

[7] I will mention the lovingkindnesses of the LORD, and the praises of the LORD, according to all that the LORD hath bestowed on us, and the great goodness toward the house of Israel, which he hath bestowed on them according to his mercies, and according to the multitude of his lovingkindnesses.

[8] For he said, Surely they are my people, children that will not lie: so he was their Saviour.

[9] In all their affliction he was afflicted, and the angel of his presence saved them: in his love and in his pity he redeemed them; and he bare them, and carried them all the days of old.

[10] But they rebelled, and vexed his holy Spirit: therefore he was turned to be their enemy, and he fought against them.

63:6 And I will tread down the people in mine anger and make them drunk in my fury, and I will bring down their strength to the earth.

63:7 I will mention the loving-kindnesses of the Lord and the praises of the Lord, according to all that the Lord hath bestowed on us and the great goodness toward the house of Israel, which he hath bestowed on them according to his mercies and according to the multitude of his loving-kindnesses.

63:8 For he said, Surely they are my people, children that will not lie; so he was their Savior.

63:9 In all their affliction he was afflicted, and the angel of his presence saved them; in his love and in his pity he redeemed them; and he bare them and carried them all the days of old.

63:10 But they rebelled and vexed his Holy Spirit; therefore, he was turned to be their enemy, and he fought against them.

[11] Then he remembered the days of old, Moses, and his people, saying, Where is he that brought them up out of the sea with the shepherd of his flock? where is he that put his holy Spirit within him?

[12] That led them by the right hand of Moses with his glorious arm, dividing the water before them, to make himself an everlasting name?

[13] That led them through the deep, as an horse in the wilderness, that they should not stumble?

[14] As a beast goeth down into the valley, the Spirit of the LORD caused him to rest: so didst thou lead thy people, to make thyself a glorious name.

[15] Look down from heaven, and behold from the habitation of thy holiness and of thy glory: where is thy zeal and thy strength, the sounding of thy bowels and of thy mercies toward me? are they restrained?

63:11 Then he remembered the days of old, Moses, and his people, saying, Where is he that brought them up out of the sea with the shepherd of his flock? Where is he that put his Holy Spirit within him,

63:12 That led them by the right hand of Moses with his glorious arm, dividing the water before them, to make himself an everlasting name,

63:13 That led them through the deep, as a horse in the wilderness, that they should not stumble?

63:14 As a beast goeth down into the valley, the Spirit of the Lord caused him to rest; so didst thou lead thy people, to make thyself a glorious name.

63:15 Look down from heaven, and behold from the habitation of thy holiness and of thy glory. Where is thy zeal and thy strength, the sounding of thy bowels and of thy mercies toward me? Are they restrained?

[16] Doubtless thou art our father, though Abraham be ignorant of us, and Israel acknowledge us not: thou, O LORD, art our father, our redeemer; thy name is from everlasting.

[17] O LORD, why hast thou made us to err from thy ways, and hardened our heart from thy fear? Return for thy servants' sake, the tribes of thine inheritance.

[18] The people of thy holiness have possessed it but a little while: our adversaries have trodden down thy sanctuary.

[19] We are thine: thou never barest rule over them; they were not called by thy name.

.64

[1] Oh that thou wouldest rend the heavens, that thou wouldest come down, that the mountains might flow down at thy presence,

63:16 Doubtless thou art our Father, though Abraham be ignorant of us and Israel acknowledge us not; thou, O Lord, art our Father, our Redeemer; thy name is from everlasting.

63:17 O Lord, why hast thou suffered us to err from thy ways and to harden our heart from thy fear? Return for thy servants' sake, the tribes of thine inheritance.

63:18 The people of thy holiness have possessed it but a little while; our adversaries have trodden down thy sanctuary.

63:19 We are thine; thou never barest rule over them; they were not called by thy name.

Chapter 64

64:1 Oh, that thou wouldest rend the heavens, that thou wouldest come down, that the mountains might flow down at thy presence,

[2] As when the melting fire burneth, the fire causeth the waters to boil, to make thy name known to thine adversaries, that the nations may tremble at thy presence!

[3] When thou didst terrible things which we looked not for, thou camest down, the mountains flowed down at thy presence.

[4] For since the beginning of the world men have not heard, nor perceived by the ear, neither hath the eye seen, O God, beside thee, what he hath prepared for him that waiteth for him.

[5] Thou meetest him that rejoiceth and worketh righteousness, those that remember thee in thy ways: behold, thou art wroth; for we have sinned: in those is continuance, and we shall be saved.

[6] But we are all as an unclean thing, and all our righteousnesses are as filthy rags; and we all do fade as a leaf; and our iniquities, like the wind, have taken us away.

64:2 As when the melting fire burneth, the fire causeth the waters to boil, to make thy name known to thine adversaries, that the nations may tremble at thy presence!

64:3 When thou didst terrible things which we looked not for, thou camest down; the mountains flowed down at thy presence.

64:4 For since the beginning of the world, men have not heard, nor perceived by the ear, neither hath the eye seen, O God, besides thee, what he hath prepared for him that waiteth for him.

64:5 Thou meetest him that worketh righteousness and rejoiceth him that remembereth thee in thy ways; in righteousness there is continuance, and such shall be saved.

64:6 But we have sinned; we are all as an unclean thing, and all our righteousnesses are as filthy rags; and we all do fade as a leaf; and our iniquities, like the wind, have taken us away.

[7] And there is none that calleth upon thy name, that stirreth up himself to take hold of thee: for thou hast hid thy face from us, and hast consumed us, because of our iniquities.

[8] But now, O LORD, thou art our father; we are the clay, and thou our potter; and we all are the work of thy hand.

[9] Be not wroth very sore, O LORD, neither remember iniquity for ever: behold, see, we beseech thee, we are all thy people.

[10] Thy holy cities are a wilderness, Zion is a wilderness, Jerusalem a desolation.

[11] Our holy and our beautiful house, where our fathers praised thee, is burned up with fire: and all our pleasant things are laid waste.

[12] Wilt thou refrain thyself for these things, O LORD? wilt thou hold thy peace, and afflict us very sore?

64:7 And there is none that calleth upon thy name, that stirreth up himself to take hold of thee; for thou hast hid thy face from us and hast consumed us because of our iniquities.

64:8 But now, O Lord, thou art our Father; we are the clay, and thou our potter; and we all are the work of thy hand.

64:9 Be not wroth very sore, O Lord; neither remember iniquity forever; behold; see, we beseech thee; we are all thy people.

64:10 Thy holy cities are a wilderness; Zion is a wilderness; Jerusalem, a desolation.

64:11 Our holy and our beautiful house, where our fathers praised thee, is burned up with fire; and all our pleasant things are laid waste.

64:12 Wilt thou refrain thyself for these things, O Lord? Wilt thou hold thy peace and afflict us very sore?

[1] I am sought of them that asked not for me; I am found of them that sought me not: I said, Behold me, behold me, unto a nation that was not called by my name.

[2] I have spread out my hands all the day unto a rebellious people, which walketh in a way that was not good, after their own thoughts;

[3] A people that provoketh me to anger continually to my face; that sacrificeth in gardens, and burneth incense upon altars of brick;

[4] Which remain among the graves, and lodge in the monuments, which eat swine's flesh, and broth of abominable things is in their vessels;

[5] Which say, Stand by thyself, come not near to me; for I am holier than thou. These are a smoke in my nose, a fire that burneth all the day.

Chapter 65

65:1 I am found of them who seek after me; I give unto all them that ask of me; I am not found of them that sought me not or that inquireth not after me.

65:2 I said unto my servant, Behold me; look upon me; I will send you unto a nation that is not called after my name, for I have spread out my hands all the day to a people who walketh not in my ways; and their works are evil and not good, and they walk after their own thoughts--

65:3 A people that provoketh me to anger continually to my face, that sacrificeth in gardens and burneth incense upon altars of brick,

65:4 Which remain among the graves and lodge in the monuments, which eat swine's flesh and broth of abominable beasts, and pollute their vessels,

65:5 Which say, Stand by thyself; come not near to me, for I am holier than thou. These are a smoke in my nose, a fire that burneth all the day.

[6] Behold, it is written before me: I will not keep silence, but will recompense, even recompense into their bosom,

[7] Your iniquities, and the iniquities of your fathers together, saith the LORD, which have burned incense upon the mountains, and blasphemed me upon the hills: therefore will I measure their former work into their bosom.

[8] Thus saith the LORD, As the new wine is found in the cluster, and one saith, Destroy it not; for a blessing is in it: so will I do for my servants' sakes, that I may not destroy them all.

[9] And I will bring forth a seed out of Jacob, and out of Judah an inheritor of my mountains: and mine elect shall inherit it, and my servants shall dwell there.

[10] And Sharon shall be a fold of flocks, and the valley of Achor a place for the herds to lie down in, for my people that have sought me.

65:6 Behold, it is written before me: I will not keep silence but will recompense, even recompense into their bosom,

65:7 Your iniquities and the iniquities of your fathers together, saith the Lord, which have burned incense upon the mountains and blasphemed me upon the hills; therefore will I measure their former work into their bosom.

65:8 Thus saith the Lord, As the new wine is found in the cluster, and one saith, Destroy it not, for a blessing is in it; so will I do for my servants' sake, that I may not destroy them all.

65:9 And I will bring forth a seed out of Jacob, and out of Judah an inheritor of my mountains; and mine elect shall inherit it, and my servants shall dwell there.

65:10 And Sharon shall be a fold of flocks, and the valley of Achor a place for the herds to lie down in, for my people that have sought me.

[11] But ye are they that forsake the LORD, that forget my holy mountain, that prepare a table for that troop, and that furnish the drink offering unto that number.

[12] Therefore will I number you to the sword, and ye shall all bow down to the slaughter: because when I called, ye did not answer; when I spake, ye did not hear; but did evil before mine eyes, and did choose that wherein I delighted not.

[13] Therefore thus saith the Lord GOD, Behold, my servants shall eat, but ye shall be hungry: behold, my servants shall drink, but ye shall be thirsty: behold, my servants shall rejoice, but ye shall be ashamed:

[14] Behold, my servants shall sing for joy of heart, but ye shall cry for sorrow of heart and shall howl for vexation of spirit.

[15] And ye shall leave your name for a curse unto my chosen: for the Lord GOD shall slay thee, and call his servants by another name:

65:11 But ye are they that forsake the Lord, that forget my holy mountain, that prepare a table for that troop, and that furnish the drink offering unto that number.

65:12 Therefore will I number you to the sword, and ye shall all bow down to the slaughter because when I called, ye did not answer; when I spake, ye did not hear, but did evil before mine eyes, and did choose that wherein I delighted not.

65:13 Therefore, thus saith the Lord God, Behold, my servants shall eat, but ye shall be hungry; behold, my servants shall drink, but ye shall be thirsty; behold, my servants shall rejoice, but ye shall be ashamed.

65:14 Behold, my servants shall sing for joy of heart, but ye shall cry for sorrow of heart and shall howl for vexation of spirit.

65:15 And ye shall leave your name for a curse unto my chosen; for the Lord God shall slay thee and call his servants by another name,

[16] That he who blesseth himself in the earth shall bless himself in the God of truth; and he that sweareth in the earth shall swear by the God of truth; because the former troubles are forgotten, and because they are hid from mine eyes.

[17] For, behold, I create new heavens and a new earth: and the former shall not be remembered, nor come into mind.

[18] But be ye glad and rejoice for ever in that which I create: for, behold, I create Jerusalem a rejoicing, and her people a joy.

[19] And I will rejoice in Jerusalem, and joy in my people: and the voice of weeping shall be no more heard in her, nor the voice of crying.

[20] There shall be no more thence an infant of days, nor an old man that hath not filled his days: for the child shall die an hundred years old; but the sinner being an hundred years old shall be accursed.

65:16 That he who blesseth himself in the earth shall bless himself in the God of truth; and he that sweareth in the earth shall swear by the God of truth because the former troubles are forgotten and because they are hid from mine eyes.

65:17 For behold, I create new heavens and a new earth; and the former shall not be remembered nor come into mind.

65:18 But be ye glad and rejoice forever in that which I create; for, behold, I create Jerusalem a rejoicing, and her people a joy.

65:19 And I will rejoice in Jerusalem and joy in my people; and the voice of weeping shall be no more heard in her, nor the voice of crying.

65:20 In those days there shall be no more thence an infant of days nor an old man that hath not filled his days; for the child shall not die but shall live to be a hundred years old; but the sinner, living to be a hundred years old, shall be accursed.

[21] And they shall build houses, and inhabit them; and they shall plant vineyards, and eat the fruit of them.

[22] They shall not build, and another inhabit; they shall not plant, and another eat: for as the days of a tree are the days of my people, and mine elect shall long enjoy the work of their hands.

[23] They shall not labour in vain, nor bring forth for trouble; for they are the seed of the blessed of the LORD, and their offspring with them.

[24] And it shall come to pass, that before they call, I will answer; and while they are yet speaking, I will hear.

[25] The wolf and the lamb shall feed together, and the lion shall eat straw like the bullock: and dust shall be the serpent's meat. They shall not hurt nor destroy in all my holy mountain, saith the LORD.

65:21 And they shall build houses and inhabit them; and they shall plant vineyards and eat the fruit of them.

65:22 They shall not build and another inhabit; they shall not plant and another eat; for as the days of a tree are the days of my people, and mine elect shall long enjoy the work of their hands.

65:23 They shall not labor in vain nor bring forth for trouble; for they are the seed of the blessed of the Lord, and their offspring with them.

65:24 And it shall come to pass that before they call, I will answer; and while they are yet speaking, I will hear.

65:25 The wolf and the lamb shall feed together, and the lion shall eat straw like the bullock; and dust shall be the serpent's meat. They shall not hurt nor destroy in all my holy mountain, saith the Lord.

[1] Thus saith the LORD, The heaven is my throne, and the earth is my footstool: where is the house that ye build unto me? and where is the place of my rest?

[2] For all those things hath mine hand made, and those things have been, saith the LORD: but to this man will I look, even to him that is poor and of a contrite spirit, and trembleth at my word.

[3] He that killeth an ox is as if he slew a man; he that sacrificeth a lamb, as if he cut off a dog's neck; he that offereth an oblation, as if he offered swine's blood; he that burneth incense, as if he blessed an idol. Yea, they have chosen their own ways, and their soul delighteth in their abominations.

[4] I also will choose their delusions, and will bring their fears upon them; because when I called, none did answer; when I spake, they did not hear: but they did evil before mine eyes, and chose that in which I delighted not.

Chapter 66

66:1 Thus saith the Lord, The heaven is my throne, and the earth is my footstool. Where is the house that ye build unto me, and where is the place of my rest?

66:2 For all those things hath mine hand made, and all those things have been, saith the Lord; but to this man will I look, even to him that is poor, and of a contrite spirit, and trembleth at my word.

66:3 He that killeth an ox is as if he slew a man; he that sacrificeth a lamb, as if he cut off a dog's neck; he that offereth an oblation, as if he offered swine's blood; he that burneth incense, as if he blessed an idol. Yea, they have chosen their own ways, and their soul delighteth in their abominations.

66:4 I also will choose their delusions and will bring their fears upon them because, when I called, none did answer; when I spake, they did not hear; but they did evil before mine eyes and chose that in which I delighted not.

[5] Hear the word of the LORD, ye that tremble at his word; your brethren that hated you, that cast you out for my name's sake, said, Let the LORD be glorified: but he shall appear to your joy, and they shall be ashamed.

[6] A voice of noise from the city, a voice from the temple, a voice of the LORD that rendereth recompence to his enemies.

[7] Before she travailed, she brought forth; before her pain came, she was delivered of a man child.

[8] Who hath heard such a thing? who hath seen such things? Shall the earth be made to bring forth in one day? or shall a nation be born at once? for as soon as Zion travailed, she brought forth her children.

[9] Shall I bring to the birth, and not cause to bring forth? saith the LORD: shall I cause to bring forth, and shut the womb? saith thy God.

66:5 Hear the word of the Lord, ye that tremble at his word: Your brethren that hated you, that cast you out for my name's sake, said, Let the Lord be glorified; but he shall appear to your joy, and they shall be ashamed.

66:6 A voice of noise from the city, a voice from the temple, a voice of the Lord that rendereth recompense to his enemies--

66:7 Before she travailed, she brought forth; before her pain came, she was delivered of a man-child.

66:8 Who hath heard such a thing? Who hath seen such things? Shall the earth be made to bring forth in one day? Or shall a nation be born at once? For as soon as Zion travailed, she brought forth her children.

66:9 Shall I bring to the birth and not cause to bring forth? saith the Lord. Shall I cause to bring forth, and shut the womb? saith thy God.

[10] Rejoice ye with Jerusalem, and be glad with her, all ye that love her: rejoice for joy with her, all ye that mourn for her:

[11] That ye may suck, and be satisfied with the breasts of her consolations; that ye may milk out, and be delighted with the abundance of her glory.

[12] For thus saith the LORD, Behold, I will extend peace to her like a river, and the glory of the Gentiles like a flowing stream: then shall ye suck, ye shall be borne upon her sides, and be dandled upon her knees.

[13] As one whom his mother comforteth, so will I comfort you; and ye shall be comforted in Jerusalem.

[14] And when ye see this, your heart shall rejoice, and your bones shall flourish like an herb: and the hand of the LORD shall be known toward his servants, and his indignation toward his enemies.

[15] For, behold, the LORD will come with fire, and with his chariots like a whirlwind, to render his anger with fury, and his rebuke with flames of fire.

66:10 Rejoice ye with Jerusalem, and be glad with her, all ye that love her; rejoice for joy with her, all ye that mourn for her,

66:11 That ye may suck and be satisfied with the breasts of her consolations, that ye may milk out and be delighted with the abundance of her glory.

66:12 For thus saith the Lord, Behold, I will extend peace to her like a river, and the glory of the Gentiles like a flowing stream; then shall ye suck; ye shall be borne upon her sides and be dandled upon her knees.

66:13 As one whom his mother comforteth, so will I comfort you; and ye shall be comforted in Jerusalem.

66:14 And when ye see this, your heart shall rejoice, and your bones shall flourish like an herb; and the hand of the Lord shall be known toward his servants, and his indignation toward his enemies.

66:15 For behold, the Lord will come with fire and with his chariots like a whirlwind, to render his anger with fury and his rebuke with flames of fire.

[16] For by fire and by his sword will the LORD plead with all flesh: and the slain of the LORD shall be many.

[17] They that sanctify themselves, and purify themselves in the gardens behind one tree in the midst, eating swine's flesh, and the abomination, and the mouse, shall be consumed together, saith the LORD.

[18] For I know their works and their thoughts: it shall come, that I will gather all nations and tongues; and they shall come, and see my glory.

[19] And I will set a sign among them, and I will send those that escape of them unto the nations, to Tarshish, Pul, and Lud, that draw the bow, to Tubal, and Javan, to the isles afar off, that have not heard my fame, neither have seen my glory; and they shall declare my glory among the Gentiles.

66:16 For by fire and by his sword will the Lord plead with all flesh; and the slain of the Lord shall be many.

66:17 They that sanctify themselves and purify themselves in the gardens behind one tree in the midst, eating swine's flesh, and the abomination, and the mouse, shall be consumed together, saith the Lord.

66:18 For I know their works and their thoughts; it shall come that I will gather all nations and tongues; and they shall come and see my glory.

66:19 And I will set a sign among them, and I will send those that escape of them unto the nations: to Tarshish, Pul, and Lud, that draw the bow, to Tubal and Javan, to the isles afar off that have not heard my fame, neither have seen my glory; and they shall declare my glory among the Gentiles.

[20] And they shall bring all your brethren for an offering unto the LORD out of all nations upon horses, and in chariots, and in litters, and upon mules, and upon swift beasts, to my holy mountain Jerusalem, saith the LORD, as the children of Israel bring an offering in a clean vessel into the house of the LORD.

[21] And I will also take of them for priests and for Levites, saith the LORD.

[22] For as the new heavens and the new earth, which I will make, shall remain before me, saith the LORD, so shall your seed and your name remain.

[23] And it shall come to pass, that from one new moon to another, and from one sabbath to another, shall all flesh come to worship before me, saith the LORD.

[24] And they shall go forth, and look upon the carcases of the men that have transgressed against me: for their worm shall not die, neither shall their fire be quenched; and they shall be an abhorring unto all flesh.

66:20 And they shall bring all your brethren for an offering unto the Lord out of all nations--upon horses, and in chariots, and in litters, and upon mules, and upon swift beasts--to my holy mountain Jerusalem, saith the Lord, as the children of Israel bring an offering in a clean vessel into the house of the Lord.

66:21 And I will also take of them for priests and for Levites, saith the Lord.

66:22 For as the new heavens and the new earth, which I will make, shall remain before me, saith the Lord, so shall your seed and your name remain.

66:23 And it shall come to pass that from one new moon to another and from one sabbath to another shall all flesh come to worship before me, saith the Lord.

66:24 And they shall go forth, and look upon the carcasses of the men that have transgressed against me; for their worm shall not die; neither shall their fire be quenched; and they shall be an abhorring unto all flesh.